HANDBOOK OF ORGANIZATIONAL STRESS COPING STRATEGIES

Dedicated to Hans Selye

HANDBOOK OF ORGANIZATIONAL STRESS COPING STRATEGIES

Amarjit Singh Sethi
Randall S. Schuler

BALLINGER PUBLISHING COMPANY
Cambridge, Massachusetts
A Subsidiary of Harper & Row, Publishers, Inc.

International Standard Book Number: 0–88410-745-0

Library of Congress Catalog Card Number: 84-3082

Printed in the United States of America

Library of Congress Cataloging in Publication Data

Main entry under title:
    Handbook of organizational stress coping strategies.

    Bibliography: p.
    Includes index.
    1. Job stress—Addresses, essays, lectures. 2. Adjustment
(Psychology)—Addresses, essays, lectures. I. Sethi, Amarjit Singh.
II. Schuler, Randall S.
HF5548.85.H36   1984   158.7   84-3082
ISBN 0–88410–745–0

CONTENTS

List of Figures   ix

List of Tables   xi

Preface   xiii

Chapter 1
Introduction to Organizational Stress Coping
Amarjit S. Sethi and *Randall S. Schuler*   1

Chapter 2
Stress and Health: A Perspective on Aging
and Retirement
Hans Selye   15

Chapter 3
Organizational Stress and Coping:
A Model and Overview
Randall S. Schuler   35

Chapter 4
Time Management and Leader Communication
Behavior *Randall S. Schuler* and *Amarjit S. Sethi*   69

v

Chapter 5
Organizational Practices for Preventing Burnout
Susan E. Jackson   89

Chapter 6
**The Role of Social Support Groups in Stress
Coping in Organizational Settings**
James A. Wells   113

Chapter 7
Meditation for Coping with Organizational Stress
Amarjit S. Sethi   145

Chapter 8
Yoga for Coping with Organizational Stress
Amarjit S. Sethi   1670

Chapter 9
Stress Coping through Biofeedback
Barbara B. Brown   183

Chapter 10
Stress Coping through Physical Activity
Maurice Jetté   215

Chapter 11
Stress and the Manager: Perspectives
John H. Howard   233

Chapter 12
Organizational Stress Management Audit
Manfred F.R. Kets de Vries   251

Chapter 13
Stress Coping Research: Methodological Issues
Terry A. Beehr   277

Chapter 14
**Organizational Stress Coping: Research Issues
and Future Directions**
Amarjit S. Sethi and *Randall S. Schuler*   301

Index   309

About the Editors   315

About the Contributors   317

LIST OF FIGURES

2-1   Hypothalamus-Pituitary-Adrenocortical Axis   23

3-1   Integrative Transactional Process Model
       of Stress in Organizations   40

3-2   Individual Cognitive Qualities (Skills)   50

4-1   The Pareto Time Principle   73

4-2   Management Activities Daily Diary   75

8-1   Eight Limbs of Yoga   172

8-2   Layers of Self along Five Sheaths in Yoga   175

8-3   Concepts of Self: Yogic and Western   176

8-4   The Yogic (Vedantic) Conception of Mind   177

10-1   Stress and the Cortical Prism   218

12-1   A Multifactorial Approach to Stress   253

12-2   Organizational Factors Contributing
       to Stress   255

13-1   The Fourfold Classification of Traditional
       Research Methods   282

13–2   Intermediary Mechanisms   288

13–3   A Sample Regression Line Representing the
Relationship between the Same Strain (Anxiety)
Measured at Two Points in Time   294

13–4   Regression-Discontinuity Research Design Using
Anxiety as a Sample Strain   296

LIST OF TABLES

3-1 Typology of Coping Strategies and Targets   56

4-1 Time Robbers   74

4-2 Conserving, Controlling, and Making Time   76

4-3 Individual Symptoms of Stress   85

5-1 Three Stages of Burnout and Their
     Accompanying Symptoms   92

5-2 Consequences of Burnout   97

6-1 Comparison of Rates of Social Support Buffering
     Effects in Three Samples   127

6-2 Results of Social Support Buffering among
     Replications across Three Samples   131

6-3 Results of Social Support Main Effects among
     Replications across Three Samples   136

8-1 Suggested Timetable for Daily Yoga   180

10-1 Relative Importance of Factors Contributing to
      Well-Being   216

10–2 Factors Contributing to the Development of the
Cortical Prism   218

10–3 Chronic Effects of Aerobic Exercise to Relieve
Stress and Counteract the Disease Process   220

10–4 Chronic Effects of Aerobic Training   225

PREFACE

Our objectives in preparing the *Handbook of Organizational Stress Coping Strategies* include: (1) bringing together the contributions of several outstanding scholars in stress and coping; (2) providing a useful textbook for university classes in health, business, science, nursing, physical education, and general education; (3) assembling a useful reference source for other stress coping scholars and practitioners; and (4) providing in a single volume a set of useful and practical strategies for coping with stress by organizations and their members.

Because our current understanding of stress is still somewhat in the developmental stage, we have chosen to avoid using one definition of stress. Consequently our authors reflect their own personal definitions of stress and organizational stress coping strategies. The strategies for coping with stress represent a diverse set of options from which organizations and organizational members can select to cope effectively with stress at both individual and organizational levels. These options include a transactional process model (Chapter 3), time management and leader communication behavior (Chapter 4), organizational practices to prevent job burnout and stress (Chapter 5), social support groups (Chapter 6), and the concept of organizational stress audit (Chapters 11 and 12). In addition, we have included four key techniques that can be used by organizational members at the individual level to cope with organizational and personal stress. These strategies include meditation, yoga, biofeedback, and physical activity (Chapters 7-10). The effectiveness of each technique depends upon an individual and organizational analysis of the stress to determine which strategy (or combination of strategies) is most appropriate.

We propose that organizational stress coping strategies are most effective when they are related to each situation and based on a careful selection process. The selection process may in turn be modified by a variety of structural and sociopsychological variables at the individual, organizational, or larger societal level.

In Chapters 13 and 14 we conclude with a discussion of research issues relevant to stress coping. Although many critical issues remain to be addressed, it is our belief that many of these strategies can be utilized now in a pro-active manner in order to prevent or minimize the occurrence or deleterious effects of organizational stress.

Finally, it is with deep sadness that we observe the death of Hans Selye, a pioneer in the research of stress and stress coping. In recognition of his immense contributions to the field, we dedicate this book to him.

A.S. Sethi
Ottawa

R.S. Schuler
New York City

1 INTRODUCTION TO ORGANIZATIONAL STRESS COPING

Amarjit S. Sethi and *Randall S. Schuler*

Stress and coping with stress in organizations are becoming increasingly important concerns in both academic research and organizational practices. Yet there is still a great deal not known about stress or coping with stress in organizations (Zaleznik, Kets de Vries, and Howard, 1977; Beehr and Newman, 1979; House, 1981; Cooper and Marshall, 1976). What is known, however, suggests that the importance given them is warranted, perhaps overdue.

THE IMPORTANCE OF STRESS AND COPING WITH STRESS IN ORGANIZATIONS

There are four major reasons why stress and coping with stress in organizations are becoming such prominent topics of discussion and research by individuals inside organizations as well as by those studying individuals in organizations (see Beehr and Schuler, 1982).

Health

The World Health Organization defines "health" as the presence of physical and psychological well-being. With this definition, a review of

1

the research on stress plainly indicates that stress my be hazardous to one's health. Some of the major health hazards associated with stress in organizations include neuroses, coronary heart disease (CHD), alimentary conditions such as dyspepsia and ulcers, cancer, asthma, high blood pressure, backaches, and the related use of alcohol and drugs. Parallel with an increased susceptibility to medical illness for those working under stressful conditions is the increased likelihood of incurring accidents on the job (for an excellent elaboration of the harmful effects on workers' health associated with stress, see Antonovsky, 1979; and Platt and Friedman, 1981).

Financial Impact

It is estimated that the economic cost of peptic ulcers and cardiovascular disease alone in the United States is about $45 billion annually (Putt, 1970; Moser, 1977). The cost to society and organizations of the stress-related symptom of backache is also high. Based on a survey conducted by the National Center for Health Statistics in 1977, backache was the fifth most common reason for visits to office-based physicians in 1975. In 1976, 14.2 percent of the disability claims filed by companies for individuals and 17.7 percent of the benefits paid involved back disorders (Warshaw, 1979). Albrecht (1979) estimates that for an organization with 2,000 employees and $60 million in sales the cost of stress (resulting in such outcomes as absenteeism, turnover, and accidents) is $3.5 million per year or $1.780 per employee.

Although these figures are only estimates of the financial impact, they do offer reasons for the growing concern over stress in organizations. Nonetheless, these data do not necessarily provide a convincing case for immediate action by organizations to reduce or even manage employee stress (Newman and Beehr, 1979; Beehr, 1980). Furthermore, employee stress may not be a result of conditions within the organization, but rather conditions outside the workplace (see for example the work on stressful life events by Holmes and Rahe, 1967; Dohrenwend and Dohrenwend, 1974; and Bhagat, 1983). This being the case, should organizations do anything more than regard the effects of stress as merely a part of doing business? It appears that many organizations have already answered this question affirmatively by developing and implementing strategies that deal with stress in organizations. Their resolve to confront the issue is based in part on the view that stress is a financial threat as well as a threat to the effectiveness of the entire organization.

Organizational Effectiveness

The increasing concern over stress shown by some organizations reflects an expanded definition of the basis on which to evaluate organizational effectiveness or success. Although many organizations still use profit or productivity as the main basis on which to evaluate how well the organization is doing, other organizations and observers of organizations recognize the need for several bases on which to make these evaluations. This need is evident from viewing organizations as open rather than closed, self-sufficient systems. With this description of organizations as open systems follow the assumptions that (1) some means must be devoted to such nongoal functions as service and custodial activities (including means employed for the maintenance of the organization itself), and that (2) employees and society have as much stake in what the organization is and does as the organization and its managers (see Steers, 1977; Katz and Kahn, 1978; and Brief, Schuler, and Van Sell, 1981).

Thus, with an open-systems view of organizations it is necessary and legitimate to evaluate organizations on the basis of employee satisfaction, health, accidents, turnover, and absenteeism, as well as efficiency, profitability, productivity, and return on investment. And since stress in organizations is related to many of these bases, stress itself becomes a necessary and legitimate concern for organizations. But even if organizations do select the open-systems view of evaluation, they are still confronted with two particularly important tradeoffs. Perhaps more apparent than real, the first tradeoff is, How much productivity must be sacrificed to achieve increased employee health? The second is, Should short-run benefits be allowed to outweigh long-run costs? These two tradeoffs are illustrated in an experiment performed by Levi (1972), in which workers were switched from a non-incentive–based pay system to an incentive system (see McLean, 1979, for a fuller description of this experiment). On the basis of a change in compensation to an incentive system, production rose an average of 113 percent without any corresponding increase in mistakes. Nearly all the workers, however, complained of head and back pains and were, in general, physically and mentally exhausted. Furthermore, tests revealed that the production of the stress hormones, noradrenaline and adrenaline, increased 27 and 40 percent respectively. These effects were manifested after only two days! The researcher in charge of this experiment highlighted the short- versus long-run tradeoff by concluding that

> one can reasonably suppose that, if this condition of stress had been allowed to continue, it would have broken out in the form of nervous complaints, increased muscular pains, low morale, a higher incidence of sick leave, and an increased turnover of personnel. The resultant losses would no doubt have been reserved for a separate ledger far away from the immaculate statistics of hourly production. But the ultimate cost, in terms of company profits, national expenditure and human values would not (Levi, 1972: 82).

Legal Compliance and Worker Compensation

Worker compensation laws now make an employer legally liable for an employee's mental illness as well as physical illness, whatever the cause, if it is aggravated, accelerated, precipitated, or triggered to the point of disability or need for medical care by any condition of the employment (McLean, 1979). Furthermore, fault or absence of fault on the part of the employee or employer has no bearing on the determination of liability of the employer for payment of worker compensation benefits (Lesser, 1967).

Thus it is only sufficient for an employee to show that an illness was precipitated by an organization event to claim compensation, regardless of other nonorganizational events (e.g., stressful life events) to which the individual may have been exposed. This argues for organizations being concerned with the effects of stress, regardless of whether the individual comes to work already stressed or not.

Organizations also need to be concerned with stress because in the United States they are legally responsible for the presence of stressful conditions, according to the Organizational Safety and Health Act (OSHA) of 1970. According to the act, the employer is liable for both physical conditions causing employee physical harm (e.g., chemical poisons and physical obstructions) and sociopsychological conditions causing employee mental or psychological harm (OSHA, 1970). Although the impact of OSHA may have been somewhat diminished by the ruling forbidding unannounced entry to organizations, it is still a potent force whose influence is likely to increase. The research counterpart of OSHA, the National Institute of Occupational Safety and Health (NIOSH), has been and is funding extensive research programs regarding stress in organizations (as an example of NIOSH funded research see Smith, Colligan, and Harnell, 1978; and Colligan and Smith, 1978).

The last decade *has* marked a significant increase in concern over occupational health and safety in Canada. Each province administers its own legislation in this field, and in recent years nearly every jurisdiction has radically revised and consolidated its legislation and administrative apparatus. These changes have been paralleled by a substantially greater commitment to the prevention of occupational illness.

While occupational stress has not been specifically singled out for attention in legislation, it is worth noting that in one Canadian province the stated purposes of the Workplace Safety and Health Act (WSHA) include "the promotion of and maintenance of the highest degree of physical, mental and social well-being of workers and the placing and maintenance of workers in an occupational environment adapted to their physiological and psychological condition" (WSHA, 1976:3). In another piece of legislation, the Act Respecting Occupational Health and Safety, the purpose includes the elimination, at the source, of dangers to the health, safety, and physical well-being of workers (AROHS, 1979). In 1978, the Canadian Centre for Occupational Health and Safety was created to serve and promote, among other things, the physical and mental health of working people in Canada (CCOHSA, 1977–1978). The legislation of each jurisdiction typically places an obligation on employers to take all precautions reasonably necessary to ensure the health of their workers.

While workers' compensation boards in Canada have generally been extremely reluctant to award compensation for illness caused by psychological stress at work, there have been several occasions in which compensation was awarded to workers who missed work due to mental illness or other stress-related diseases attributable to their work (CCOHS, 1982).

Although organizations should be concerned with stress, not all are. Indeed, many organizations are either unconcerned with it or do nothing about it. But even in those organizations that are concerned, managers recognize that not everyone appears to be under stress or that much of what their employees identify as stress is really caused by off-the-job stressors. Consequently, these managers are reluctant to develop organizational stress coping programs. In these organizations, then it is up to the worker to develop individual stress coping strategies.

Because both organizations and individuals need to be concerned with stress, we have incorporated chapters addressing both organizational and individual stress and coping strategies. This is not to say, however, that programs designed to help individuals deal with stress apart from or even within the organization cannot be of concern to organizations. Indeed, many of the organizational stress coping strategies are as applicable to individuals when they are inside the organization as when they are outside. But organizational stress coping strategies are especially applicable to individuals when they are inside the organization. For example, a stress management program to improve supervisory communication skills is only useful in an organizational context. Similar to organizational stress coping, individual stress coping strategies are applicable to individuals whether they be part of an organization or not. While an organization would not sponsor an individual stress management program under our definition, individuals can benefit from the programs in activities both inside and outside the job. In addition, most individual stress management programs can be implemented outside the organization.

Because individuals spend so much of their time in organizations and because the space of this book is limited, we have chosen to emphasize organizational stress and coping strategies. We also believe that organizations should, when appropriate, implement stress coping programs. Nonetheless, several important individual stress coping strategies are included here that can be utilized by organizational members in coping with both personal and organizational stress.

WHAT IS STRESS?

Stress has been and continues to be defined in numerous ways. For example, Selye (1936: 32) defines stress as "the nonspecific response to any demand." Stress, according to French, Rogers, and Cobb (1974: 72) is "a misfit between a person's skills and abilities and demands of the job, and a misfit in terms of a person's needs supplied by the environment." Beehr and Newman (1978: 669) define job stress as "a condition wherein job-related factors interact with the worker to change (disrupt or enhance) his/her psychological or physiological condition such that the person (mind and/or body) is forced to deviate from normal functioning." McGrath (1976: 1352) defines stress in terms of a set of conditions having stress in it: "Stress involves an interaction of person and environment. Something happens 'out there' which presents a person with a demand, or a constraint or an opportunity for behavior." And Schuler (1982: 6) defines stress as "a dynamic situation of uncertainty involving something important." This definition is detailed in Chapter 3.

Because there is insufficient research to support conclusively any of these definitions, we have chosen to allow each of our authors to use his or her own preferred definitions of stress. And although our authors have taken us up on this liberty and use, either implicitly or explicitly, numerous definitions, they all concur on the importance of stress and the need for individuals and organizations to develop strategies to cope with it.

WHAT IS COPING?

As with stress, coping is defined in several ways. According to Lazarus and Launier (1978: 293), coping is defined as "efforts, both action oriented and intrapsychic, to manage (i.e., to master, tolerate, reduce and minimize) environmental and internal demands and conflicts among them which tax or exceed a person's resources." Based on this definition, Lazarus and his associates (for example, Folkman, Schaefer, and Lazarus, 1979) describe four strategies of coping (all essentially process-oriented cognitive strategies): (1) information search, (2) direct action, (3) intrapsychic modes, and (4) inhibition of action. These strategies are used either to mediate person-environment relationships in an instrumental or problem-solving mode or to control selectively individual stress responses in a palliative mode. In essence, coping functions as a decision-making/problem-solving activity to regulate responses to stress.

Pearlin and Schooler (1978) state that coping refers to behavior that protects people from being psychologically harmed by problematic social experiences. Coping protects by (1) eliminating or modifying stressors, (2) perceptually controlling the meaning of the stress experience and thus neutralizing its problematic character, or (3) keeping emotional consequences within manageable bounds. McGrath

(1970) defines coping as an array of covert and overt behavior patterns by which the organism can actively prevent, alleviate, or respond
to stress-inducing circumstances. Schuler (1984), recognizing the
positive as well as the negative aspects (outcomes) of stress, defines
coping as a process of analysis and evaluation to decide how to protect
oneself against the diverse effects of any stressor and its associated
negative outcomes yet to take advantage of its positive outcomes. This
definition is expanded in Chapter 3.

Thus, coping performed either on the individual or the organizational
level includes stress *prevention* and stress *management* strategies. To
differentiate whether they are individual stress coping strategies or
organizational stress coping strategies depends on where they are
done, by whom, and for whose primary benefit. We anticipate, however, that regardless of the coping strategy used, not only will the individual and the organization benefit, but so will the society in which
these two co-exist.

To ensure that neither the richness of the varied definitions of coping nor the variety of coping strategies is diminished in any way, we
have again allowed our authors the liberty of addressing individual
and organizational coping as they choose. We will briefly outline
their contributions.

OVERVIEW OF CHAPTERS

Because the literature and research regarding stress and stress coping
are so extensive and yet relatively unintegrated, one of our three major objectives in editing this book is to bring together within one
volume as much expertise as possible. Our next objective is to give
the reader a single source on stress coping strategies that will be as
useful, authoritative, up-to-date, and all-encompassing as possible.
Our third objective is to present stress coping strategies that can be
performed at the individual level and at the organizational level.
This, we feel, enhances the usefulness of this *Handbook*.

Before briefly describing the content of each chapter, we wish to
express our appreciation to all of our authors. We feel that they have
helped us immensely in meeting our three major objectives.

In Chapter 2, Hans Selye describes stress as a flow of stressors,
mediated by numerous internal and external conditioning factors,
that results in heightened arousal, and eventual disturbance, of the

system's homeostatic steady state. Attempts to restore homeostasis, both at a physiological and psychological level, pass through a general adaptation syndrome (GAS) of alarm, resistance, and exhaustion, which is considered by Selye as a universal biological defense reaction aroused by any physically noxious agent. For Selye, stress remains a nonspecific response of the body to any demand made upon it regardless of whether the stimulus or demand is pleasant or unpleasant. Selye, however, also incorporates specificity into his discussion of stress. To quote Selye:

> As emphasized nearly 20 years ago in the first edition of *The Stress of Life,* specificity and nonspecificity are always relative, in the sense that few (if any) agents produce only one change, and the number of "side effects" varies. However, alterations produced by only one or a few agents are conveniently referred to as "specific," in opposition to those that affect many organ systems indiscriminately. Stress is by definition nonspecific in its causation; that is, it is "the response of the body to any demand" just as is energy utilization, though its phenotypes may be vastly different, depending upon the previously mentioned conditioning factors.
>
> Of course, administration of CRF, ACTH, or corticoids may elicit certain manifestations generally ascribed to stress, in a highly specifically manner. The same may be said about some drugs (e.g., amphenone) which specifically interfere with the stress mechanism itself. However, this hardly could justify abandoning the concept of nonspecificity, any more than the fact of an albino Negro or a deeply pigmented Caucasian Addisonian would justify the distinction between black and white races in anthropology (Selye, 1976: 74).

In Chapter 3, Schuler offers a transactional process model of organizational stress and a transactional process model of organizational stress coping. As part of these two models, which are compatible, definitions of stress and coping are provided. Although the discussion of stress and coping is related to organizational contexts, people within organizations could still benefit individually from using some of the strategies described. After Schuler presents the models of stress and coping, he suggests what actions can be taken by organizations to help cope with the stress often generated by organizational conditions. These suggestions are somewhat general in scope. More specific strategies for organizational stress coping follow in later chapters.

Several specific coping strategies are described by Schuler and Sethi in Chapter 4. The two described in most detail include changing supervisory communication behaviors and practicing time management techniques. While organizations promote personal training programs to improve supervisory communication and time management skills, so too can individuals. It is probably more beneficial, however, for these skills to be presented to individuals in programs sponsored by the organization. Specific directions for increasing these skills are provided.

In Chapter 5, Jackson discusses organizational stress coping practices designed to prevent job burnout, a type of stress normally applied to human services, especially social service, law enforcement, and nursing. Characteristic of these professions or occupations is a set of intensive interpersonal relationships with clients. Often in dealing with these clients, the professional has limited control over how the client actually utilizes the assistance provided. Continued exposure to these conditions can result in burnout; that is, depersonalization, emotional exhaustion, and a feeling of low personal accomplishment.

After reviewing the research on burnout, Jackson suggests several techniques that organizations can use (even if they are not solely in the human services area) to help prevent burnout. The techniques presented and extensively described include Kramer's anticipatory socialization, performance feedback, and participation.

In Chapter 6, Wells describes in detail the concept of social support groups and distinguishes between the "task clarification" and "buffering" roles that groups can play to help individuals minimize the effects of stress. This buffering role is central to the team social support groups. Wells then describes how social support groups operate and how they can be developed and promoted within the organization.

The next two chapters are by Sethi. In Chapter 7, he discusses the importance of meditation and emphasizes that it can be a particularly useful organizational coping strategy when used in conjunction with other strategies such as biofeedback (Brown), fitness (Jetté), and time management (Schuler and Sethi). After reviewing some of the research that has been done on the effectiveness of meditation, Sethi explains various types, including transcendental meditation (TM), clinically standardized meditation (CSM), Benson's relaxation response, zen meditation, Sikh meditation, and diagnostic meditation. He concludes by describing the relationship between meditation and other coping techniques dealt with in this book.

The positive psychophysiological effects of yoga are presented by Sethi in Chapter 8. After defining and explaining the types of yoga, the author makes several specific recommendations for its use.

Following Sethi's two chapters is Brown's description of biofeedback. As with yoga and meditation, there are several different types, or more accurately, methodologies of biofeedback. Brown describes these and provides a historical account of them. Basically she describes two categories of methods and then four modalities. The mechanisms of biofeedback are then presented along with the caveat that there is, at this time, a significant gap between biofeedback concepts and research. Conclusions and recommendations regarding biofeedback as a stress coping strategy are therefore made with caution.

In Chapter 10, Maurice Jetté discusses the fitness movement in North America and points out recent research findings related to exercise and its effectiveness, at both individual and organizational levels. Basing his findings on the Canada Fitness Survey (1982), the largest and most comprehensive study of physical activity ever undertaken anywhere in the Western world, Jetté explains the importance of physical activity on three counts: (1) as a basic component in the pursuit of health—to maintain optimal weight, to improve cardio-respiratory fitness (aerobic power), and to enhance physical working capacity; (2) as a socially acceptable method for the organism to rid itself of potentially harmful biochemical secretions released during emotional stress; and (3) as a leisure and social activity to provide general relaxation and a feeling of well-being. Jetté proposes specific guidelines for initiating aerobic exercise programs and their utility in combating stress. He examines organizational fitness programs and shows the specific benefits of these programs to organizations for reducing job tension and improving productivity.

In Chapter 11, John Howard provides practical guidelines in coping with job stress for managers, and, using his research work in Canada, examines the effectiveness of various techniques for coping with job tension. In Chapter 12, Kets de Vries introduces the concept of stress audit, and discusses the causal, mediating, and end-result variables in coping with organizational stress.

In the last two chapters, research issues and future directions are suggested. In Chapter 13, Beehr discusses the research issues related to stress and coping with stress. An important premise Beehr makes is that there is a relative scarcity of research on stress and coping. Consequently, before our understanding of these areas can advance, more research is necessary.

Then he presents a fourfold classification of research methods that can be used to research stress coping along with useful research designs and statistical procedures. Appropriately, he discusses the ethical issues attendant in stress coping research and the difficulties involved due to the intermediary mechanisms between stressors and stress. Beehr, however, does provide guidelines on how these issues and difficulties can be addressed.

In the closing chapter, Sethi and Schuler discuss further issues associated with coping and suggest some directions for future work in the form of six testable hypotheses and several, more general stress research topics. Consistent with Beehr's premise, Sethi and Schuler suggest that while a great deal of stress coping research has been done, more needs to be done to advance the state of our knowledge and understanding.

REFERENCES

Albrecht, K. 1979. *Stress and the Manager.* Englewood Cliffs, N.J.: Prentice-Hall.

Antonovsky, A. 1979. *Health, Stress and Coping.* San Francisco: Jossey-Bass.

An Act Respecting Occupational Health & Safety (AROHS). 1979. S.Q. 1979, c. 63, section 2. Canadian.

Beehr, T.A. 1980. "Organizational Strategies for Managing Job Stress." Paper presented at the Midwest Academy of Management, Cincinnati.

Beehr, T.A., and J.E. Newman. 1978. "Job Stress, Employee Health, and Organizational Effectiveness: A Facet Analysis, Model and Literature Review." *Personnel Psychology* 31: 665–699.

Beehr, T.A., and R.S. Schuler. 1982. "Stress in Organizations." In *Personnel Management,* edited by K.M. Rowland and G.R. Ferris. Boston: Allyn and Bacon.

Bhagat, R.S. 1983. "Effects of Stressful Life Events Upon Individual Performance Effectiveness and Work Adjustment Processes Within Organizational Settings: A Research Model." *Academy of Management Review* 8 : 660–671.

Brief, A.P.; R.S. Schuler; and M. Van Sell. 1981. *Managing Stress.* Boston: Little, Brown and Company.

Canadian Centre for Occupational Health and Safety Act (CCOHSA). 1977–78 S.C., c. 29, section 5(1)(a).

Canadian Centre for Occupational Health and Safety. (CCOHS). 1982. Document no. 0479U (Unpublished) Hamilton, Ontario.

Canada Fitness Survey. 1982. Canada Fitness: Preliminary Findings of the 1981 Survey. Ottawa.

Colligan, M., and M. Smith. 1978. "A Methodological Approach for Evaluating Outbreaks of Mass Psychogenic Illness in Industry." *Journal of Occupational Medicine* 20: 6–15.

Cooper, C.L., and J. Marshall. 1976. "Occupational Sources of Stress: A Review of the Literature Relating to Coronary Heart Disease and Mental Ill Health." *Journal of Occupational Psychology* 49, 11–28.

Dohrenwend, B.S., and B.P. Dohrenwend, eds. 1974. *Stressful Life Events.* New York: John Wiley and Sons.

Folkman, S., and R.S. Lazarus. 1980. "An Analysis of Coping in a Middle Aged Community Sample." *Journal of Health and Social Behavior* 21: 219–239.

Folkman, S.; C. Schaefer; and R.S. Lazarus. 1979. "Cognitive Processes as Mediators of Stress and Coping." In *Human Stress and Cognition,* edited by V. Hamilton and D.M. Warburton. Chilchestor, England: John Wiley and Sons.

French, J.R.P., Jr.; W. Rogers; and S. Cobb. 1974. "Adjustment as a Person-Environment Fit." In *Coping and Adaptation: Interdisciplinary Perspectives,* edited by G.V. Coelho, D.A. Hamburg, and J.S. Adams. New York: Basic Books.

Holmes, T.H., and R.H. Rahe. 1967. "Social Readjustment Rating Scale." *Journal of Psychosomatic Research* 11: 213–218.

House, J.S. 1981. *Social Support and Stress.* Reading, MA: Addison-Wesley Publishing Company.

Katz, D., and R.L. Kahn. 1978. *The Social Psychology of Organizations* (2nd ed.). New York: John Wiley and Sons.

Lazarus, R.S., and R. Launier. 1978. "Stress-Related Transaction Between Person and Environment." In *Perspectives in Interactional Psychology,* edited by Pervin and Lewis, pp. 287–327. New York: Plenum.

Lesser, P.J. 1967. "The Legal Viewpoint." In *To Work is Human,* edited by A. McLean. New York: Macmillan.

Levi, T. 1972. *Stress and Distress in Response to Psychosocial Stimuli.* Elmsford, N.Y.: Pergamon Press, Inc.

McGrath, J.E., ed. 1970. *Social and Psychological Factors in Stress.* New York: Holt, Rinehart and Winston.

McGrath, J.E. 1976. "Stress and Behavior in Organizations." In *Handbook of Industrial and Organizational Psychology,* edited by M.D. Dunnette. Chicago: Rand McNally College Publishing Company.

McLean, A.A. 1979. *Work Stress.* Reading, Ma.: Addison-Wesley Publishing Company.

Moser, M. 1977. "Hypertension: A Major Controllable Public Health Problem—Industry Can Help." *Occupational Health Nursing,* August: 19–26.

Newman, J.F., and T.A. Beehr. 1979. "Personal and Organizational Strategies for Handling Job Stress: A Review of Research and Opinion." *Personnel Psychology* 32: 1–43.

Pearlin, K.I., and C. Schooler. 1978. "The Structure of Coping." *Journal of Health and Social Behavior* 19: 1–21.

Platt, S.M., and S.B. Friedman. 1981. "Psychosocial Factors in Infectious Disease." In *Psychoneurommunology,* edited by R. Ader. New York: Academic Press.

Putt, A.M. 1970. "One Experiment in Nursing Adults with Peptic Ulcers." *Nursing Research* 19: 484–494.

Schuler, R.S. 1982. "An Integrative Transactional Process Model of Stress In Organizations." *Journal of Occupational Behavior* 3: 5–19.

Schuler, R.S. 1984. "Integrative Transactional Process Model of Coping with Stress in Organizations." In *Human Stress and Cognition in Organizations: An Integrative Perspective,* edited by T.A. Beehr and R.S. Bhagat. New York: John Wiley and Sons.

Selye, H. 1936. "A Syndrome Produced by Diverse Nocuous Agents." *Nature* 138: 32.

Selye, H. 1976. *The Stress of Life.* New York: McGraw-Hill.

Smith, M.J.; J.M. Colligan; and J.J. Harnell. 1978. *A Review of Psychological Stress Research of the National Institute for Occupational Safety and Health, 1971 to 1976.* Cincinnati: NIOSH Research Report.

Steers, R.M. 1977. *Organizational Effectiveness.* Santa Monica, Ca.: Goodyear Publishing.

Warshaw, L.J. 1979. *Stress Management.* Reading, Ma.: Addison-Wesley Publishing Company.

The Occupational Safety and Health Act (OSHA), Public Law 91-596, December 29, 1970. United States of America.

The Workplace Safety and Health Act WSHA, S.M., 1976, C. 63, as amended sections 2(2)(a), 2(2)(d).

Zaleznik, A.; M.F.R. Kets de Vries; and J. Howard. 1977. "Stress Reactions in Organizations: Syndromes, Causes and Consequences." *Behavioral Science* 22: 151–161.

2 STRESS AND HEALTH: A PERSPECTIVE ON AGING AND RETIREMENT

Hans Selye

Stress is a natural element of life. It is everywhere: we cannot avoid it, nor would it be desirable if we could. Though often a cause of disease, it is nonetheless essential for health. How stress affects us depends largely on how we handle it. For this reason, I have developed guidelines to help us use stress to our best advantage.

The concepts expressed here and the ensuing implications for individuals are supported by biologic research into the great laws that regulate the body's resistence to any type of injury and help maintain life in the face of all kinds of adversity. Though I have arrived at these concepts through my own research on stress, in formulating my recommendations I have also leaned heavily on previously known facts. Foremost among these are observations about the evolution of natural selfishness in human beings, their need for security and for the expression of whatever drives motivate them, and the frustrating choice between seeking immediate gratification and attaining long-range goals.

WHAT IS STRESS?

To start with, let us analyze the concept of biologic stress, which was my main inducement for formulating the view that the best motto of behavior is to act in such a way as to "*earn* thy neighbor's love."

15

Stress is associated with a great variety of essentially dissimilar problems, such as surgical trauma, burns, emotional arousal, mental or physical effort, fatigue, pain, fear, the need for concentration, the humiliation of frustration, the loss of blood, intoxication with drugs or environmental pollutants, or even with the kind of unexpected success that requires an individual to reformulate his lifestyle. While all these are quite different problems, they produce a stereotyped pattern of biochemical, functional, and structural changes essentially involved in coping with any type of increased demand upon vital activity, particularly adaptation to new situations.

All endogenous or exogenous agents that make such demands are called *stressors*. Distinguishing between their widely differing specific effects and the common biologic response that they elicit is the key to a proper understanding of biologic stress.

From the point of view of its stressor activity, it is even immaterial whether the agent or situation being faced is pleasant or unpleasant; all that counts is the intensity of the demand for readjustment or adaptation that it creates. Sorrow and joy are completely different; in fact, they are opposite each other, yet their stressor effect—the nonspecific demand for readjustment to a new situation—is the same.

At first it is difficult to see how such essentially different things as cold, heat, drugs, hormones, sorrow, and joy could provoke an identical biologic reaction. Nevertheless this is the case. It can now be demonstrated by highly objective, quantitative biochemical and morphologic parameters that certain reactions are totally nonspecific and common to all types of agents, whatever their superimposed specific effects may be. The most important step in the scientific analysis of stress phenomena is the conceptual distinction between the specific and the nonspecific consequences of any demand made on the body.

Stress is not the same as emotional arousal or nervous tension. It occurs in experimental animals even after total surgical deafferentation of the hypothalamus, which eliminates all neurogenic input. It can occur during anesthesia in people as well as in lower animals. It can occur even in plants, which have no nervous system. On the basis of these considerations I have recommended the following definition: *Stress is the nonspecific response of the body to any demand.*   First, we must understand nonspecificity, with regard to which the concept of stress is not without precedent. All machines, whether animate or inanimate, require energy for their activities, be these constructive or destructive. In fact, we shall see that biologic stress is closely linked to, though not identical with, energy utilization. This explains its apparently paradoxical, yet inseparable combination with the specific effects of the particular agent that creates a need for adaptive work. Any demand made on the body must be for some specific activity, and yet the demand is inseparably associated with nonspecific phenomena (that is, energy utilization), just as in the inanimate world specific demands made upon machines to increase or decrease room temperature, to produce light or sound, to accelerate or decrease motion are invariably dependent upon energy utilization.

In everyday life we must distinguish between two types of stress effects, namely *eustress* (from the Greek *eu* or good—as in euphony, euphoria, eulogy) and *distress* (from the Latin *dis* or bad—as in dissonance, disease, dissatisfaction), depending upon whether stress is associated with desirable or undesirable effects.

In view of these considerations it is also quite obvious that there cannot be *different types of stress*, although the effects of stressors are almost invariably different. There is no "specific stress"; this expression is a contradiction in terms. Such terms as emotional stress, surgical stress, flying stress, failure stress, cold stress, sleep deprivation stress, gravitational stress, swimming stress, social stress, and so on are acceptable only if we clearly understand that they are mere abbreviations for the stress produced by this or that factor.

What stress is not.   There are so many confusing and contradictory definitions of stress that it will be useful to add a few remarks stating clearly what it is not. *Stress is not merely nervous tension.* This fact must be emphasized, since most laymen and even many scientists tend to identify biological stress with nervous exhaustion or intense emotional arousal. Indeed, quite recently, Dr. John W. Mason, a former president of the American Psychosomatic Society and one of the most distinguished investigators of the psychologic and psychiatric aspects of biological stress, devoted an excellent essay to an analysis of my stress theory. He suggested that the common denominator of stressors may simply be activation of "the physiological apparatus involved in emotional or arousal reactions to threatening or unpleasant factors in the life situation as a whole" (1975a: 8). In man, with his highly developed nervous system, emotional stimuli are in fact the most common stressors—and, of course, these would be encountered most frequently in psychiatric patients. However, it must not be forgotten that stress reactions do occur in lower animals that have no nervous sytem, and even in plants.

Stress is not always the nonspecific result of damage.   It is immaterial whether a stressor is pleasant or unpleasant, its stressor effects depend merely on the intensity of the demand made upon the adaptive capacity of the body. Any kind of normal activity—a game of chess or even a passionate embrace—can produce considerable stress without causing harmful effects.

Stress is not something to be avoided.   In fact, it is evident from the definition given earlier in this chapter that it cannot be avoided. In common parlance, when we say someone is "under stress," we actually mean someone is under excessive stress or distress, just as the statement "he is running a temperature" refers to an abnormally high temperature, that is, fever. Some heat production is essential to life.

Similarly, no matter what you do or what happens to you, there arises a demand for the necessary energy required to maintain life, to resist aggression, and to adapt to constantly changing external influences. Even while fully relaxed or asleep, you are under some stress. Your heart must continue to pump blood, your intestines to digest that night's dinner, and your muscles to move your chest for respiration. Even your brain is not at rest while you are dreaming.

Complete freedom from stress is death.   It has already been mentioned that stress can be associated with pleasant or unpleasant experiences. The physiological stress level is lowest during indifference, but it *never* falls to zero, which would mean death. Pleasant as well as unpleasant emotional arousal is accompanied by an increase in physiological stress, but not necessarily distress. On the other hand, deprivation of stimuli and excessive stimulation are also accompanied by an increase in stress, sometimes to the point of distress.

Contrary to public opinion, we must not—and indeed cannot—avoid stress. However, we can meet it efficiently and enjoy it by learning more about its mechanism and adjusting our philosophy of life accordingly.

EVOLUTION OF THE STRESS CONCEPT

It must have occurred even to prehistoric man that there was something common in the loss of vigor and the feeling of exhaustion that overcame him after hard labor, prolonged exposure to cold or heat, loss of blood, agonizing fear, or any kind of disease. He may not have been conscious of the uniformity of his response to anything that was too much for him, but when the feeling came he must have realized that he had exceeded the limits of what he could reasonably handle; in other words, that "he had had it."

Man soon must have also discovered that whenever faced with a prolonged and strenuous task that he was not used to—be it swimming in cold water, lifting rocks, or going without food—he passes through three states: at first the experience is a hardship; then he becomes habituated; and finally he cannot stand it any longer. He did not think of this three-phase response as a general law regulating the behavior of living beings faced with an exacting task. The immediate necessities of finding food and shelter kept him too busy to meditate about such concepts as homeostasis, the maintenance of the *milieu intérieur*, or biologic stress. Yet the vague outlines of all this were there, ready to be analyzed and translated from intuitive feeling into the precise terms of science, a language that can be appraised by the intellect and tested by the critique of reason.

How could different agents produce the same result? Is there a nonspecific adaptive reaction to change as such? In 1926, as a second year medical student, I first came across the problem of a stereotyped response to any exacting task. The story of its elucidation has been told many times; although it is still unfinished, the salient points follow.

I began to wonder why patients suffering from the most diverse diseases have so many signs and symptoms in common. When people suffer from a severe loss of blood, an infectious disease, or advanced cancer, they lose appetite, muscular strength, and the ambition to accomplish anything. Usually the patients also lose weight, and even their facial expression betrays that they are ill. What is the scientific basis for what I thought of at the time as the "syndrome of just being sick"? Could the mechanism of this syndrome be analyzed by modern scientific techniques? Could it be reduced to its elements and be expressed in the precise terms of biochemistry, biophysics, and morphology?

In 1936 this problem presented itself again, now under conditions more suited to scientific analysis. At the time, I was working in the Biochemistry Department of McGill University, trying to find a new hormone in extracts of cattle ovaries. I injected the preparations into rats to see if their organs would show unpredictable changes that could not be attributed to any known hormone. Much to my satisfaction, even the first and most impure extracts caused a set of organ changes, characterized by enlargement and hyperactivity of the adrenal cortex, atrophy of the thymus gland and lymph nodes, and the appearance of gastrointestinal ulcers. The close interdependence of the three types of changes implied a definite syndrome. The alterations varied from slight to pronounced and depended only upon the amount of extract injected.

As we have now begun to run into some technical terms, let me explain them. The adrenals are endocrine glands situated just above each kidney and consist of two parts: an outer layer or cortex and an inner layer or medulla. The cortex produces hormones that I called *corticoids* (such as cortisone), whereas the medulla secretes adrenalin and related hormones. All play important roles in the response to stress. The thymus (a large lymphatic organ in the chest) and the lymph nodes (such as can be felt in the groin and armpits) form a single system usually referred to as the thymicolymphatic apparatus, which is mainly involved in immune defense reactions.

At first I ascribed all these changes to a new sex hormone in the extracts I was using. But soon I found that all toxic substances—crude extracts of kidney, spleen, or even a toxicant not derived from living tissue—produced the same syndrome. Animal experiments also showed that the same set of organ changes that were caused by the glandular extracts could be produced by cold, heat, infection, trauma, hemorrhage, nervous irritation, and many other stimuli.

General Adaptation Syndrome

Gradually, my classroom concept of the "syndrome of just being sick" came back to me. I realized that the reaction I had produced with my impure extracts and toxic drugs was an experimental replica of this syndrome. Adrenal enlargement, thymicolymphatic involution, and gastrointestinal ulcers were the omnipresent signs of damage to the body when under attack. The three changes thus became the first known objective indices of stress and the basis for the development of the general adaptation syndrome (GAS) or biological stress syndrome.

The characteristic changes constituting the *alarm reaction* (the first part of the GAS), however, evidently did not comprise the entire response. Upon continued exposure of an organism to any noxious agent capable of eliciting this reaction, a stage of adaptation or resistance ensues. In other words, no organism can be maintained continuously in a state of alarm. If the agent is so damaging that continued exposure becomes incompatible with life, the animal dies during the alarm reaction within the first hours or days. If it can survive, this initial reaction is necessarily followed by the *stage of resistance*. The manifestations of this second phase are quite different from—indeed, often the exact opposite of—those characterizing the alarm reaction. For example, during the alarm reaction, the cells of the adrenal cortex discharge their secretory granules into the bloodstream and thus become depleted of corticoid-containing lipid storage material. In the stage of resistance the cortex becomes particularly rich in secretory granules, whereas in the alarm reaction there is hemoconcentration, hypochloremia, and anabolism, with a return toward normal body weight.

Surprisingly, after still more exposure to the noxious agent, the acquired adaptation is lost again. The animal enters a third phase, the *stage of exhaustion*, which follows inexorably if the stressor is severe enough and is applied for a sufficient length of time.

This triphasic nature of the GAS gave us the first indication that the body's adaptability, or *adaptation energy*, is finite, since under constant stress, exhaustion eventually ensues. We still do not know precisely what is lost, except that it is not merely caloric energy, since food intake is normal during the stage of resistance. One would think that once adaptation has occurred and ample caloric energy is available, resistance should go on indefinitely. This is not the case. Just as any inanimate machine gradually wears out, the human machine sooner or later becomes the victim of constant wear and tear. These three stages are suggestive of childhood (with its characteristic low resistance and excessive responses to any kind of stimulus), adulthood (during which the body has adapted to most commonly encountered agents and resistance is increased), and senility (characterized by loss of adaptability and eventual exhaustion). Hence, we suspect some relationship between stress and aging—and therefore the need to use one's adaptation energy wisely, not to waste it but to use it generously for the enhancement of our lives.

Numerous additional biochemical and structural changes of previously unknown origin have been traced to nonspecific stress since 1936. Among these, special attention has been given to clinicians to changes in the chemical constituents of the body and to nervous reactions.

Considerable progress has also been made in the analysis of the hormonal mediation of stress reactions. It is now generally recognized that the emergency discharge of adrenalin represents only one aspect of the acute phase of the initial alarm reaction to stressors. At least equally important in the maintenance of homeostasis—the body's stability—is the hypothealamus-pituitary-adrenocortical axis, which probably participates in the development of many disease phenomena as well (Figure 2-1). This axis is a coordinated system consisting of the hypothalamus (a brain region at the base of the skull) that is connected to the pituitary gland (hypophysis), which regulates adrenocortical activity. The stressor excites the hypothalamus (through pathways not yet fully identified, but probably consisting of endorphin-like polypeptides) to produce a substance that stimulates the pituitary to discharge the hormone ACTH (*a*drenocortico*t*rophic *h*ormone) into the blood. ACTH, in turn, induces the external, cortical portion of the adrenal to secrete corticoids. These elicit thymus changes, such as atrophy of the lymph nodes, inhibition of inflammatory reactions, and production of sugar (a readily available source of energy). Another typical feature of the stress reaction is the development of peptic ulcers in the stomach and upper intestine (duodenum). Their production is facilitated by an increased level of corticoids in the blood, but the autonomic system also plays a role in eliciting ulcers.

As soon as any agent acts upon the body (thick outer frame of Figure 2-1), the resulting effect will depend upon three factors (broad vertical arrows pointing to the upper horizontal border of the frame). All agents possess both nonspecific stressor effects (solid part of arrow) and specific properties (interrupted part of arrow). The latter are variable and characteristic of each individual agent; they are inseparably attached to the stressor effect and invariably modify it. The other two heavy vertical arrows pointing toward the upper border of the frame represent exogenous and endogenous conditioning factors that largely determine the reactivity of the body. It is clear that since all stressors have some specific effects, they cannot elicit exactly the same response in all organs. Furthermore, even the same agent will act differently in different individuals, depending upon the internal and external conditioning factors that determine their reactivity.

Under the influence of conditioning factors, which can be internal (genetic predisposition, age, or sex) or external (treatment with certain hormones, drugs, or dietary factors), the GAS can be "derailed"

Figure 2-1.   Hypothalamus-Pituitary-Adrenocortical Axis.

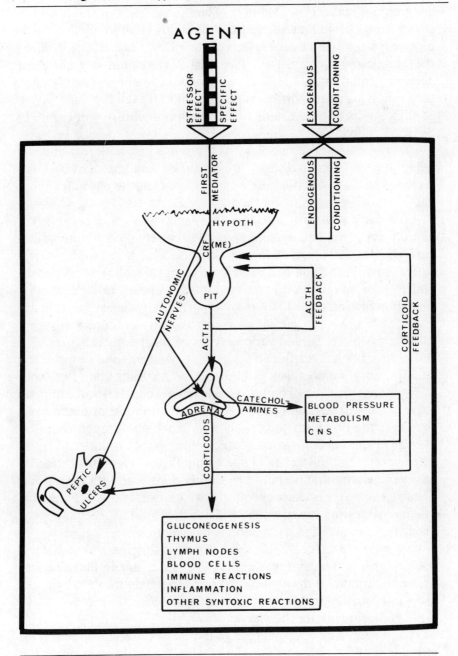

and a normally well-tolerated degree of stress can become pathogenic and cause diseases of adaptation. Then those parts of the body are selectively affected that are particularly sensitized both by these conditioning factors and by the effects of the eliciting agent. This explains the seemingly contradictory fact that: (1) qualitatively different agents of equal toxicity (or stressor potency) do not necessarily elicit the same syndrome in different people; and (2) even the same degree of stress, induced by the same agent, may produce different lesions in different individuals.

The concept of conditioning, in the sense just outlined, and the hypothesis that certain diseases are caused by derailments of the GAS mechanism, have clarified the relations between the physiology and pathology of stress in many fields.

As we have seen, any kind of activity sets our stress mechanism in motion, though it will depend upon the accidental conditioning factors whether the heart, kidney, gastrointestinal tract, or brain will suffer most. In the body, as in a chain, the weakest link breaks down under stress although all parts are equally exposed to it. Some diseases in which stress usually plays a particularly important role are high blood pressure, cardiac accidents, gastric or duodenal ulcers (the "stress ulcers"), and various types of mental disturbances.

The biochemical analysis of the stress syndrome showed that the equilibrium of an organism or homeostasis, depends upon two types of reactions: syntoxic (from the Greek *syn* or together) and catatoxic (from the Greek *cata* or against). Apparently, to resist different toxic stressors, the organism can regulate its reactions through chemical messengers and nervous stimuli which either pacify or incite to fight. The syntoxic stimuli act as tissue tranquilizers, creating a state of passive tolerance that permits a peaceful coexistence with aggressors. The catatoxic agents cause chemical changes mainly through the production of destructive enzymes, which actively attack the pathogen, usually by accelerating its metabolic degradation.

In the course of evolution the body probably learned to defend itself against all kinds of aggressors (whether arising in the organism or the environment) through mechanisms that help it tolerate the aggressor (syntoxic) or destroy it (catatoxic). Among the most effective syntoxic hormones are the *glucocorticoids*.

That it should be advantageous to inhibit or interfere with such essentially useful defense (catatoxic) reactions as inflammation or the rejection of foreign tissues is unexpected. The main purpose of inflammation is to localize irritants (for example, microbes) by putting a barricade of inflammatory tissue around them to prevent their spread into the blood, which could lead to sepsis and even death. The suppression of the basic defense reaction is an advantage, however, when a foreign agent is itself innocuous and causes trouble only by inciting inflammation. In such cases, inflammation itself is what we experience as a disease. Thus, in many patients who suffer from hay fever or extreme inflammatory swelling after an insect sting, suppression of defensive inflammation is essentially a cure, because the invading stressor agent is not in itself dangerous or likely to spread and kill. In the case of grafts, it may even be lifesaving.

In this connection we must distinguish between direct and indirect pathogens. Direct pathogens cause disease regardless of the body's reaction, whereas indirect pathogens cause damage only because they provide exaggerated defensive responses.

If a man accidentally exposes his hand to a strong acid, alkali, or boiling water, damage will occur regardless of his reactions, because these are all direct pathogens. They would damage even the hand of a dead man, who obviously could not put up any defense reactions. Most common inflammatory irritants, including allergens, are essentially indirect pathogens: they cause disease only through the purposeless defense reactions they stimulate.

Immunologic reactions, which lead to the destruction of microbes, grafts, and other foreign tissues, undoubtedly evolved as useful defensive mechanisms against potentially dangerous foreign materials. When the attack against the foreign agent is unnecessary or even harmful—as in the case of many allergens, heart transplants, and so on—man can improve upon the wisdom of Nature by suppressing this hostility. When the aggressor is dangerous, the defensive reaction should not be suppressed but, if possible, increased beyond the normal level. This can be achieved, for example, by catatoxic substances that carry the chemical message to the tissues to destroy the invaders even more vigorously than would normally be the case.

STRESS AND AGING

According to stress theory, there is an intimate relationship between aging and adaptability. Some of the hypotheses about this relation originated from observations in everyday life. If one looks at photographs of people who have been in concentration camps, one can see an expression resembling that of an old person. Apparently, the prolonged and severe demands, both physical and psychological, imposed within these places elicit the prematurely aged condition. Moreover, people who were old before entering the camps withstand the hardship far less than do the young.

There is also considerable experimental evidence to support the view that adaptability to changed environments declines with age. For example, it has been proven that age influences the adaptability of rats to cold and mechanical trauma, though the mechanisms responsible are not yet fully understood.

In the terms of medical science, aging appears to reflect all the stress that has acted upon the body during a lifetime. Each period of stress, especially if it results from frustrating, unsuccessful struggles, leaves some irreversible chemical scars, which gradually hamper successful adaptation, eventually making it impossible. These scars accumulate to constitute the signs of aging.

For a more detailed discussion of biologic stress, see *The Stress of Life* (Selye, 1976) and *Stress in Health and Disease* (Selye, 1976), upon which the foregoing summary is based.

Aging and Adaptability

Although it is difficult to prove that in animals every transient exposure to stress shortens the lifespan, several experiments have shown that this does occur when stressors are continuously applied. When animals, forced to undergo uninterrupted exposure to damaging agents (cold, forced muscular exercise, drugs), enter the stage of exhaustion, they become unusually sensitive to any additional damage. This nonspecific depletion of resistance is also characteristic of senile animals. The GAS resembles an accelerated, "telescope" version of a normal lifespan.

It has long been assumed that the phenomenon of aging must have a specific cause and that if we could only discover what this is, it would be possible to stop the clock and perhaps even to turn it back. Attractive as it may sound, there is no evidence to support this belief. As far as we know, our reserve of "adaptation energy" is an inherited, finite amount, which cannot be regenerated; and according to the stress theory of aging, the cause of its depletion is nonspecific.

One might view adaptation energy as the ability to remove the chemical scars of life. Each biologic process leads to some chemical changes whose end-products are usually soluble or subject to destruction and elimination. Whenever this form of restoration is rapid, and recovery complete, our tissues undergo little change—we remain "young." However, an infinitesimally small percentage of all biologic reaction-products are insoluble, or at least less rapidly removable than their rate of deposition; the so-called "aging pigments," calcium deposits, cross-linked proteins, and many other products of biologic activity belong to this class. Excessive accumulation suffices to block the machinery. It could induce the changes we consider characteristic of aging by the mere presence of ever-larger amounts of inert waste products and the consequent inability to produce indispensable vital ingredients at the proper rate. Such processes largely account for the progressive hardening of old blood vessels. As these lose their elasticity, the blood pressure must rise to maintain circulation through them despite their stiffness and narrowing. The resulting hypertension, in turn, causes a predisposition to cardiovascular accidents, particularly strokes.

Another mechanism that leads to the final exhaustion of adaptability during senility is the cumulative effects of continuously losing small bits of irreplaceable tissue (in the brain, heart, etc.), usually owing to injuries or minor vascular ruptures. In the young, these defects are readily compensated by the ample supply of remaining healthy tissue; but through a long life, our tissue reserves are used up, and eventually these losses are replaced by scar tissue, adding to the "chemical scars" of the piled-up metabolic debris.

The molecular basis for aging has been discussed by many workers. Alterations of DNA, protein synthesis, membranes, and RNA have been invoked as factors of early change.

In recent years, studies of cellular lifespan in cell culture have assumed great importance, and the concept that the number of divisions of somatic cells is limited has received ample confirmation. This idea would seem to represent a model of aging *in vitro*; nonetheless, we can assume that the relevant aging depend also on structural relationships among extracellular material, blood vessels and cells, relationships not contemplated in *in vitro* studies. In fact, the extracellular changes may be the primary ones.

The pattern and rate of aging may be modified by pharmacologic agents and by altering endocrine balance or environment. In experimental animals, retardation of growth by restriction of dietary intake prolongs their lifespan and decreases the incidence of many chronic diseases. On the other hand, a number of environmental stresses, especially ionizing radiation, shorten lifespan and increase the rate of aging (Trujillo et al., 1962).

The observation that animals exposed to ionizing radiation die at an early age, with a syndrome of premature senility, attracted considerable attention. It was proposed that aging is the consequence of the cumulative effect of mutations in somatic cells. These mutations take place in the genes and in their regulators so that errors of protein synthesis ensue. The evidence for this somatic mutation theory has been widely discussed in recent years, but it has not led to agreement; some investigators consider mutation merely as a factor accompanying the aging process.

Calciphylaxis

A direct attack upon the problems of aging has become possible through the concept of calciphylaxis, a biologic mechanism through which the body can selectively send calcium to certain organs or prevent the calcification of tissues, depending upon conditions (Selye, 1965a, 1968).

It has long been known that, in old people, there is some derangement in the distribution of calcium. The bones become brittle and lose calcium, while various soft tissues attract calcium salts and thereby become hardened. Thus calcium may accumulate in the arteries (arteriosclerosis), in the crystalline lens of the eye (cataract), around the joints, in tendons, and in many other tissues. Among the many factors that can interfere with calciphylactic responses is the exposure to systemic stress prior to sensitization. Local stress, on the other hand, may produce calcification under certain well-established conditions. If a rat is calciphylactically sensitized by the oral administration of a single dose of the vitamin-D derivative dihydrotachysterol (DHT), simultaneous application of trauma to various tissues will not cause any local calcinosis. But if a critical period (in this case, 24 hours) is allowed to elapse and then some hair is plucked out, this mild trauma produces massive petrification of the epilated region. If, after similar sensitization, the shoulder or hip joint is traumatized, for example by extreme rotary movements, periarticular calcium deposition results and motion in the affected joints becomes very limited and painful.

It has been assumed as a self-evident fact that calcium deposition must be secondary to some "dystrophic" tissue damage that characterizes aging. However, in the course of our work on calciphylaxis we noted that, in young animals, the induction of certain types of calcium metabolism disturbances may result in a variety of changes typical of aging, such as a generalized calcification of the arterial system, loss of elasticity and wrinkling of the skin, loss of hair, thymicolomphatic involution, atrophy of the skeletal muscles and the sex organs, dental anomalies, and sometimes cataracts, similar to those seen in senile animals.

This "progeria-like syndrome" (progeria is a rare congenital disease in which whole symptoms resemble many of the features of aging) can be prevented if the animals are previously given small doses of calciphylactic challengers, such as certain metallic salts. These observations suggest that the experimental "aging" of the progeria-like syndrome is not the cause but the consequence of a disturbance. However, we still cannot state with certainty whether this syndrome is fundamentally related to the process of aging, because we have no way of diagnosing premature aging except through its resemblance to natural senility.

Research

Even if there is little reason to suspect that an all-embracing concept of aging could ever be formulated, we might still succeed in clarifying the biochemical basis of the loss of adaptive capacity that sooner or later effects all living tissues and becomes increasingly less amenable to restoration either through rest or through the caloric energy of food. The most practical approach to this type of study appears to be the stimulation and acceleration of diverse vital activities by exposing experimental animals to constant stress; this enables us to determine objectively the effect of wear upon longevity as well as upon the structure and chemical composition of tissues, and provides an experimental model on which to test the influence of potentially protective agents.

It remains to be seen to what extent animal experiments will help us combat spontaneous aging, but there can be no doubt that really significant progress concerning the problems of the aged will not come by merely supplying them with food, shelter, and social games; it will come rather through basic research into the phenomenon of senescence.

To Die of Old Age

Although I have performed over 1,000 autopsies, I have never seen a person who died of old age. In fact, I do not think anyone has ever died of old age. To make this feasible would be the ideal accomplishment of medical research (if we discount the unlikely event of someone discovering how to regenerate adaptation energy). It would mean that all the organs of someone's body had given out simultaneously, merely by having been used too long. This is never the case. Death invariably occurs because one vital part has worn out too early in proportion to the rest of the body. Life, the biologic chain that holds our parts together, is only as strong as its weakest link. With this break our parts can no longer be held together as an organism. (Note that I did not say "our parts die," because this is not necessarily so. In tissue cultures, isolated cells of a human being can go on living for a long time after the body as a whole has died. It is only the complex organization of all our cells into a single individual that necessarily vanishes when one indispensable part breaks down.)

People, then, do not die of old age but rather of the diseases incident to it. It is undoubtedly true that life develops according to a definite program coded in the genes of the individual somatic cells; but at the same time, deterioration takes place in the body at an ever-increasing rate, and at present we cannot distinguish the pathologic conditions accompanying old age from the normal process of senescence. There is no authenticated record of anyone living longer than about 120 years. This figure may be regarded as the optimum lifespan that man might attain by living in perfect harmony with natural laws. There are many factors at work here, of course, and I am far from saying that just by following a certain lifestyle, one automatically lives that long. Yet there is little doubt that the average human lifetime is still capable of being considerably prolonged. I shall have more to say about this in the next section, where I discuss, in connection with the problems of retirement, a science-derived code of behavior that specifically addresses itself to the management of that fixed store of energy, "adaptability."

RETIREMENT

There is a great difference between biologic and chronologic age. Chronologic age is easy to understand and determine in quantitative terms. It merely represents the number of years that we have spent in this world. Biologic age is harder to measure but a much more important concept. There are many people who, at forty-five, have the mentality and motivation customarily associated with advanced age; they would prefer to and should retire from their jobs, provided they have the means to do so. Others still adore life at eighty and are perfectly able to act in a manner which makes them useful to themselves and to society; in this regard we need only think of the achievements in old age of Thomas Mann, Michelangelo, Pablo Picasso, Arturo Toscanini, and Bertrand Russell.

Successful activity, no matter how intense, leaves you with comparatively few aging scars. It causes stress, but little if any distress. On the contrary, it provides you with the exhilarating feeling of youthful strength, even at a very advanced age. Work wears you out mainly through the frustration of failure. Many of the most eminent among the hard workers in almost any field lived a long life. They overcame their inevitable frustrations by the great preponderance of success.

Of course, none of these men "worked" in the sense of work as something one has to do to earn a living but does not enjoy. Rather, one might say that they lived a life of constant leisure by always working at what they liked to do. It is true that few people belong to this category of the creative elite. In a way, such success in meeting the challenge of stress cannot serve as a basis for a general code of behavior. But you can live longer and more happily by working hard along modest lines if you have found the right activity and are reasonably successful at it.

Admittedly, age imposes constraints, but if we can adapt to new conditions as they present themselves, we can be content with our lives no matter what our age. Nature has endowed us with numerous compensatory mechanisms, and when one channel is blocked, we are able to develop another.

For activity and rest to be judiciously balanced, every person must analyze his own constitution. To lie motionless in bed all day is no relaxation for what I call the "racehorse" type; nor is conventional retirement a reward for someone who likes to work. With advancing years, most people require increasingly more rest, but the process of aging does not progress at the same speed in everybody. Many valuable people, who could still have given several years of useful work to society, have been made physically ill and prematurely senile by enforced retirement at an age when their requirements and abilities for activity were still high. This tragedy is so common that it has been given a name: *retirement disease.*

All work and no play is certainly harmful for anyone at any age; but then what is work and what is play? Fishing is hard work for the professional fisherman, but anyone else might go fishing to unwind. Play, in other words, can be as demanding and productive as you please. Its essential feature is that it serves as a diversion of our energies from usual channels, giving the latter a chance to recuperate.

Yet I recognize that not everyone is the racehorse type, and that retirement is often desirable and necessary. For example, failing health, or the desire to explore new areas of life in a serene and unhurried fashion, would be good reasons to retire. As with so many other things, how retirement affects us depends largely on how we take it and what we make of it. It is certainly a great change that, until we are adjusted to it, involves considerable stress. But it is not wholly beyond our control whether this stress does us good or bad. A very old man may be unhappy, bitter, and a burden to those close to him because of his constant complaints, or he may always be radiating optimism and anxious to be useful to his relatives and friends by sharing with them the fruits of his long experience.

Coming from one who never retired, advice on coping with this situation may seem out of place. But retirement is not very different from many other periods of our life to which we must adjust. The same principles of stress management apply. What follows is a brief outline of the results of my lifelong inquiry into the nature, mechanisms, and prophylaxis of stress—a code of behavior based on objective research and designed to minimize distress and maximize eustress, my term for the type of stress that is beneficial (see also Selye, 1974).

1. *Find your own natural predilections and stress level.* People differ with regard to the amount and kind of work they consider worth doing to meet the demands of daily life and to assure their future security and happiness. In this respect, all of us are influenced by hereditary predispositions and the expectations of our society. Only through planned self-analysis can what we really want be established. Many people suffer all their lives because they are too conservative to risk a radical change and break with traditions.

2. *Altruistic egoism*. The selfish hoarding of the goodwill, respect, esteem, support, and love of our neighbor is the most efficient way to give vent to our pent-up energy and create enjoyable, beautiful, or useful things.

3. *Earn thy neighbor's love*. This motto, unlike "Love thy neighbor as thyself," is compatible with man's biological structure, and although it is based on altruistic egoism, it could hardly be attacked as unethical. Who would blame those who want to assure their own homeostasis and happiness by accumulating the treasure of other people's benevolence toward them? Yet this makes them virtually unassailable, for nobody wants to attack and destroy those upon whom he depends.

Even those who accept the value of my code as a means of facing the adversities inflicted by psychological reactions often doubt that it can be applied to extreme situations—for instance, coping with incurable disease or advanced age. Yet on the basis of my own experience, I believe that the three maxims above can be just as useful in dealing with life's worst crises as in handling everyday problems.

Some may find helpful a condensation of my philosophy, which has guided me through stress, aging, and pseudo-retirement:

Fight for your highest attainable aim
But do not put up resistance in vain.

REFERENCES

Marx, J. 1974. "Aging Research: Pacemakers for Aging." *Science* 186: 1196–1197.

Mason, J.W. 1975a. "A Historical View of the Stress Field. Part I." *Journal of Human Stress* 1, no. 1: 6–12.

Mason, J.W. 1975b. "A Historical View of the Stress Field. Part II." Journal of Human Stress, no. 2: 22–36.

Selye, H. 1936. "A Syndrome Produced by Diverse Nocuous Agents." *Nature* 138: 32.

Selye, H. 1952. *The Story of the Adaptation Syndrome.* Montreal: Acta, Inc.

Selye, H. 1965a. "Calciphylaxis: the Key to Aging?" *Norden News* 40: 6.

Selye, H. H. 1965b. "Man after 65: Resource or Burden?" *Medical Opinion and Review* 1: 80.

Selye, H. 1966. "The Future in Aging Research." In Shock, *Perspectives in Experimental Gerontology,* Springfield, Ill.: Charles C. Thomas.

Seyle, H. 1968. "Calciphylaxis and Aging." *Archives of Otolaryngology* 88: 294.

Selye, H. 1974. *Stress Without Distress*. New York: Lippincott.

Selye, H. 1975. "Confusion and Controversy in the Stress Field." *Journal of Human Stress* 1, no. 2: 37–44.

Selye, H. 1976a. *Stress in Health and Disease*. Reading, Ma.: Butterworths.

Selye, H. 1976b. *The Stress of Life*. New York: McGraw-Hill.

Selye, H. 1976c. "Stress Without Distress." *Proceedings of Symposium on Society, Stress and Disease: Aging and Old Age*. Stockholm, June 14–19.

Selye, H. 1979. *The Stress of My Life*. New York: Van Nostrand Reinhold.

Selye, H., and B. Tuchweber. 1976. "Stress and Aging." *Proceedings of Symposium on Society, Stress and Disease: Aging and Old Age*. Stockholm, June 14–19.

Taché, J., and H. Selye. 1978. "On Stress and Coping Mechanisms." In *Stress and Anxiety*, Vol. 5, edited by C.D. Spielberger. Washington: Hemisphere Publishing Corporation.

Thomae, H. 1968. "Psychological and Social Aspects of Aging." *Gerontology* 1, (Spring): 43–55.

Thompson, G.B. 1973. "Work Versus Leisure Roles: An Investigation of Morale Among Employed and Retired Men." *Journal of Gerontology* 28: 339–344.

Trujillo, T.T.; J.F. Spalding; and W.H. Langham. 1962. "A Study of Radiation-Induced Aging: Response of Irradiated and Nonirradiated Mice to Cold Stress." *Radiation Research* 16: 144–150.

3 ORGANIZATIONAL STRESS AND COPING: A MODEL AND OVERVIEW

Randall S. Schuler

Job stress is of rapidly growing concern to organizational researchers and managers because of its cost to both the individual and the organization alike (Schuler, 1980a; McLean, 1979; Greenwood, 1978). Together with this concern is the tendency for many, and in some cases almost all, traditional organizational phenomena to be indentified as stressors. Job satisfaction and level of performance, in turn, are being viewed as symptoms or outcomes of stress. Nevertheless, not all aspects of organizations are stressors, although they have the potential to be so, nor are satisfaction and performance the only stress symptoms which should be of concern to researchers and practitioners.

Because stress can be so costly, researchers and management should focus their attention on the identification of potential environmental stressors in organizations and develop strategies by which individuals can most effectively manage or reduce their stress. This responsibility is not an easy one. The task can be facilitated, however, by offering a precise definition of stress in organizations. The

Portions of this chapter have been taken from two previous sources by the author, namely a chapter entitled "Integrative Transactional Process Model of Coping with Stress in Organizations," in *Human Stress and Cognition in Organizations: An Integrative Perspective,* edited by T.A. Beehr and R.S. Bhagat. (New York: Wiley, 1984) and a chapter with T.A. Beehr entitled "Current and Future Perspectives on Stress in Organizations," in *Personnel Management: New Perspectives,* edited by Rowland and Ferris. (Boston: Allyn & Bacon, 1982).

definition presented here is critical because it will specify those aspects of an organizational environment that actually function as stressors. It will also serve as a foundation upon which to construct a model of stress so that these environmental stressors can be integrated and thus more effectively dealt with by management and employee.

The purposes of this discussion, then, are to: (1) offer a definition of organizational stress; (2) present an integrative transactional process model of organizational stress that includes previous research and literature on the subject; (3) review the literature and research on what the major environmental stressors for individuals within an organizational setting are; (4) offer a definition of coping; and (5) present an integrative transactional process model of coping with stress.

WHAT IS ORGANIZATIONAL STRESS?

Based upon many earlier definitions of organizational stress and others not reviewed here (e.g., Cox, 1978; and McLean, 1979), stress is defined here as *a perceived dynamic state* involving uncertainty about *something important.* The dynamic state can be associated with opportunities, constraints, or demands (McGrath, 1976). States of opportunity are perceived by the individual as offering the potential fulfillment of important needs and values, while states of constraint block or prevent fulfillment of these needs and values. States of demand, such as noise, heat, and toxic chemicals, issue from the physical environment and influence important needs and values both perceptually and objectively (Schuler, 1980a; Beehr and Schuler, 1982).

This definition incorporates several important aspects of organizational stress:

1. Organizational stress can be positive (an opportunity) or negative (a constraint or demand). For example, a promotion can be perceived as a positive stress if the employee thinks that the promotion will lead to a valuable outcome but is unsure of succeeding. Negative stress occurs when an individual, realizing that a job is meaningless and cannot satisfy any important values, feels uncertain over a means of quitting.
2. Organizational stress results from a transaction between the environment (see Lazarus, 1978 for a discussion of the differences

between viewing the person-environment as a transaction as opposed to an interaction). The environment presents a set of dynamic conditions or potential stressors that can be perceived as opportunities, constraints, or demands. What is important to one person may not be important to another because each individual may have different needs and values. Resolution of stressful conditions, therefore, involves a high degree of uncertainty.

3. Organizational stress can be associated wtih physical as well as sociopsychological conditions. The stress associated with the physical conditions, however, is less perceptual than that associated with the sociopsychological conditions. Nevertheless, perceptions of certain physical conditions are extremely critical in the level of stress they may elicit; for example, spatial relationships and safety conditons.

4. Organizational stress is an additive concept across situations and over time: the larger the number of events perceived as stressful, the greater the stress experience (Theorell, 1978). Holmes and Rahe (1967) found that individuals with more severe illnesses had experienced more stressful events in the months preceding their illnesses than individuals with fewer severe illnesses. In addition to the importance of the accumulation of stressful events over time, their study also supported the notion that both positive events (e.g., getting a new job) and negative events (e.g., losing one's job) can be associated with stress. Making both these types of events stressful is the uncertainty, the importance, and the desire for resolution associated with them.

5. Organizational stress and the desire for resolution are precipitated by events that cause a disruption of homeostasis, either physiological or psychological. Demanding conditions in the environment disrupt physiological homeostasis, and the body involuntarily seeks to restore homeostasis. A classic explanation of stress, for example, maintains that under conditions of physical threat the body produces increased blood sugar, adrenaline, and noradrenaline to provide the individual with the energy necessary for a "flight or fight response" (Cannon, 1929). The physical activity of the flight or fight response then utilizes the stress-produced physiological responses, the body is restored to homeostasis and the physical threat is removed. Unfortunately, in cases of job constraint or opportunity associated with sociophysiological

stress conditions, the body also responds involuntarily with physiological reactions similar to those associated with physical stress conditions. However, it is less likely that the increased blood sugar, adrenaline, and noradrenaline will be utilized through any physical exertion to restore the sociopsychological disequilibrium caused by the situation of opportunity or constraint. If other strategies for dealing with the stress are not utilized, long-run wear and tear on the body will occur as the body fights to restore physiological homeostasis. Diseases of adaptation are often the result (Selye, 1956).

Thus, organizational stress is a perceived, dynamic state of uncertainty about something important to the individual. It can be both positive and negative. Most importantly, however, it is a dynamic condition most individuals seek to avoid, resolve, or take advantage of. Putting this definition into the context of a model of stress will elaborate each of these aspects of stress in organizations and place organizational stress coping strategies in perspective.

Integrative Transactional Process Model of Stress in Organizations

A model of stress in organizations is important not only because it provides an awareness of the existence of stressors and how they work, but also because it shows what the outcomes of stress are and how qualities of individuals influence their stress in organizations.

A transactional approach to stress indicates that the relationships revealed in the model are reciprocal rather than linear. An individual experiences stress from one's own perception of the environment as set against one's unique skills, needs, and characteristics. Thus, what is a stressor for one person may not be for another. An individual's response to the stress may alleviate the stress or provoke even more stress. It is therefore important to treat the components of the stress model as being multidirectional so that all the components can be viewed in terms of either cause or effect (Lazarus, 1978).

"Process" refers to what happens over time or across stressors. It is composed of two elements: (1) the actual interchange between the person and the environment (full of potential stressors), and (2) the person's responses over time to the stress experienced. Thus, stress is not just a dynamic situation of importance involving uncertainty, but one which evokes individual responses that occur over time. The model is "integrative" since it has been developed from the literature and research in several diverse areas, and because a study of stress requires an interdisciplinary approach.

The components of the transactional process model are the environmental stressors, individual characteristics and individual short-term, intermediate, and long-term responses. Responses are categorized into physiological, psychological, and behavioral. These components are illustrated in Figure 3-1.

Only the organizational stressors, the "causes" of stress, are discussed in this chapter. These, in turn, are the targets of organizational coping strategies as presented later in this chapter and in Chapters 4, 5, and 6.

Review of the Research on Organizational (Environmental) Stressors

Because several excellent reviews and compilations of the research on stress in organizations currently exist (Cooper and Marshall, 1976; Cox, 1978; Beehr and Newman, 1978; Caplan, Cobb, French, Van Harrison, and Pinneau, 1975; McLean, 1979; Shostak, 1980; Schuler, 1980a; and Van Sell, Brief, and Schuler, 1981), in this section we will review a limited body of research in order to highlight what has been done, with particular emphasis on the definition and conceptualization of stress in organizations. Research that has focused on organizational conditions associated with stress will be reviewed first. Stress research uniquely related to occupational groups will also be highlighted since it identifies an important body of research and concern.

The organizational (environmental) conditions most frequently identified and researched as stressors are: (1) role characteristics, (2) job qualities, (3) relationships at work, (4) organizational structure, and (5) physical qualities. As shown in Figure 3-1, however, there are several other environmental stressors. Those examined here, however, tend to be among the most commonly researched in the study of stress.

Role Characteristics.   Role characteristics have been one of the most widely investigated organizational conditions in stress research. Selected

Figure 3-1. Integrative Transactional Process Model of Stress in Organizations.

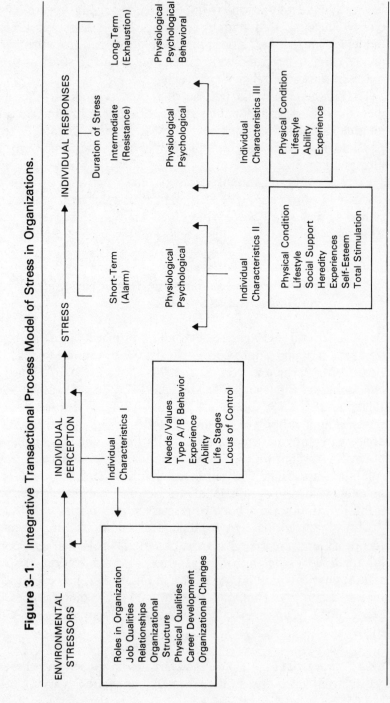

Source: Adapted from Schuler (1982).

role characteristics most frequently researched include role ambiguity, role conflict (person-role, inter sender, and intra sender), role overload (quantitative and qualititative), role underload (quantitative and qualitative), and role-status in congruency. Each of these role characteristics has been shown to be associated with stress (French and Caplan, 1973; Kahn et al., 1964; French, 1974). As suggested by Kahn et al. (1964) and French (1974), among others, some of these role characteristics, particularly conflict and ambiguity, tend to prevent an individual from attaining or completing a task. This prevention probably represents a constraint on an individual's need to achieve and be productive (Seashore, 1972). In addition to its relationship to an individual's need for achievement, role ambiguity also appears to be directly associated with an individual's need for certainty and predictability. It is perhaps because of this dual need relationship that role ambiguity often tends to be more highly related to stress than does role conflict. (See Van Sell, Brief, and Schuler, 1981 for a review of the literature on role conflict and ambiguity.)

Role overload and underload appear to be directly associated with an individual's need for stimulation (Levi, 1967, 1972). Typically, situations of overload are associated with too much stimulation, and situations of underload are associated with too little stimulation (Levi, 1972). Either situation is associated with high stress (French, 1974; Frankenhaueser and Gardell, 1976), although qualitative overload (e.g., responsibility for people rather than things) may be the more stressful (Wardwell, Hyman, and Bahnson, 1964; French and Caplan, 1973; French, 1974). Research suggests that role underload represents a constraint, while role overload represents a demand (Terryberry, 1968). Qualitative role overload is more stressful than quantitative overload because it involves people, thus increasing the importance of resolution.

Two important areas related to role characteristics in organizations are the mid-career crisis and the work-nonwork relationship. Although mid-career crisis is only one aspect of career development, the entire area of which could be investigated here, the mid-career aspect seems critical for individuals in organizations. The mid-career crisis, as defined here, represents any one of several conditions that occurs midway through an individual's career: overpromotion (the Peter Principle), underpromotion, status incongruence, lack of job security (obsolescence), and thwarted ambition (Cooper and Marshall, 1976). These conditions, in varying degrees, appear to be most directly related to an individual's needs for achievement, interpersonal recog-

nition, certainty, and security. Research certainly suggests the importance of those mid-career conditions associated with an individual's
stress (Erikson, Pugh, and Gunderson, 1972; Brook, 1973; and Kleiner
and Parker, 1963).

Occasionally related to the mid-career crisis is the work-nonwork
relationship. This relationship may include conflict between roles,
such as that faced by some career-oriented females (Hall, 1972; Hall
and Gordon, 1973), and conflict outside the organization, such as life
and family crises, the effects of which may influence the work role
(Pahl and Pahl, 1971; Dohrenwend and Dohrenwend, 1974; Gowler
and Legge, 1975). The needs of the individual that are most likely to be
influenced by these work-nonwork conditions are certainty, achievement, security, and interpersonal recognition and acceptance.

Job Qualities.   The job qualities commonly associated with stress are
work pace or control, and work underload and work overload (both
qualitative and quantitative). Although only limited research exists
regarding work underload, French and Caplan (1973) list at least nine
different psychological and physiological responses associated with
qualitative and quantitative overload: job dissatisfaction, job tension,
lowered self-esteem, threat, embarrassment, high cholesterol levels, increased heart rate, skin resistance, and increased smoking. Qualitative
overload is a condition wherein job duties appear to exceed an individual's abilities. This, of course, is compatible with our definition
of stress. Conversely, qualitative underload fails to supply sufficient
needs to the individual. Quantitative overload is a condition of having
too many job demands. With either overload condition, it becomes
uncertain whether or not an individual can meet all the responsibilities
the job demands. In either case of work underload, the individual may
desire that more needs be satisfied, but remains uncertain as to how to
correct the situation. Several needs appear to be left unsatisfied by
either underload or overload conditions, among the most common being a sense of challenge, meaningfulness, and self-control.

Work pace, particularly who or what controls the pace of the work,
is another important potential stressor in organizations. Machine pacing is a work condition in which the speed of operation and production
are controlled to some extent by a source other than the employee.
With employee pacing, the individual has control of the operations.
The effects of machine pacing can be severe. Frankenhaeuser and
Gardell (1976) reported that workers on machine-paced jobs felt ex-

haustion at the end of the shift and were unable to relax soon after work due to the increased levels of adrenaline secretion during working hours. Caplan et al. (1975) recorded that assembly line workers reported the highest level of severity of stress responses out of the twenty-three white- and blue-collar occupations studied.

Relationships at Work. Supervisors are often stressors for individuals in organizations. "Two major subjective stresses that blue-collarites associate with supervision involve the enervating pettiness of various work rules and the enervating nature of relentless pressure for more and more production" (Shostak, 1980: 49). In both cases, the worker is denied freedom of control and the need for recognition and acceptance as an individual. As a result, employees often try to bend or violate rules in order to regain some control of their work situation.

Relationships with co-workers have also been found to induce stress, especially when poor relations exist and lead to low trust, low supportiveness, low interest in listening to and trying to deal with problems that confront the organizational member (French and Caplan, 1973). Mistrust of co-workers has been found to be positively related to role ambiguity and inadequate communications which result in low job satisfaction and in feelings of a job-related threat to one's well-being (Kahn et al. 1964; French and Caplan, 1973; Buck, 1972). In addition, Kahn et al. (1964) reported that poor relations with one's subordinates were highly related to feelings of threat among colleagues and superiors.

Regarding relationships with clients, research on job burnout among human service professionals has identified several features of the relationship between service providers and their clients that contribute to stress. For example, the percentage of time a physician spent in direct contact with patients was directly related to the emotional exhaustion experienced by the physician (Maslach and Jackson, 1981). In many service occupations, the ability of the professional to respond successfully to clients' needs is limited by bureaucratic regulations and uncooperative clients. Recognition that success vis-à-vis the client is only partially under one's control can lead to a feeling of helplessness (Seligman, 1975). This, combined with strong feelings of personal responsibility for failures and infrequent feedback successes, makes service providers easy targets of job stress (Maslach and Jackson, 1982; Jackson and Maslach, 1982).

Organizational Structure.   Few aspects of the organizational structure have been examined in stress research. The two frequently studied aspects of structure include participation (centralization-decentralization), and occupational type or level in the organization. An individual's participation in the decisionmaking process, especially when these decisions bear on the employee's own work, should enhance the meaningfulness of the job and provide a sense of responsibility, autonomy, certainty, predictability, and a measure of ownership (French and Caplan, 1973; Schuler, 1980a). Similar relationships would exist whether the individual's participation is one-on-one with the manager or is with other group members such as found in the autonomous work groups (Susman, 1976). Because of the large number of needs related to participation, it is not surprising to find many studies discovering the benefits of participation in reducing stress (Buck, 1972; Kasl, 1973; Schuler, 1980b).

Physical Qualities.   Physical qualities of an organization refer to the physical conditions that surround the individual: the presence of pathogenic agents, such as poisons and chemicals; noise; space; privacy; and visibility. Each of these physical conditions in the workplace is associated with an individual's needs, whether those needs operate for a minimum of biological functioning, such as physical safety, or for purposes of autonomy, ownership, and interpersonal needs (Manning, 1965; Selye, 1976; Sundstrom, 1977; Rousseau, 1978; Oldham and Brass, 1979). The results of research on the significance of privacy and crowding generally suggest that individuals value some degree of privacy in the workplace, as is found in traditional office layouts rather than the open plan of some office layouts (Sundstrom, 1977; Oldham and Brass, 1979). The need for privacy, personal ownership, and control over one's environment appear to play an important role in successful job performance.

Occupations and Stress

HELP WANTED: World's busiest airport seeks radar jockies for unusually stimulating, high-intensity environment. Must be able to direct at least 12 aircraft at one time and make instant decisions affecting the safety of thousands. No degree required, but prior experience as traffic cop, seeing-eye dog, or God helpful. Severe stress will jeopardize sanity and result in early termination from job, but employer will absorb cost of medical and psychiatric care. (*Psychology Today,* February 1977, p. 71)

Although this ad never appeared, it does illustrate one of the most stressful occupations—air-traffic control. The stressors of this occupation are grueling pace (beyond the immediate control of the controller), split-second decisions (time pressure), and the constant threat of mid-air collisions. In addition, there are numerous conflicts between the employers and the Federal Aviation Administration. The results are predictable: ulcers, high blood pressure, arthritis, colitis, headaches, allergies, upset stomachs, alcoholism, depression, and acute anxiety (Martindale, 1977).

"Stress in the work lives of America's 35 million workers [blue collar] appears to have three major sources: anxiety over joblessness; anxiety over workplace accidents or work-linked illnesses and anxiety over workrole insults to one's adulthood" (Shostak, 1980: 12). And there is the added stress of wanting to do a job one way but being told to do it another way. "For years and years, it was most important to the company that we give excellent service. But it's more important now to get it finished than to get it right, and the guy who considers himself a real craftsman can no longer be a craftman" (*Business Week,* June 25, 1979, p. 96).

Stress for white collar workers (especially managers) has been associated with decisionmaking and its consequences, responsibility for people, heavy demands for cooperation between superiors and subordinates, time pressure, fear of failure, fear of poor performance, mid-career crisis from lack of promotion, and management of a workforce with rapidly changing values (McLean, 1979; Warshaw, 1980; Wahlund and Nerell, 1978; Cooper, 1979).

Although research on occupational groups indicates that different stressors are more important in the stress of one group than in another, perhaps one of the most important conclusions is that the blue-collar workers do not necessarily suffer from fewer stress responses than white-collar workers. If anything, some white-collar workers probably suffer from less stress, or at least enjoy it more, than some blue-collar workers. Nevertheless, both groups are concerned with dealing with the stress they do have; that is, with coping.

WHAT IS COPING?

According to Lazarus and Launier (1978: 293), coping is defined as "efforts, both action-oriented and intrapsychic, to manage (i.e., to master, tolerate, reduce and minimize) environmental and internal demands and conflicts among them which tax or exceed a person's resources." Based on this definition, Lazarus and his associates (see Folkman, Schaefer, and Lazarus, 1979) describe four strategies of coping (all essentially process-oriented cognitive strategies): (1) information search; (2) direct action; (3) intrapsychic modes; and (4) inhibition of action. These strategies are used either to mediate person-environment relationships or to control selectively individual stress responses in a palliative mode. For example, an individual may take direct action and talk to the supervisor who is sending ambiguous messages. Or the individual may decide not to take direct action and avoid seeing the supervisor as much as possible. The strategy selected and its use may be a function of individual differences such as cognitive complexity, problem-solving and decision-making skills, experience, personality, and total stress.

Pearlin and Schooler (1978) state that coping refers to behavior that protects people from being psychologically harmed by problematic social experience. Coping protects by (1) eliminating or modifying stressors; (2) perceptually controlling the meaning of the stress experience, and thus neutralizing its problematic character; or (3) keeping emotional consequences within manageable bounds. McGrath (1970) defines coping as an array of covert and overt behavior patterns by which the organism can actively prevent, alleviate, or respond to stress-inducing circumstances.

Drawing upon these definitions, coping is defined here as a process of analysis and evaluation to decide how to protect oneself against the adverse effects of any stressor and its associated negative outcomes, and at the same time take advantage of its positive outcomes. This definition has several important aspects.

1.   Coping is an intentional, cognitive act of analyzing the perceived qualities or conditions in the environment that are associated with a stressful experience. In essence, this is Lazarus's primary appraisal process during which time the individual asks, "What is it?"; Does it offer harm, threat, or benefit?"; and "Is it important?" Thus an individual may experience stress without really having thoroughly evaluated or analyzed the stressor, that is, its associated uncertainty and importance. In coping, however, it is necessary that the individual begins this analysis and evaluation explicitly or what amounts to problem-solving and decisionmaking.

2.   The challenge and effort involved in this process of analysis and evaluation are determined in part by the "structural ambiguity" of the situation, that is, the degree to which the stressor is identified, uncertainty over the outcomes, and its importance (Shalit,

1977). Clearly and correctly identifying these characteristics become important in determining how effective a selected coping strategy will be. As structural ambiguity increases, coping effectiveness is influenced by the level of an individual's cognitive complexity in dealing with complex situations (for a fuller discussion of this relationship see Driver and Streufert, 1969; Hamburg and Adams, 1967; and Lazarus, 1966). The greater an individual's cognitive complexity, the easier it is for the individual to differentiate a complex situation and then integrate the appropriate information for effective coping. Increased cognitive complexity facilitates effective analysis, problem-solving, and decisionmaking.

3. Stress can be associated with uncertain positive or negative outcomes as long as they are important to the individual. It is with regard to negative outcomes that an individual copes in order to protect. It is with stressful situations having positive outcomes that an individual engages in coping to take advantage. But the process of coping applies in either case.

4. Coping strategies are actions based on an analysis and evaluation of the stressor, with particular attention paid to the importance and uncertainty associated with it. The strategy selected should be influenced by an analysis and evaluation of the personal and environmental resources and constraints in addition to personal values and needs. Strategy selection should also reflect the immediate and future costs and benefits. For example, some types of coping strategies may reduce negative physiological consequences (see Gal and Lazarus, 1975 for a review of studies indicating these findings). An individual may find leaving a stressful or demanding job more costly than the potential benefits associated with a new job. An important aspect of the strategy selection process is an evaluation of the potential effectiveness of the various strategies that can be used. Only by incorporating this range of possibilities can the true costs and benefits of strategies be estimated.

5. Costs and benefits of coping strategies imply criteria upon which to evaluate the effectiveness of strategies. Criteria may include: (a) physiological and psychological well-being (Pearlin and Schooler, 1978); (b) success in altering the source of stress; (c) success in attaining the opportunity associated with a stress condition; (d) success in removing the condition associated with a constraint, (i.e., gaining the ability to anticipate stress conditions so as to reduce their potential adverse effects); (e) gaining

the skills and the ability needed to analyze and evaluate stress situations in order to develop appropriate strategies more quickly; (f) the time it takes to develop an effective strategy; (g) the number of iterations it takes in developing, implementing, and evaluating strategies to find one that is acceptable; (h) the impact of a current strategy selection on future coping strategy selections; and (i) the extent to which valid information is obtained and processed in the analysis and evaluation of a stressful condition. (For a thorough review of possible strategy analysis and evaluation based on the functions of coping see Haan, 1977; Menninger, 1963; Vaillant, 1971; Janis and Mann, 1977; Cohen and Lazarus, 1973; White, 1974; Mechanic, 1962; Burke and Weir, 1980; and Folkman and Lazarus, 1980).

6. This definition of coping provision has been made for a typology of coping strategies. Since developing a typology is integral to coping strategy development and selection, this aspect of coping is discussed more extensively after the presentation of the coping model.

7. Coping, like stress, is highly dependent on the individual's perception of the environment and, as with stress, involves a transaction with that environment. Coping is thus a process of gathering and evaluating information, generating alternatives, weighing (through cost-benefit analysis) and selecting alternatives, implementing these alternatives (strategies), evaluating the effectiveness of the strategy selected and then, if necessary, considering additional strategies. Coping therefore requires an analysis of one's own needs and values as much as an analysis of the situation. In this transaction between the person and environment both may change, perceptually if not objectively.

8. Finally, this definition of coping is tied closely to the definition and model of stress. It is also integrated with the work that has been done in several diverse areas of research, such as medicine, psychology, nutrition, and organizational behavior. By recognizing its integrative nature the coping process may be better understood and more effective coping strategies prescribed (Burke and Weir, 1980.)

Integrative Transactional Process Model of Coping in Organizations

Based upon the above definition of coping and the definition and model of stress in organizations, the following model of coping is presented. As shown in Figure 3-2, several major aspects constitute the process of coping in organizations: (1) the coping trigger; (2) primary appraisal; (3) secondary appraisal; (4) strategy development and selection; (5) strategy implementation; (6) strategy evaluation; and (7) feedback.

Coping Trigger. An individual begins to engage in coping once a situation is perceived as stressful and a response is felt. Almost instantaneously with the perception of stress, the individual experiences a short-term physiological response (for discussion of this response see Mason, 1975; Selye, 1956). Although the individual may not have conspicuously and methodically interpreted the environmental stressor in terms of uncertainty and importance (Schuler, 1980a; 1982), the short-term physiological response is experienced nonetheless. Because of the discomfort associated with this physiological response the body seeks to restore itself to its natural state of homeostasis (Cannon, 1929). This physical discomfort triggers the individual to find a solution to the stressful condition, and the search for resolution of this condition begins (Figure 3-2).

Primary Appraisal. This aspect involves generating answers to three basic questions: (1) What is the relevant stressor? (2) Where is the uncertainty?, and (3) Is it really important? These questions are essentially those which form part of Lazarus's primary appraisal process. For Lazarus this process initiates the coping process. For the model of coping presented here, however, this aspect of coping initiates a systematic evaluation of a stress event that has already occurred and for which the individual has experienced a short-term physiological or psychological response as shown in Figure 3-1.

These three questions of the primary appraisal process directly link coping with the definition of stress presented above. To the first question, the individual seeks to locate which of the seven potential stressors identified in Figure 3-1 might be associated with the individual's discomfort. The degree of uncertainty associated with the stressor is then determined. The individual tries to determine if the uncertainty is associated with the effort-performance relationship or with the performance-outcome relationship. An individual's success in accurately perceiving and determining the degree, as well as the type, of uncertainty can be critical in the development of coping strategies. An individual's ability to perceive the relevant information in

Figure 3-2. Individual Cognitive Qualities (Skills).

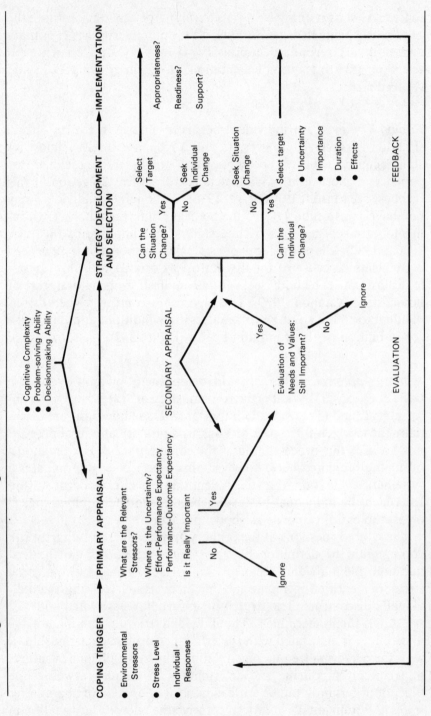

Source: Adapted from Schuler (1982).

the environment is therefore important in the coping model, together with individual cognitive qualities of cognitive complexity, and problem-solving and decisionmaking ability.

If the cause of discomfort is judged to be unimportant the coping process is terminated. If the answer to the final question in the primary appraisal is "yes" and the stressful condition is deemed to be really important, then the secondary appraisal process begins.

Secondary Appraisal. To begin an analysis of why the stressful situation is significant requires that the individual recognize the needs and values that have been identified as associated with stress (Schuler, 1980a). This analysis is critical because it not only attempts to determine if a situation is really important, but also, why it is important. The individual must determine the needs and values associated with this situation. Such an identification is important in the development of coping strategies and their relative appropriateness.

After the question of "why" has been addressed, the question of "Is it still important?" must be answered. After this second query the answer may be negative, and the coping process is terminated. But if the response is affirmative, the final question in the secondary appraisal process must be asked: "What can or should be changed, the situation or the individual?" The answer to this question initiates the strategy development process. It should be noted that during the primary and secondary appraisal processes, the individual may wish to involve other individuals in the analysis of the environment and the individual's needs and values. For example, an employee may perceive that the supervisor is sending ambiguous messages and so must decide what strategy to take to deal with this situation. Although a direct-action strategy of talking with the supervisor may appear reasonable, colleagues with previous experience may know that the supervisor would perceive this action as a direct threat to the supervisor's ability to communicate. Consequently, if the individual asks colleagues their advice on what to do, the path of direct action may not be selected. Others can be useful in providing much-needed information to make coping as effective as possible.

Strategy Development and Selection. This aspect of coping is what Lazarus refers to as secondary appraisal. His secondary appraisal essentially answers the question, "What should I do now?" The answer to this is critical in developing ways to deal with the stressful situation. Although many responses to this question have already been identified, the purpose here is to offer a typology of the strategies that can be considered in attempts to reduce the stressfulness of situations for individuals. This typology is presented after discussing strategy implementation, strategy evaluation, and feedback.

Strategy Implementation.   Strategy implementation should consider the cost and benefit of alternative strategies, readiness for change, and support. Analysis of the costs versus benefits of alternative coping strategies should specify what is needed to implement each strategy and what is to be gained from each strategy. Essentially this is a utility analysis as suggested by Landy, Farr, and Jacobs (1982). Implementation must include an analysis of the readiness for change and what it will take for the appropriate level of readiness to occur. For example, an individual may decide that the best way to deal with the stress of being unemployed is by getting a job and that this requires further education. Yet the individual is not ready to go back to school. Deciding to return to school, though potentially most effective over the long run, may prove to be ineffective as long as the individual is not motivated to learn. If, for example, the individual believes that getting a degree in accounting is the best thing to do but not at this time, it is still possible to determine the things that are necessary before readiness is established. In this case, the individual may begin by entering into an independent reading program in accounting to see how it feels to read and study again.

In addition to readiness, support conditions must be established. If group support is necessary to implement a strategy for an individual, the group must be available and ready. If an individual decides to lose weight as a way of dealing with social rejection, success may be made much easier by joining a weight-reducing club. The organization can be generally helpful in assisting its employees in coping with stress by building and maintaining social support groups (House, 1981). The unconditional support provided by these groups serves to increase an individual's self-esteem and self-confidence, both of which can reduce the stressfulness of situations and increase the effectiveness of the individual's coping efforts.

If an organization can assist individuals in coping with stress, so it can also prove to be a roadblock. It may, for example, prevent the formation of social support groups, prohibit its employees from taking continuing education courses on company time, or it may not provide tuition reimbursement assistance.

Strategy Evaluation. After the chosen strategy has been implemented, its effects must be evaluated. This can be done at the organizational, group, and individual levels. Currently, evaluation of coping strategies is rare at best (Newman and Beehr, 1979). Evaluation, however, is critical in order to determine if opportunities have been utilized and constraints successfully removed.

Criteria for evaluating coping strategies include the three classes of outcomes of stress shown in Figure 3-1: physiological, psychological, and behavioral. Since these three classes of outcomes are so diverse, their use requires evaluating coping effectiveness along several methodological lines (see McGrath, 1976; Burke and Weir, 1980). Physiological outcomes require medical methodologies such as measures of heart rate, blood pressure, catecholamines, and cholesterol. Psychological outcomes require methodologies such as interviews and questionnaires, while behavioral outcomes require industrial engineering and personnel methodologies in order to measure employee performance, safety, absenteeism, and turnover.

Extensive evaluation would, consequently, require the efforts of a team of researchers. Most individuals and organizations, however, would be likely to use fewer than all three classes of outcomes. Individuals, for example, may base the success of their coping efforts on how well they feel psychologically. Organizations may attempt to evaluate their efforts to help employees cope by examining the rate of absenteeism. Although there is nothing inherently wrong with evaluations this restricted, the real effects of a coping strategy may be understated or result in a strategy being evaluated as unsuccessful. Since such results would likely have a serious impact on the future use of a coping strategy, evaluation using all three sets of outcomes should be done whenever possible.

A final consideration in strategy evaluation is determining the appropriate time to gather the three classes of outcomes. As illustrated in Figure 3-1, it is probable that the effects of a coping strategy will occur over time with some physiological and psychological effects occuring before some behavioral effects. Employees are likely to become dissatisfied with their jobs before deciding to quit. Similarly employees are likely to experience tension and anxiety before having ulcers. Although these and other relationships seem plausible, little evidence exists as to their order of occurrence. However, because an understanding of their relationships appears critical to an evaluation of any coping strategy, extensive research in this area is warranted.

Feedback. Completion of the strategy evaluation stage results in feedback to the individual, group, or organization. Since evaluation occurs over time, so will feedback of the results. For purposes of rigorously evaluating the effectiveness of coping strategies, evaluation and feedback should be done formally by the individual and the organization, but individuals can provide their own informal evaluation.

Individuals are perhaps best able to make informal judgments about whether they have coped successfully, especially when using psychological criteria such as job satisfaction, esteem, and involvement. They may, however, be less able to make informal judgments regarding physiological criteria such as blood pressure, and may even be inappropriate sources of judgments concerning the performance level of a unit in the organziation or even their own performance. Consequently, formal evaluation by others is appropriate and necessary. This formal, outside evaluation can then be made available to the individual or the organization.

Feedback serves the individual and the organization by providing information, especially over time, about the effectiveness and efficiency of various coping strategies. This, of course, is useful for dealing with future stress episodes, and can assist the individual or organization in determining the utility of alternative coping strategies. When feedback is provided, it is important that certain facts be established: for example, the individuals who were involved, the strategy that was used, the conditions under which the strategy was implemented, and the history of coping. This feedback information enhances future coping strategies undertaken by the individual alone or conducted by the organization for its employees.

Feedback to the individual, whether based upon informal or formal evaluation, can be critical to an individual's self-esteem. To the extent the strategy was effective, the individual's self-esteem will be positively influenced. This, in turn, may serve to enhance the individual's problem-solving and decisionmaking skills, and enable the individual to be even more effective in dealing with stress in the future.

Now that the transactional process coping model has been considered, it is important to develop a typology of the strategies that can be used to cope with stress.

Typology of Coping Strategies

The typology begins with an analysis of the situation and the individual. The critical questions here are: (1) Will the situation be changed or modified, and if so, how? and (2) How can the individual manage or change? As a consequence of these questions, a typology consisting of four categories can be used to classify coping strategies. These categories are shown in Table 3–1.

Since we are specifically addressing coping strategies for stress in organizations, the typology is based upon either the organization or aspects of it changing, or the individual managing or changing. Only a few individuals in an organization may be perceiving stress, due perhaps to unique on-the-job conditions, hereditary characteristics, or off-the-job stress conditions (Bhagat, in press). Organizationally-based coping strategies may then be inappropriate, and it is likely that aspects of the organization will not be changed. Strategies dealing with the stress in this example must therefore focus on the individual either managing or changing. Note, however, that individuals need not develop strategies on their own. The organization, perhaps through the personnel department, may assist the employee in developing successful coping strategies (Beehr and Schuler, 1982).

In circumstances where many individuals are experiencing stress and exhibiting its symptoms, changing the organization is appropriate. It is also likely to be much more effective if the organization were to change (and thus reduce the negative symptoms of stress such as absenteeism or low performance), than to rely on each individual to develop effective coping strategies. Based upon the major consideration of the number of people who are experiencing stress in the organization, either the organization or the individual will be the primary focus of implementing coping strategies. If it is decided that many individuals are experiencing stress, the organization should change; if the stress experience applies to only a few individuals, it is the individuals who should change.

The Organization.   If the organization is to be changed, one must ascertain the most effective strategy. The choice will depend upon the particular stressor. As Hall (1972) indicates, several strategies may be taken to deal with just one stressor, but some are likely to be more effective than others. Thus information is needed on both the stressor and the availability and efficacy of strategies related to that stressor.

Table 3-1. Typology of Coping Strategies and Targets.

Situational (Organizational)		Individual	
Targets	Reduce Uncertainty	Reduce Importance	Reduce Effects
Roles in organization	Experience	Denial	Dietary
Job qualities	Training	Avoidance	Exercise
Relationships	Education	Withdrawal	Meditation
Organizational structure	Colleague interaction	Projection	Social support
Physical qualities	Confrontation		groups
Career development			
Organizational change			

There are seven major aspects of organizations, previously identified as potential environmental stressors, that may be changed: organizational structure, relationships, roles, change processes, physical environment, career development, and intrinsic job qualities (see Cooper and Marshall, 1976; and Beehr and Schuler, 1982 for a fuller discussion of all of these).

Within each of these seven aspects there are several specific conditions generally associated with stress. Space prohibits a full elaboration of each aspect, but a discussion of one will illustrate the complexity involved. Within the organizational structure there are six conditions typically associated with stress:

1. Lack of participation
2. No sense of belonging
3. Poor communications
4. Restrictions on behavior
5. Lack of opportunity for advancement
6. Inequity in pay and performance evaluation

For discussions of these conditions see Cooper and Marshall (1976); Coch and French (1948); French and Caplan (1973); Cameron (1971); McLean (1979); Drabek and Haas (1969); Jacobson (1972); and Galbraith (1977). Based on these six conditions one or several coping strategies could be used to reduce or eliminate the stress associated with them. These strategies include:

1. Clarification of policies regarding transfer and promotion
2. Decentralization and increased participation
3. Change in the selection and placement policies
4. Change in the communication procedures and networks in the organization
5. Change in the reward system
6. Utilization of training and development programs
7. Clarification of the performance evaluation system
8. Development and utilization of permanent and temporary work groups
9. Change in shift patterns and job rotation policies

These strategies and their relation to the six organizational structure conditions are extensively covered by Brief, et al. (1981). The same level of detail for the other six organization aspects is provided in the same source. The reason for the potential efficacy of the strategies is that (1) they reduce the uncertainty perceived by individuals in the organization resulting from the organizational stressors; and (2) they are the most appropriate strategy for the stress identified in the organization. The appropriateness of these strategies initially depends on correctly answering the first questions in the primary appraisal: "What is the relevant stressor?" and "Where is the uncertainty?" If this appraisal indicates that the organizational structure is really the stressor, further analysis should be performed to determine which specific structure condition is the stressor. The choice may then be made from among the possible alternative strategies listed above (1-9).

This discussion suggests that there is one best strategy: simply find the source of the stress and pick the coping strategy that fits that source. This, however, would be premature for several reasons. In actuality, individuals often experience stress from several sources. The stressors are generally highly interdependent—dealing successfully with only one is almost impossible. Several need to be dealt with concurrently. Furthermore, there are probably several strategies for each stressor, not just one per condition of each stressor as implied in the above discussion. Each of these several strategies is also potentially effective. The contingencies that determine effectiveness, however, remain to be identified.

The Individual. If a rather limited number of individuals are identified as being under stress, having the individual change or manage the stress may be more appropriate. There are three major sets of strategies. One set is aimed at the uncertainty associated with the stressful condition. Strategies to reduce uncertainties include additional experience, training, and education. Assistance from individuals who have information related to the stressful condition can also be an effective strategy to reduce the uncertainty. In essence these strategies represent ways to gain control over the situation so that fewer uncertain situations result (Thompson, 1981). For example, if an individual is experiencing stress over the uncertainty of not knowing how to perform a task, appropriate training can eliminate this uncertainty. Or if an individual is uncertain about the appropriate behavior in an organization, interaction among colleagues can provide information that enables the individual to define the appropriate role. The sooner this action is taken, the shorter the duration of the experienced stress and its effects. The duration of the stress can also be reduced by minimizing the importance of the situation.

When it is not feasible or appropriate for the employee to change in order to reduce the uncertainty of the situation, the individual can engage in strategies that reduce the importance of the situation and diminish the impact of the effects of stress. These strategies are also referred to as palliative strategies (Lazarus, 1978).

Reducing the importance of stress can involve denial, avoidance, withdrawal, and projection (Folkman, Schaefer, and Lazarus, 1979). Strategies may include taking advantage of the main or buffering effects of social support groups (House and Wells, 1978), dietary changes, physical exercise, meditation (Frew, 1977), feedback, and muscle relaxation exercises (Benson, Beary, and Carroll, 1974).

With so many strategies available, the question arises, "Which strategy will be selected?" The choice depends on several factors: (1) the potential and perceived costs and benefits of each strategy; (2) environmental constraints or support; (3) individual experience; and (4) individual attributes. The potential costs and benefits of a strategy can be determined by an individual in many ways. Appropriateness depends upon the situation. If the individual is experiencing stress because of uncertainty over how to perform a job, which, if performed well, can lead to a promotion, the individual can determine the costs (in dollars and time) of receiving the necessary training, and then judge the benefits (in dollars and self-satisfaction) of knowing how to do the job, and thus earn the promotion. The organizational environment may help determine the strategy chosen by the support, or lack of support, that it provides. If, for example, the organization provides tuition reimbursement to individuals for taking training or education classes, individuals may find (through cost/benefit analysis) that training is an attractive coping strategy.

Individual experiences are also likely to influence strategy selection. If an employee has previously and successfully coped with role ambiguity by talking to a supervisor, the worker is likely to do the same thing when experiencing this form of stress again. If an individual has experienced failure with a particular strategy, it is likely that strategy will be avoided in the future.

Individual attributes likely to influence strategy selection include problem-solving and decisionmaking skills, cognitive complexity, self-esteem, Type A personality, and an individual's total skills. There are individual differences in problem-solving and decisionmaking skills. These differences are, in turn, influenced by an individual's level of cognitive complexity (Driver and Streufert, 1969; Hamburg and Adams, 1967; Milburn, 1981). Individuals who rank high in these skills are more likely to diagnose and analyze stressful conditions more effectively than individuals who do not. The former are also more likely to select effective coping strategies.

Individuals with high self-esteem are likely to be more confident and willing to engage in direct confrontation to seek information to reduce uncertainty than individuals with low self-esteem. Those with low self-esteem are also likely to have a low sense of personal efficacy and consequently withdraw from stressful situations. They may do this even after correctly diagnosing the situation and realizing that direct confrontation is better.

An individual's current level of stress may also have an impact on the selection of strategies. As shown by Anderson (1976), problem-solving activities (those which seek to incorporate more information and decisionmaking) are more likely to be involved at low and moderate levels of stress. At higher levels of stress, emotional activities displace problem-solving activities. It is important to keep in mind that cognitive processes pertaining to coping with stress of long-term duration are different from those pertaining to coping with stress with short-term duration (Weick, 1979; Doob, 1971). The theory of Abramson, Seligman, and Teasdale (1978) concerning learned helplessness can be tied into our notion of duration of some stressful events. Stressful events requiring long-term and repeated coping and adaptive resources may lead a person to experience lack of control over the event and the environment because success seems to be elusive. Such lack of control over important outcomes could develop into depression (Abramson, Seligman, and Teasdale, 1978). In turn, this depression is likely to result in a withdrawal from active coping and a reduced sense of personal efficacy. The phenomenon of learned helplessness seems more likely to occur in those individuals who seek control and quick solutions to problems, such as the Type A personality (Sanders and Milkus, 1980).

Thus, and this is a key point, some individuals may not implement the appropriate coping strategy because they cannot diagnose the situation or because they are not able to implement the most appropriate strategy. Of course, use of an inappropriate strategy could also be due to a lack of correct information. Whatever the specifics, however, there is evidence to suggest that not everyone always selects the best coping strategy. For example, Lazarus (1978: 33) observed that

one of the most common ways women coped with the threat of having discovered a breast lump was a pattern of avoidance-denial which resulted in delay in seeking medical evaluation. If the growth were malignant, excessive delay could result in metastasis and a much poorer medical outlook. Similarly, Hackett and Cassem (1975) observed men who, during symptoms of a heart attacks, did vigorous pushups or ran up and down some flights of stairs, on the reasoning that they could not be having a heart attack since the exercise didn't kill them. These men were trying to feel better psychologically (palliation) at the expense of taking the adaptive action of getting medical attention. As it turned out, they were, indeed, having a heart attack and they did survive but the coping process clearly endangered their lives.

SUMMARY

Stress in organizations is becoming an important concern for both individuals and organizations because of its severe deleterious effects. Since reducing or managing stress is the essence of coping, an understanding of coping can aid in attaining the benefits of dealing with stress successfully.

It is proposed here that effective coping depends upon an individual's cognitive skills. These skills enable an individual to analyze a stress situation, develop and select a coping strategy, implement the strategy, and then get feedback on its effects in order to evaluate it. The transactional process model of coping describes each of these steps in detail so individuals can take a methodical approach in coping with stress. This model can also assist organizations in helping their employees. Basically, however, effective coping depends on reducing the uncertainty or importance associated with a situation, reducing the length of the stress situation, or reducing the effects on the individual experiencing the stress.

Since effective coping depends on utilizing the appropriate strategy, a discussion of possible strategies and situations for potential application was presented. These strategies and situations were framed in a typology to suggest a starting point for strategy development and selection. Critical to our understanding of coping is the evaluation of the typology of coping strategies. This evaluation is complex; nevertheless the evaluation can be done. Since the criteria for evalution are so diverse, an interdisciplinary team of researchers may be necessary to conduct an effective evaluation of coping strategies.

REFERENCES

Abramson, L.Y.; M.E.P. Seligman; and J.D. Teasdale. 1978. "Learned Helplessness in Humans: Critique and Reformulation." *Journal of Abnormal Psychology* 87: 49–74.

Anderson, D.R. 1976. "Coping Behaviors and Intervening Mechanisms in the Inverted-U–Stress Performance Relationship." *Journal of Applied Psychology* 61: 30–34.

Beehr, T.A., and J.E. Newman. 1978. "Job Stress, Employee Health, and Organizational Effectiveness: A Facet Analysis, Model and Literature Review." *Personnel Psychology* 31: 665–669.

Beehr, T.A., and R.S. Schuler. 1982. "Current and Future Perspectives on Stress in Organizations." In *Personnel Management: New Perspectives,* edited by Rowland and Ferris. Boston: Allyn and Bacon.

Benson, H.; J.F. Beary; and M.P. Carroll. 1974. "The Relaxation Response." *Psychiatry* 37: 37–46.

Bhagat, R.S. 1983. "Effects of Stressful Life Events Upon Individual Performance Effectiveness and Work Adjustment Process within Organizational Settings: A Research Model." *Academy of Management Review.* 8, 660–671.

Brief, A.P.; R.S. Schuler; and M. Van Sell. 1980. *Managing Job Stress.* Boston: Little, Brown.

Brook, A. 1973. "Mental Stress at Work." *The Practitioner* 210: 500–506.

Buck, V. 1972. *Working Under Pressure.* London: Staples.

Burke, R.J., and T. Weir. 1980. "Coping with the Stress of Managerial Occupations." In *Current Concerns in Occupational Stress,* edited by C.L. Cooper and R.L. Payne, pp. 299–335. London: John Wiley and Sons.

Cameron, C. 1971. "Fatigue Problems in Modern Industry." *Ergonomics* 14: 713–718.

Cannon, W.B. 1929. "Organization for Physiological Homeostasis." *Physiological Review* 9: 339–430.

Caplan, R.D., and K.W. Jones. 1975. "Effects of Workload, Role Ambiguity and Type A Personality on Anxiety, Depression and Heart Rate." *Journal of Applied Psychology* 60: 713–719.

Caplan, R.D.; S. Cobb; and J.R.P. French. 1975. "Relationships of Cessation of Smoking with Job Stress, Personality and Social Support." *Journal of Applied Psychology* 60: 211–219.

Caplan, R.D.; S. Cobb; J.R.P. French, Jr.; R.U. Van Harrison; and S.R. Pinneau, Jr. 1975. "Job Demands and Worker Health." National Institute of Occupational Safety and Health Research Report.

Coch, L. and J.R.P. French. 1948. "Overcoming Resistance to Change." *Human Relations* 11:512–532.

Cohen, F., and R.S. Lazarus. 1973. "Active Coping Processes, Coping Dispositions and Recovery from Surgery." *Psychosomatic Medicine* 35: 375–389.

Cooper, C.L., and J. Marshall. 1976. "Occupational Sources of Stress: A Review of the Literature Relating to Coronary Heart Disease and Mental Ill Health." *Journal of Occupational Psychology* 49: 11–28.

Cooper, C.L. 1979. Sources of Managerial (di)stress. Unpublished paper, University of Manchester.

Cox, T. 1978. *Stress.* Baltimore: University Park Press.

Dohrenwend, B.S., and B.P. Dohrenwend. 1974. *Stressful Life Events.* New York: John Wiley and Sons.

Doob, L. 1971. *Patterning of Time.* New Haven: Yale University Press.

Drabek, T.E., and J.E. Haas. 1969. "Laboratory Simulation of Organizational Stress." *American Sociological Review* 34: 223–238.

Driver, M., and S. Streufert. 1969. "Integrative Complexity: An Approach to Individuals and Groups as Information-processing Systems." *Administrative Science Quarterly* 14: 272–285.

Erikson, J.; W.M. Pugh; and E.K. Gunderson. 1972. "Status Congruency as a Predictor of Job Satisfaction and Life Stress." *Journal of Applied Psychology* 56: 523–525.

Folkman, S. 1980. "An Approach to the Measurement of Coping." Paper presented at the Research Conference on Current Issues in Occupational Stress: Theory, Research and Intervention, York University, Toronto.

Folkman, S., and R.S. Lazarus. 1980. "An Analysis of Coping in a Middle Aged Community Sample." *Journal of Health and Social Behavior* 21: 219–239.

Folkman, S.; C. Schaefer; and R.S. Lazarus. 1979. "Cognitive Processes as Mediators of Stress and Coping." In *Human Stress and Cognition,* edited by V. Hamilton and D.M. Warburton. Chilchestor, England: John Wiley and Sons.

Frankenhaeuser, M., and B. Gardell. 1976. "Underload and Overload in Working Life: Outline of a Multidisciplinary Approach." *Journal of Human Stress* 2: 35–45.

French, J.R.D. 1974. "Person Role Fit." In *Occupational Stress,* edited by A. McLean. Springfield, Ill.: Charles C. Thomas.

French, J.R.P., and R.D. Caplan. 1973. "Organizational Stress and Individual Strain." In *The Failure of Success,* edited by A.J. Murrow, pp. 30–66. New York: American Management Associations.

French, J.R.P.; W. Rogers; and S. Cobb. 1974. "Adjustment as a Person Environment Fit." In Coping and Adaptation: Interdisciplinary Perspectives, edited by G.V. Coelho; D.A. Hamburg; and J.F. Adams. New York: Basic Books.

Frew, D.R. 1977. Management of Stress. Chicago: Nelson-Hall.

Gal, R., and R.S. Lazarus. 1975. "The Role of Activity in Anticipating and Confronting Stressful Situations." Journal of Human Stress 2: 4–20.

Galbraith, J. 1977. Organization Design. Reading, Ma.: Addison-Wesley.

Gastorf, J.W.; J. Suls; and G.S. Sanders. 1980. "Type A Coronary-Prone Behavior Pattern and Social Facilitation." Journal of Personality and Social Psychology 38: 773–780.

Gowler, D., and K. Legge. 1975. Managerial Stress. London: Gower Press.

Greenwood, J.W. 1978. "Management Stressors" in Reducing Occupational Stress. Cincinnati: NIOSH Research Report.

Haan, N. 1977. Coping and Defending. New York: Academic Press.

Hackett, T.P. and H. Cassem. 1975. "Psychological Management of the Myocardial Infarction Patient, Journal of Human Stress, 1, 25–38.

Hall, D.T. 1972. "A Model of Coping with Role Conflict: The Role Behavior of College-Educated Women." Administrative Science Quarterly 17: 471–486.

Hall, D.T., and F.E. Gordon. 1973. "The Career Choices of Married Women: Effects on Conflict, Role Behavior and Satisfaction." Journal of Applied Psychology 58: 42–48.

Hamburg, D.A., and J.E. Adams. 1967. "A Perspective on Coping: Seeking and Utilizing Information in Major Transactions." Archives of General Psychiatry 17: 277–284.

Holmes, T.H., and R.H. Rahe. 1967. "Social Readjustment Rating Scale." Journal of Psychosomatic Research 11: 213–218.

Holmes, T.S., and T.H. Holmes. 1970. "Short-term Instrusions into the Life Style Routine." Journal of Psychosomatic Research 14: 121–132.

House, J.S. 1981. Social Support and Stress. Reading, Ma.: Addison-Wesley.

House, J.S., and J.A. Wells. 1978. "Occupational Stress and Health." Reducing Occupational Stress. Cincinnati: NIOSH Research Report.

Howard, J.H.; P.A. Rechnitzer; and Cunningham, D.A. 1975. "Coping with Job Tensions—Effective and Ineffective Methods." Public Personnel Management 1: 317–326.

Jackson, S.E., and C. Maslach. 1982. "After-effects of Job-Related Stress: Families as Victims." Journal of Occupational Behavior 3: 63–77.

Jacobson, D. 1972. "Fatigue-producing Factors in Industrial Work Preretirement Attitude." Occupational Psychology 46: 193–200.

Janis, I., and L. Mann. 1977. Decision Making. New York: The Free Press.

Kahn, R.L.; D.M. Wolfe; R.P. Quinn; J.D. Snoek; and R.A. Rosenthal. 1964. Organizational Stress: Studies in Role Conflict and Ambiguity. New York: John Wiley and Sons.

Kasl, S.V. 1973. "Mental Health and the Work Environment." *Journal of Occupational Medicine* 15: 509–518.

Klein, S.M. 1971. *Workers Under Stress.* Lexington: University Press of Kentucky.

Kleiner, R.J., and S. Parker. 1963. "Goal Striving, Social Status, and Mental Disorder." *American Sociological Review* 28: 189–203.

Landy, F.J.; J.L. Farr; and R.R. Jacobs. 1982. "Utility Concepts in Performance Measurements." *Organizational Behavior and Human Performance* 30: 15–40.

Lazarus, R.S. 1966. *Psychological Stress and the Coping Process.* New York: McGraw-Hill.

Lazarus, R.S. 1978. "The Stress and Coping Paradigm." Paper presented at the conference on the Critical Evaluation of Behavioral Paradigms for Psychiatric Science, Glendon Beach, Oregon, November 3–6.

Lazarus, R.S. 1979. "Positive Denial: The Case for not Facing Reality." *Psychology Today,* November: 44.

Lazarus, R.S., and R. Launier. 1978. "Stress-Related Transaction Between Person and Environment." In *Perspectives in Interactional Psychology,* edited by Perrin and Lewis, pp. 287–327. New York: Plenum.

Levi, T. 1967. *Stress: Sources, Management and Prevention; Medical and Psychological Aspects of the Stress of Everyday Life.* New York: Liveright.

Levi, T. 1972. *Stress and Distress in Response to Psychosocial Stimuli.* Elmsford, N.Y.: Pergamon Press, Inc.

Manning, P. 1965. *Office Design: A Study of Environment.* Liverpool: University of Liverpool.

Martindale, D. 1977. "Sweaty Palms in the Control Tower." *Psychology Today,* February: 71.

Maslach, C., and S.E. Jackson. 1981. "The Measurement of Experienced Burnout." *Journal of Occupational Behaviour* 2: 99–113.

Maslach, C., and S.E. Jackson. 1982. "Burnout in Health Professions: A Social Psychological Analysis." In *Social Psychology of Health and Illness,* edited by G. Sanders and J. Suls. Hillsdale, N.J.: Lawrence Erlbaum.

Mason, J.W. 1975. "A Historical View of the Stress Field. Part I." *Journal of Human Stress* 1: 6–12.

McGrath, J.E. 1976. "Stress and Behavior in Organizations." In *Handbook of Industrial and Organizational Psychology,* edited by M.D. Dunnette. Chicago: Rand McNally College Publishing Company.

McGrath, J.E., ed. 1970. *Social and Psychological Factors in Stress.* New York: Holt, Rinehart and Winston.

McLean, A.A. 1979. *Work Stress.* Reading, Mass.: Addison-Wesley.

Mechanic, D. 1962. *Students Under Stress.* New York: The Free Press of Glencoe.

Menninger, K. 1963. *The Vital Balance: The Life Process in Mental Health and Illness.* New York: Viking.

Milburn, T.W. 1981. *Maximizing Degrees of Freedom Over Time as a Principal of Rational Behavior.* Unpublished paper, Ohio State University.

Newman, J.F., and T.A. Beehr. 1979. "Personal and Organizational Strategiesfor Handling Job Stress: A Review of Research and Opinion." *Personnel Psychology* 32: 1–43.

Oldham, G.R., and D. Brass. 1979. "Effects of an Office Physical Layout and its Effects on Employee Attitudes." *Administrative Science Quarterly* 24: 267–284.

Pahl, J.M., and R.E. Pahl. 1971. *Managers and Their Wives.* London: Allen Lane.

Pearlin, L.I. 1979. *The Life Cycle and Life Strains.* Paper presented at the American Sociological Meeting, Boston.

Pearlin, L.I., and C. Schooler. 1978. "The Structure of Coping." *Journal of Health and Social Behavior* 19: 2–21.

Rousseau, D.M. 1978. "Characteristics of Departments, Positions, and Individuals: Contexts for Attitudes and Behavior." *Administrative Science Quarterly* 23: 521–540.

Sanders, G.S., and F.S. Milkis. 1980. "Type A Behavior, Need for Control, and Reactions to Group Participation." *Organizational Behavior and Human Performance* 24: 194–216.

Schuler, R.S. 1980a. "Definition and Conceptualization of Stress in Organizations." *Organizational Behavior and Human Performance* 24: 115–130.

Schuler, R.S. 1980b. "A Role and Expectancy Perceptions Model for Participation in Decision Making." *Academy of Management Journal* 23: 331–340.

Schuler, R.S. 1982. "An Integrative Transactional Process Model of Stress in Organizations." *Journal of Occupational Behavior* 3: 5–19.

Seashore, S.E. 1972. "A Survey of Working Conditions in the United States." *Studies in Personnel Psychology* 4: 7–19.

Selgiman, E.E.P. 1975. *Helplessness: On Depression, Development, and Death.* San Francisco: Freeman.

Selye, H. 1956. *The Stress of Life.* New York: McGraw-Hill.

Selye, H. 1973. "The Evolution of the Stress Concept." *American Scientist* 61: 692–699.

Selye, H. 1975. "Confusion and Controversy in the Stress Field." *Journal of Human Stress* 1: 37–44.

Selye, H. 1976. *The Stress of Life* (rev. ed.). New York: McGraw-Hill.

Shalit, B. 1977. "Structural Ambiguity and Limits to Coping." *Journal of Human Stress* 3 (December): 32–45.

Shostak, A.B. 1980. *Blue Collar Stress.* Reading, Ma.: Addison-Wesley.

Sundstrom, E. 1977. "Interpersonal Behavior and the Physical Environment." In *Social Psychology,* edited by L. Wrightman. Monterey, Ca.: Brooks/Cole.

Susman, G.I. 1976. *Autonomy at Work.* New York: Praeger Publisher.

Terryberry, S. 1968. "The Organization of Environments." Unpublished Ph.D. dissertation, Ann Arbor, Mi.: University Microfilms.

Theorell, T. 1978. "Workload, Life Change and Myocardial Infarction." *Reducing occupational stress.* Cincinnati: NIOSH Research Report.

Thompson, S.C. 1981. "Will It Hurt Less If I Can Control It? A complex answer to a simple question." *Psychological Bulletin* 90: 89-101.

Vaillant, G. 1971. "Theoretical Hierarchy of Adaptive Ego Mechanisms." *Archives of General Psychiatry* 24: 107-18.

Van Sell, M.; A.P. Brief; and R.S. Schuler. 1981. "Role Conflict and Role Ambiguity: Integration of the Literature and Directions for Future Research." *Human Relations* 34: 43-71.

Wahlund, I., and G. Nerell. 1978. "Stress Factors in the Working Environments of White-collar Workers." *Reducing occupational stress.* Cincinnati: NIOSH Research Report.

Wardwell, W.I.; M.M. Hyman; and C.B. Bahnson. 1964. "Stress and Coronary Disease in Three Field Studies." *Journal of Chronic Diseases* 17: 73-84.

Warshaw, L.J. 1980. *Stress Management.* Reading, Ma.: Addison-Wesley.

Weick, K. 1979. *Social Psychology of Organizing* (2nd edition.) Reading, Ma.: Addison-Wesley.

White, R. 1974. "Strategies of Adaptation: An Attempt at Systematic Description." In *Coping and adaptation,* edited by G. Coelho; D.A. Hamburg; and J.E. Adams. New York: Basic Books.

4 TIME MANAGEMENT AND LEADER COMMUNICATION BEHAVIOR

Randall S. Schuler and *Amarjit S. Sethi*

As reviewed in the preceding three chapters, there are numerous sources of stress for individuals in organizations including those related to the organizational structure, interpersonal relationships, roles, organizational change, physical environment, career development, and intrinsic job qualities (Schuler, 1980, 1982; Newman and Beehr, 1979). Within each of these seven aspects several specific conditions are generally associated with organizational stress. For example, in an organizational structure there are six typical conditions: (1) lack of participation; (2) no sense of belonging; (3) poor communication; (4) restrictions on behavior; (5) lack of opportunity for advancement; and (5) inequity in pay and performance evaluation.

Based on these six conditions or targets of organizational structure, several organizational coping strategies can be used, including: (1) clarification of policies regarding transfer and promotions; (2) decentralization and increased participation; (3) change in selection and placement policies; (4) change in the communication procedures and networks in the organization; (5) change in reward systems; (6) utilization of training and development programs; (7) statement of the performance evaluation system; (8) development and utilization of permanent and temporary work groups; and (9) change in shift patterns and job rotation policies.

Each of these strategies and their relation to the six structure conditions are extensively discussed by Brief, Schuler, and Van Sell (1981). The essence of the strategies is that they reduce the uncertainty caused by organizational stressors, provide individuals with more conditions able to fulfill their needs and values, and remove demands or constraints that prevent them from fulfilling important needs and values. The appropriateness of these strategies initially depends on the results of the primary appraisal. For example, if the results identify organizational structure as the stressor, the choice may then be made among the nine possible alternative targets for organizational structure listed in Chapter 3.

Thus, the number of possible, though not necessarily the most feasible or effective, organizational coping strategies that can be developed and used by individuals in an organization is extensive (Albrecht, 1979; Beehr, 1980; Cooper and Payne, 1978, 1980). Since space prohibits an examination of them all, we will focus in this chapter on two coping strategies for individuals in organizations. The first is time management and it can be effective for everyone. The second, supervisory and managerial communication behaviors, is aimed more exclusively at supervisors and managers.

In the following chapters, other potentially useful coping strategies are examined in detail including social support groups and burnout strategies.

WHAT IS TIME MANAGEMENT?

Time management is a process that enables an individual to accomplish or achieve the tasks or goals necessary for successful job performance. Within this process are several necessary phases, the essential point of them being to identify those needs and wants of the individual in terms of importance and then to match them with the time and resources available or potentially available to the individual. The tasks or goals an individual needs to achieve are prescribed by the organization for the individual to remain at the current job position. The tasks or goals an individual wants to achieve are self-imposed. They are based on the individual's value system and are related to one's long-term career. Thus an individual may perform far beyond the required level perhaps because the individual really wants to do a good job or because doing a good job will lead to a valued promotion.

The real importance and necessity of time management arises because many individuals have too many tasks they "need to do." Even if they can do them they still have things they desire to do but can't find the time for. The relationship between stress and time management now falls into play. If an individual is not able to attain or fulfill a need or desire, according to the stress definition, the individual experiences stress. With time management an individual is more likely to attain or fulfill a need or desire. Before explicating this relationship further, however, it is important to look more fully at the common stumbling blocks to time management and then discuss the things necessary for effective time management.

Stumbling Blocks to Time Management. Most individuals who claim they don't have enough time to do what they need or want to do really think they are doing a good job or at least trying hard. Our society tends to value more highly those individuals who exert a lot of effort to succeed, but in fact fail, than those individuals who appear not to try as hard, but succeed. Thus, time management problems are almost viewed by many individuals not as something to reduce, but as a battle scar to be displayed proudly. Let us assume, however, that individuals do desire to alleviate or manage their time management problems. What are the stumbling blocks most of them encounter in fulfilling this desire?

A major stumbling block is a lack of awareness of one's job, duties, authority, and responsibility levels. Upon closer inspection, the individual trying hard to succeed is often doing a task that is not a part of the job description or a task that is relatively unimportant. Individuals often fail to utilize the skills or time of others because they didn't realize they had the power or authority to obtain their assistance. Time management problems due to the unawareness of responsibility levels can occur when an individual is required to do two or more tasks, for which the individual feels responsible, at the same time. The individual is in conflict and can't get done what's really necessary in a given time period. This last phrase is extremely important because it highlights the fact that time management problems only exist in relation to a specified amount of time. If time were not a constraint, there would be no time management problems. Thus people who are confortable with "mañana" find time management a foreign word.

Another important stumbling block to effective time management is the inability to prioritize tasks. Many individuals fail to prioritize because they are unaware of their job duties. Others fail to prioritize because they are unaware of prioritization practices (Friedman and Rosenman, 1974). An essential practice is categorizing duties, for example, grouping duties into trivial, routine, and innovative. Another practice is to separate those duties that only the individual can perform from those for which the individual can delegate and hold others accountable. With those duties that only the individual can do, it is necessary to rank their relative importance. It is an essential practice to set up time tables; for example, a Gantt chart indicating time periods and extent of completion of the related duty. In briefly describing prioritization, it is more apparent why individuals may be unaware of them. Failure to prioritize is a real source of time management problems especially when combined with the Pareto Principle.

The Pareto Principle is a stumbling block because, as shown in Figure 4–1, most individuals spend 80 percent of their time on duties that are related to only 20 percent of the results of the total job. Most individuals, often because they fail to prioritize, spend much of their time on the wrong duties. Thus, if there is a time constraint, they are faced with doing the 80 percent of the duties that are easy and quick to do. There is quick feedback in terms of whether a duty is completed or not. But even if an individual is doing the appropriate time allocation, "the best laid plans of mice and men often go astray."

An individual's plans often go astray because of time robbers, as indicated in Table 4–1. Time robbers are events, incidents, or situations that, if repeated often enough, tend to eat unduly into one's time. They are not necessarily wasteful or undesirable, but they do cut into time that could be better spent. Again, many individuals encounter these time robbers every day and fail to do anything about them. As a result they fail to accomplish what they need or want to do.

These stumbling blocks appear to be common sources of time management problems for many individuals working at frantic paces, appearing to be in real binds, drinking a lot of coffee, and making themselves and others nervous and tense. So what can be done about these stumbling blocks? More specifically, what are the practices necessary for effective time management?

Effective Time Management Practices.   A key practice is awareness: (1) awareness of one's job duties, authority, responsibility, and their importance; (2) awareness of one's own skills, needs, and abilities; and (3) awareness of how one currently allocates oneself. Suggested techniques for doing this involve keeping daily and weekly logs of activities

Figure 4-1.   The Pareto Time Principle.

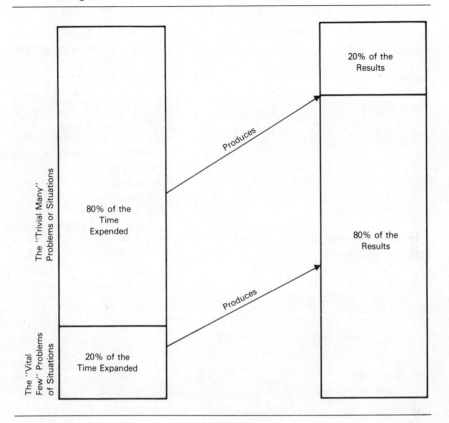

with a detailed analysis of what, who, where, and how much time is involved in each of the activities. A sample daily log is provided in Figure 4-2. Another technique involves reviewing one's job description with one's supervisor, and perhaps co-workers and subordinates. Occasionally individuals find it necessary to bring together all those individuals who have expectations, or ask favors, or make demands on them. These sessions can help clarify job, authority, and responsibility expectations that these individuals have for the focal individual, and can also help reduce the conflict potential from these various "role" senders.

Frequently, time management problems arise because an individual simply doesn't want to do the job. This lack of motivation may be due to a mismatch between the individual's skills, needs, or abilities.

Table 4-1.   Time Robbers.

Meetings	Late Arrivals and Cancellations
Correspondence	Subordinates Needing Attention
Visitors	Attempts to Reach Other Managers for Consultation
Reports	Need for Discussion and Correction of Inadequate Work by Subordinate
Travel (Official Trips)	"Breaking in" of New Employees
Questionnaires	Community Activities
Committee Work	"Standing By" for Scheduled Meetings with Bosses or Other Managers
Gripes, Complaints, Morale Situations	Clarification of Misunderstandings of Policies or Instructions
Inaccessible Records	New Projects that seem to "Break in" on the Work Load
Searches for Needed Information	
Emergency Situations; Trouble-Shooting	
Overinvolvement in Personal Problems of a Subordinate	
Telephone	

Source: Adapted from Steward (1978: 172).

A final technique related to awareness is in the daily log of activities. A individual may be an ineffective time manager but only in certain situations In analyzing the daily log, attention should be given to situations that can b regarded as either ineffective or effective. The effective situations may revea use of effective time management practices that can then be applied to othe situations.

Assuming an individual has a high level of awareness in the areas discussed it is important to consider all or parts of the aspects of these three processes (1) conserving time; (2) controlling time; and (3) making time. Examples o each of these processes are shown in Table 4-2. Because each of these pro cesses is too extensive for a general discussion here, two aspects of makin time should be elaborated because of their importance: delegation and goe setting.

Many managers fail to delegate as much as they should and could. Th "could" results from a lack of job awareness, and the "should" results fron personal preferences and styles of managing. Personal preferences are im portant because they prevent individuals from effectively utilizing and de

Figure 4-2.   Management Activities Daily Diary.

LOCATION OF INCIDENT

My office

Supervisor's office

Subordinate's office

Other

Starting time _____

Ending time _____

Duration _____

ALLOCATION OF TIME

WHO?		HOW?		WHAT?		FUNCTION?	
Superiors	_____	Formal meeting	_____	Accounting/ Finance	_____	Planning	_____
Peers	_____					Organizing	_____
Subordinates	_____	Informal meeting	_____	Marketing/ Sales	_____	Staffing	_____
Other internal contact	_____	Telephone	_____	Production	_____	Directing	_____
		Social	_____	Personnel	_____	Reporting	_____
External contact	_____	Reading	_____	R&D	_____	Budgeting	_____
		Writing	_____	Public relations	_____		
		Reflecting	_____		_____		
				General management	_____		

KIND OF INCIDENT

Is this incident an interruption?   _____ Yes   _____ No

Could it have been delegated?   _____ Yes   _____ No

Source: Adapted from Bonoma and Slevin (1978: 16).

Table 4-2.   Conserving, Controlling, and Making Time.

Conserving Time
Speed reading; reading for the highlights
Using electronics or mechanization such as intercom, tapes, push-button
Drafting of key points of letter rather than writing it in fully
Doing business during coffee breaks and the like
Using form letters
Curtailing duration of meetings
Using library abstracts, digests
Good note-taking on new or complicated matters
Blocking out time for dictation, answering phone calls, and the like
Using reminders, color tabs, alerts
Cutting down on lengthy lunches
Clustering reading matter into stacks to be read today, by the end of the week, with no set time limi
Better physical layout to curtail walking and possible interruptions
Avoiding "clerking" for your secretary

Controlling Time
Better, more realistic scheduling
Having secretary "screen" and in other ways save your time
Awareness of cyclical periods such as contract renewals, inspections due, quarterly reports, and so o
Alertness to deadlines
Budgeting weekly or monthly time
Consolidating dates for travel, conferences, and the like
Good feedback: knowing who's working on what and state of progress
Effective, firm correction of employee errors, mistakes, slip-ups, unwise commitments
Avoiding procrastination—doing it now
Reducing internal office bickering, personality clashes
Questioning regular meetings
Doing preventive management to ward off repeated "crises"
Learning to say "no" to some invitations; sending someone as your representative
Probing reasons for absenteeism and its effects on staff workloads
Avoiding perfectionism fetish; accepting high standards

Making Time
More effective planning
Better listening, advising
Candid appraisal of subordinates' performance
Coaching, on-the-job training, and development of subordinates
Improved communication
Effective delegation to subordinates
Getting competent assistance on high-priority matters
Being more decisive
Improving organization: modifying, simplifying, consolidating, eliminating procedures
Questioning the need for certain functions: do they contribute at all to profitability?
Handling morale situations in time and systematically
Clarifying policies, program requirements, authority
Resolving line-staff misunderstandings
Adapting to "management by objectives" concepts, goal setting
Updating standards of performance for your subordinate managers

Source: Adapted from Stewart (1978: 168–169).

veloping their employees and themselves. Assuming one is aware of one's job duties, authority, and responsibility, and prefers to delegate, what are the important principles of good delegation? The principles are: (1) definition of what's expected and perhaps how it's to be done; (2) specification of the level of initiative or type of authority the individual is given; (3) appropriate controls on the performance of the delegated individual; and (4) feedback to the delegated individual on the results of the duties performed. Each of these principles may be discussed at length, but suffice it to say, effective delegation can't exist without all of them.

The last major effective time management practice to be discussed is goal setting. This essential activity involves setting down on paper the things that an individual really wants or needs to achieve. It is best to list first the goals that one wants to attain in one's lifetime—they can range from job-related goals such as having a good family, a good marriage, a new vocation, and so on. Then one makes another list of goals to attain in the next three years. Next, it is important to list each set of goals and identify any conflicts that may exist among the goals in each of the lists. Measurable performance indicators should be identified for each goal. Specific behaviors that are needed to attain each of the goals should then be listed. For example, in order to attain the goal of having a good family life, one may decide one needs to spend two nights a week with family members. There may be several behaviors for each goal. After this, it is necessary to state current strengths and weaknesses that enable or prevent the individual from engaging in the behavior needed to reach each goal.

TIME MANAGEMENT AND STRESS

Time management practice raises several important questions for managers and organizations. If someone uses time management and actually gets more done in less time should the individual be rewarded more? Are there enough job duties to warrant time management programs, since they do take time, effort, and money to learn? What are the gains and losses of all employees really understanding their jobs? Do the managers actually want to delegate, or will this be seen as a loss of power? Thus there are several crucial questions and issues that should be addressed when considering the use of time management.

Implications aside, however, the advantages of time management are significant, both from the individual and organizational points of view. Generally, time management means less stress for individuals, and that means more effective, satisfied, and healthy individuals and thus more effective, adaptive, and healthy organizations (Warshaw, 1979; Burke and Weir, 1980; Beehr and Schuler, 1982).

LEADER COMMUNICATION BEHAVIORS

Stress results from many activities, events, and behaviors that we experience in our daily lives and especially in the organizations where we spend so much of our time. The effects of stress, unfortunately, are usually as unfavorable for us as for the companies in which we work. Stress can come from the pressures of deadlines, from too many things to do, or from the last minute customer. Generally stress arises from not knowing what to do or when to do it, from new work that conflicts with existing work, from our values, or just the number of work hours in a day. Stress also arises when we feel we don't have the ability to do the job. Stress also comes from not knowing how well we are doing (Beehr and Newman, 1978; Schuler, 1980). The phrase "management by exception" is really a stress-inducing principle. It suggests that we won't be informed of how "well" we are doing, but simply how "unwell" we are doing. In other words, we need to do something badly to get information or feedback about how we're doing. Thus, stress often results from a lack of communication or a lack of the right type of communication at the right time. The right type of communication by the supervisor at the right time may, therefore, be an important way to reduce stress.

If we look at some important leader communication behaviors that reduce stress, we can then describe how and why these behaviors work. Research suggests that if you practice the following behaviors appropriately, you will be a better supervisor and have employees who are much more involved in their work, more satisfied with both you and their jobs, and more likely to perform better quality work because their stress levels are lower.

There are many categories of leader communication behaviors, but there are seven that are important here because of their impact on employee stress. All of these behaviors can be practiced by supervisors or managers; it is just a matter of being aware of these behaviors and the situation of the employee.

Achievement communication behavior by the supervisor conveys statements of goals, challenge, confidence, and high expectations to the employee. Such a statement may be, "You know, Sam, that I really feel you can do this job, even though it is especially complex and difficult." Achievement communication behavior builds self-worth in the employee and suggests you are confident the worker has the ability to do the job. Knowing one has the ability to do the job can reduce or eliminate a potentially stressful situation.

This communication behavior is especially important to new employees, to employees whose jobs generally exceed their abilities, or to employees facing new or unpredictable job situations. The specific effect of this behavior is to increase workers' perception of their ability to do a job the way they think best, not the way the supervisor thinks best.

Ego deflation communication behavior is the reverse of achievement communication behavior. As suggested by the title, this leader behavior reduces the employee's feelings of self-worth and self-confidence, and makes the employee feel incapable of doing anything. Ego deflation communication is captured in this statement of a supervisor to an employee: "You know, I can never trust you to do it right!" A non-verbal communication of ego deflation would be to watch closely or check-up on an employee. The phrase, "He's always on my back," is a classic description of ego deflation communication by a supervisor.

Ego deflation communication reduces one's concept of one's ability to do the job. Stress is induced because the employee perceives an inability to do what is expected. Both ego deflation and achievement communication behavior tend to be self-fulfilling. That is, if the supervisor expects and acts as though the employee can perform, the employee usually does, but if the supervisor doesn't expect and act as if the employee can succeed, even the same employee doesn't.

Contingent approval communication behavior aids the employee in knowing what is expected and how well the worker is doing. The supervisor communicates a contingent approval by praising or otherwise rewarding the employee when performance is good. The approval or reward given by the supervisor is contingent or dependent upon the employee's performance. The phrase, "That's really a good job, Mary," is an example of contingent approval communication. That phrase lets Mary know how well she is doing and also that she is performing as expected. This communication behavior tends, however, to be historically oriented, not future-oriented. If jobs are constantly changing, the employee who receives only contingent approval may be in a state of uncertainty about future expectations, since past behaviors and rewards may not continue.

Contingent approval communication generally acts to increase the employee's perceptions of what's expected (especially in situations that don't change much) and perceptions of what's rewarded. These perceptions in turn will help reduce stressful situations. It's also helpful if the employee knows what's not rewarded.

Contingent disapproval communication behavior lets the employee know what is not rewarded, or more specifically, what results in punishment or disapproval. A supervisor engaging in this communication behavior may tell an employee, "You really loused up that job," or "I could have done that better myself." The employee suffers from negative or embarrassing feedback from the supervisor because the performance level wasn't up to par. In order to get the most benefit from this communication behavior, the supervisor should specify the exact behavior or performance of the employee that was below par. Frequently, because the supervisor wasn't specific enough the employee doesn't know the source of the reprimand. In addition to being related to specific behavior, the contingent disapproval should be aimed only at the behavior or performance of the employee, not at the employee as a person—such as "You're really a crummy worker."

Contingent disapproval and approval communication require the supervisor to be aware of the employee's accomplishments. The employee may be left to decide how to do the job, but the supervisor should appraise the final results so that reward or punishments can be provided. Effective use of contingent communications also requires that performance indicators exist and are understood by both the supervisor and the employee. Taking time to develop performance standards and to observe or to be aware of employee performance results is well worthwhile. These communication behaviors minimize stress levels for the employee.

Participative communication behavior of the supervisor can be helpful in establishing future goals for the employee or deciding how best to do a job. This communication behavior usually refers to decisions that should be made and can refer to how and when to do things and what can and should be done. This behavior is especially useful when the employee is faced with a difficult job or when the job changes without new performance levels and goals being established. Used under these conditions, participative communication behavior can clarify what is expected and what is rewarded and can even reduce some conflicts because the supervisor and employee discuss and iron out inconsistencies or conflicts. Participation could even be extended to include more than two supervisors and is then perhaps the most useful tool in reducing conflict.

Participation, used in situations where it clarifies what is expected, or rewarded, or where it reduces conflict, is functional and legitimate. Participation also reduces conflicts by determining the employee's values so that the supervisor may consider these in job assignments. Participation in situations that are not changing or that are relatively simple may not be legitimate, but rather a "con job" by the supervisor.

There are occasions, however, when an employee, regardless of the situation, would prefer simply to be told what to do. Little or no participative communication may then be in order. A supervisor, therefore, needs to diagnose both the situation and the employee before utilizing participative communication. However, when the situation warrants participation, the supervisor benefits as much as the employee because of insights and skills that the employee provides to the decisions to be made (Coch and French, 1948). When the employee wants to be told what to do, then directive or instrumental communication behavior is appropriate.

Directive communication behavior is especially appropriate when the employee wants directions and guidance or when circumstances warrant it. Some such circumstances are when the employee is just joining the organization, when changes are being made by others and need to be communicated to the employee, and when time pressure may preclude participation. Directive communication also may prove appropriate when the employee is not performing well because the employee doesn't really know the desired performance. When directive communication is used with contingent disapproval, the combination is sometimes called scolding and instructing communication behavior. This behavior is used frequently by coaches to get the best performances from their players in a short period of time.

Directive communication behavior sounds like, "Here's what I want you to do today." Directive behavior may refer to both what to do and what the goals are, as well as how to get to them: for example, "Here's what I want you to do today, and here's how I want you to do it." If the employee doesn't want or have the information to determine what to do or how to do something, directive communication behavior is appropriate. The end result is an employee who better knows what is expected and how to do it. Directive communication can also help reduce conflict when directions take the form of ordering and specifying the importance of goals and providing the time and resources to do what is expected.

For many of the leader communication behaviors to work, to clarify expectations, and ultimately to reduce stress, the communications have to be accepted by the employee. If the employee doesn't accept the communication, the effect on stress is lost. The employee's trust of the supervisor is necessary for acceptance. But what fosters trust? Considerate or supportive communication behavior does.

Supportive communication behavior indicates concern for the employee as a person, not as an instrument of production. This quality helps increase the level of trust between the supervisor and the employee. Supportive communication is really necessary for the preceding six leader communication behaviors to be effective. For a supervisor to be good, it's necessary to be supportive. A supportive supervisor may say to an employee: "Good morning, Ruth. How are you feeling today?" Non-verbal supportive communication includes keeping commitments, being on time, and removing some barriers of distinction between supervisor and employee.

Supportive communication has nothing directly to do with an employee knowing what is expected, how to do something, or what is rewarded. Its impact on employee stress is indirect and increases trust between supervisor and employee so that other leader communication behaviors that do directly influence employee stress are facilitated.

These seven leader communication behaviors have been discussed as though a supervisor could choose any one set of the behaviors and not the others. Although this might be possible, in reality most supervisors engage in several communication behaviors. It should be emphasized that effective supervisors are distinguished from ineffective or less effective supervisors by practicing appropriate leader communication behavior—and a sufficiently high level of that behavior—so that stressful conditions are reduced. For example, the more the employee wants participation and the more complex or changing the job conditions, the more appropriate is participative leader communication behavior. Similarly, all other leader communication behaviors have a range or a number of levels. It's usually not just a matter of behaviors being there or not being there, but how much is there.

It was suggested that all supervisors could practice or engage in leader communication behaviors. This highlights the fact that any supervisor can be effective. However, some supervisors may have more difficulty practicing some behaviors primarily because of style of interaction, or personal values and preferences. Some supervisors may possess an interaction style that tends to make them quiet, or avoid confrontation or problem-solving. They may avoid participation that causes conflict or may need to justify uncomfortable actions. Most supervisors have values or preferences on how to be supervisors ranging from directive and autocratic to laissez-faire. These preferences could be based on culture, upbringing, assumptions about people, or experience. Each supervisor should know preferences and examine how they relate to the seven communication behaviors. A supervisor may have a set of values or preferences that conflict with some leader communication behaviors. In the short-run, the supervisor can engage in the appropriate leader communication behavior regardless of values, but, over the long-run, continued conflict would be too stressful. The supervisor should seek a situation or type of employee where the appropriate leader communication behavior is consistent with personal values.

On a more general level, each supervisor, to utilize successfully any of the leader communication behaviors, should have the basic skills of good listening and good communicating, and skills in receiving and giving specific task-related feedback, non-verbal communicating, and diagnosing a situation. Good communication skills embody several characteristics: (1) seeking to clarify your ideas before communicating; (2) examining the true purpose of each communication; (3) considering the total physical and human environment whenver you communicate; (4) consulting with others, when appropriate, in planning communications; (5) being aware, while you communicate, of the overtones as well as the basic content of your message; (6) taking the opportunity, when it arises, to convey something of help or value to the employee; (7) following up your communication; (8) being sure your actions support your communications; (9) seeking not only to be understood but to be understanding—being an effective listener.

Efficient and effective listening skills include: (1) action listening; (2) listening for total meaning; (3) listening to feeling; and (4) avoiding the stumbling blocks to listening that include: pre-judging, jumping to conclusions, assuming that others think as you do, the wandering mind, the closed mind, wishful hearing, plural meaning, excessive talking, absence of humility, fear and absence of good feedback.

The characteristics of good feedback are its being: (1) specific rather than general; (2) focused on behavior, rather than the person; (3) considerate of the needs of the receiver; (4) directed at behavior which the receiver can do something about; (5) solicitous; (7) well-timed; (8) involved with the amount of communication the receiver can use; (9) concerned with what is said or done, not why; and (10) checked to insure clear communication.

Finally, the ability to diagnose a situation by determining the employee's perception of the clarity of what is expected, the level of conflict, and the behaviors rewarded and punished is crucial. The supervisor can both ask the employee and give a questionnaire to the employee to determine these perceptions. Regardless of the method of gathering information, the supervisor must do it fairly frequently—especially if there is a high turnover of employees. Good, effective supervision is not merely the practice of appropriate leader communication behaviors, good listening skills, and good feedback skills, but the continuous practice of these behaviors and skills.

SUMMARY

The number of alternative organizational coping strategies to develop when the organizational stressors can be changed is rather extensive. Final selection of the appropriate strategy or strategies must rest on the cost/benefit analysis of each. An analysis of the feasibility and cost/benefit of various coping strategies should include the specification of what is needed to implement each strategy. Implementation must include an analysis of the readiness for change (by either the organization or the individual), and what it will take for the appropriate level of readiness to transpire.

In addition to readiness, support conditions must be established (Payne, 1980; House, 1981; House and Wells, 1978; Gastorf, Suls, and Sanders, 1980). If group support is necessary to implement a strategy for an individual, the group must be available and ready. If the leadership of the organization requires change, the reward systems of the organization may also need to be changed to ensure that the leadership change will occur and its effects maintained.

Table 4-3.   Individual Symptoms of Stress.

1. *Physiological*
   Short-term: heartrate, GSR, respiration, headache
   Long-term: ulcer, blood pressure, heart attack
   Non-specific: Adrenaline, nonadrenaline, thymus deduction, lymph
                 deduction, gastric acid production, ACTH production

2. *Physiological Responses (Affective and Cognitive)*
   Fight or withdrawal
   Apathy, resignation, boredom
   Regression
   Fixation
   Projection
   Negativism
   Fantasy
   Forgetfulness
   Tendency to misjudge people
   Uncertainty about whom to trust
   Inability to organize self
   Inner confusion about duties or roles
   Dissatisfaction
   High intolerance for ambiguity, inability to deal well with new or strange situations
   Tunnel vision
   Tendency to begin vacillating in decisionmaking
   Tendency to become distraught with trifles
   Inattentiveness: loss of power to concentrate
   Irritability
   Procrastination
   Feelings of persecution

3. *Behavioral*
   a. Individual consequences
      Loss of appetite
      Sudden noticeable loss or gain of weight
      Sudden change of appearance:
      Decline/improvement in dress
      Sudden change of hair style and length
      Difficult breathing
      Sudden change of smoking habits
      Sudden change in use of alcohol
   b. Organizational Consequences
      Low performance—quality/quantity
      Low job involvement
      Loss of responsibility
      Lack of concern for organization
      Lack of concern for colleagues
      Loss of creativity
      Absenteeism
      Voluntary turnover
      Accident proneness

After the chosen strategy has been implemented, its effects must be evaluated. This can be done at the organizational, group, and individual levels. Currently, evaluation of coping strategies is sparse at best (Newman and Beehr, 1979; Beehr, 1980; Beehr, Chapter 13 of this book). This stage, however, is critical to determine if opportunities have been taken advantage of and demands or constraints successfully removed.

Criteria for evaluation can include the three classes of outcomes of stress shown in Table 4-3: physiological, psychological, and behavioral. Since the behavioral outcomes include consequences of importance to the individual as well as the organization, these three classes of outcomes are potentially appropriate for coping evaluation at all three levels. They are also appropriate for evaluation of the coping strategies to be presented in the following chapters.

REFERENCES

Albrecht, K. 1979. *Stress and the Manager.* Englewood Cliffs, N.J.: Prentice Hall.

Beehr, T.A. 1980. "Organizational Strategies for Managing Job Stress." Paper presented at the Midwest Academy of Management, Cincinnati.

Beehr, T.A., and J.E. Newman. 1978. "Job Stress, Employee Health, and Organizational Effectiveness: A Facet Analysis, Model and Literature Review." *Personnel Psychology* 31: 664–669.

Beehr, T.A., and R.S. Schuler. 1982. "Current and Future Perspectives on Stress in Organizations." In *Personnel Management: New Perspectives,* edited by Rowland and Ferris. Boston: Allyn and Bacon.

Bonoma, T.V., and D.P. Slevin. 1978. *Executive Survival Manual.* Boston: CBI.

Brief, A.P.; R.S. Schuler; and M. Van Sell. 1981. *Managing Stress.* Boston: Little, Brown and Company.

Burke, R.J., and R. Weir. 1980. "Coping with Stress of Managerial Occupations." In *Current Concerns in Occupational Stress,* edited by Cooper and Payne, pp. 299–335. London: John Wiley and Sons.

Coch, L., and J.R.P. French. 1948. "Overcoming Resistance to Change." *Human Relations* 11: 512–532.

Cooper, C.L., and R. Payne, eds. 1978. *Stress at Work.* London: John Wiley and Sons.

Cooper, C.L., and R. Payne, eds. 1980. *Current Concerns in Occupational Stress.* London: John Wiley and Sons.

Friedman, M., and R.H. Rosenman. 1974. *Type A Behavior and Your Heart.* New York: Alfred A. Knopf.

Gastorf, J.W.; J. Suls; and G.S. Sanders. 1980. "Type A Coronary-Prone Behavior Pattern and Social Facilitation." *Journal of Personality and Social Psychology* 38: 773–780.

House, J.S. 1981. *Work Stress and Social Support.* Reading, Mass.: Addison-Wesley.

House, J.S., and J.A. Wells. 1978. "Occupational Stress and Health." In *Reducing Occupational Stress,* edited by McLean, Black and Colligan. Cincinnati: NIOSH Research Report.

Newman, J.F., and T.A. Beehr. 1979. "Personal and Organizational Strategies for Handling Job Stress: A Review of Research and Opinion." *Personnel Psychology* 32: 1–43.

Payne, R.L. 1980. "Organizational Stress and Social Support." In *Current Concerns in Occupational Stress,* edited by Cooper and Payne. London: John Wiley and Sons.

Schuler, R.S. 1980. "Definition and Conceptualization of Stress in Organizations." *Organizational Behavior and Human Performance* 24: 194–216.

Schuler, R.S. 1982. "An Integrative Transactional Process Model of Stress in Organizations." *Journal of Occupational Behavior* 5: 3–12.

Steward, Nathaniel. 1978. *The Effective Woman Manager.* New York: John Wiley and Sons.

Warshaw, L.J. 1979. *Stress Management.* Reading, Ma.: Addison-Wesley.

5 ORGANIZATIONAL PRACTICES FOR PREVENTING BURNOUT

Susan E. Jackson

As recently as ten years ago, the word "burnout" was included in the vocabularies of very few people, though the feelings we now call burnout were undoubtedly as pervasive as they are today. During the late 1970s and the early 1980s, both the general public and the scientific community began to recognize that burnout and its consequences were serious issues of widespread concern. Popular sources such as *Time* magazine and *Psychology Today* began to describe vividly the symptoms of frustration, exhaustion, and cynicism that were being experienced by people such as teachers, nurses, police, and others in the human service professions. More recently, reports have appeared that suggest these same burnout symptoms are prevalent among managers and executives in business settings.

A perusal of articles in the popular press reveals that often little distinction is made between what is now labelled burnout and what has previously been referred to simply as stress, but an examination of the research literature on burnout reveals that those who are studying the phenomenon consider burnout to be a unique type of stress reaction experienced by people who have jobs that require extensive contact with other people. In fact, most of the research completed to date has focused primarily on the consequences of burnout among those who work in the human service professions (see Perlman and Hartman, 1982, for a review). Unlike many occupations in which the employee spends most of the work day dealing with inanimate objects, human service workers spend almost all of their time interacting with people. Furthermore, the people these workers are involved with are usually in a state of need, a fact that has led some to refer to human service providers as "helping professionals." The nature of the relationship that exists between a helping professional and patients or clients generates special pressures and dependencies that are typically not experienced by people whose interactions at work are carried out in the context of business organizations. Some of these pressures and dependencies are similar to those experienced by people in supervisory positions, however, since supervisors are often called upon to help employees resolve or cope with both job-related and personal difficulties.

The specific work environment in which one is embedded is a major determinant of the burnout a person experiences, so that environment must be well understood before suggestions can be made for how to help workers cope with, reduce, or prevent burnout. This chapter will focus on those aspects of organizations that determine the likelihood that their employees will experience burnout. (Since most burnout research has been done in human service organizations, examples here are drawn from them. It is expected, however, that burnout research in other types of organizations will produce similar results.) Based on our knowledge about the causes of burnout, suggestions will then be made for how organizations can help prevent employee burnout. First, however, burnout needs to be more specifically defined.

WHAT IS BURNOUT?

Burnout can be thought of as a psychological process—a series of attitudinal and emotional reactions—that a person goes through as a result of job-related experiences. Often the first sign of burnout is a feeling of being emotionally exhausted from one's work. When asked to describe how she feels, an emotionally exhausted employee might say she feels drained or used-up, that she is at the end of her rope and is physically fatigued. Waking up in the morning may be accompanied by a feeling of dread at the thought of having to put in another day on the job. For someone who was once enthusiastic about her job and idealistic about what she could accomplish, feelings of emotional exhaustion may come somewhat unexpectedly, though to an outsider looking at the situation, emotional exhaustion would be seen as a natural response to an extended period of intense interaction with people and their problems.

Extreme emotional exhaustion can be very debilitating both on and off the job, so people who are experiencing it must find some way to cope. One common coping reaction is to put psychological distance between one's self and one's clients and to decrease one's personal involvement with them. In moderation, this reaction may be an effective method for creating "detached concern," but when engaged in to excess, the employee may begin to dehumanize or depersonalize the clients. People who have reached the extreme end of the depersonalization continuum report feeling they have become calloused by their jobs and that they have grown cynical about their clients. Unfortunately, for the friends and family of an employee who has reached this stage, the cynical and uncaring attitudes that develop toward clients may be generalized to nonclients as well, having a negative effect on all of the person's social interactions.

In addition to emotional exhaustion and depersonalization, a third and final aspect of burnout is a feeling of low personal accomplishment. Many human service professionals begin their careers with great expectations that they will be able to improve the human condition through their work. After a year or two on the job, they begin to realize they are not living up to these expectations. There are many systemic reasons for the gap that exists between the novice's goals and the veteran's accomplishments, and these include unrealistically high expectations due to a lack of exposure to the job during training, constraints placed on the worker through the rules and regulations of an immutable bureaucracy, inadequate resources for performing one's job, clients who are frequently uncooperative and occasionally rebellious, and a lack of feedback about one's successes. These and other characteristics of human service organizations almost guarantee that employees will be frustrated in their attempts to reach their goals, yet the workers may not recognize the role of the system in producing this frustration. Instead, the worker may feel personally responsible and possibly a failure. When combined with emotional exhaustion and depersonalization, low personal accomplishment may reduce motivation to a point where performance is in fact impaired, leading to further experienced failure. Because these three signs of burnout usually occur in sequence, it is useful to conceptualize them in stages, as shown in Table 5-1.

This conceptualization of burnout as a series of three stages through which a person is likely to progress underlies much of the theorizing and research of psychologists studying the phenomenon, but because no longitudinal studies have been conducted to track people as they progress through their careers, the sequencing of these stages is not well-documented. What is well-documented is that a person may be experiencing one of the three components of burnout but not the other two (Golembieski, 1981; Maslach and Jackson, 1981a). Recognizing that burnout is a multifaceted concept has two important implications for those who want to design programs to help people cope with, or alleviate, burnout symptoms. First, it suggests that individuals who are qualitatively quite different may respond quite differently. For example, one person may be emotionally exhausted but not feel cynical or calloused toward clients; another may feel calloused toward clients without feeling emotional or physical fatigue. Because these two people are experiencing different aspects of burnout, different solutions will be needed to help them. Secondly, be-

Table 5-1.   Three Stages of Burnout and their Accompanying Symptoms.

Emotional Exhaustion	Depersonalization	Low Personal Accomplishment
feel drained by work	have become calloused by job	cannot deal with problems effectively
feel fatigued in the morning	treat people like objects	am not having a positive influence on others
feel burned out	don't care what happens to people	cannot understand others' problems or empathize with them
frustrated	feel others blame you for their problems	
don't want to work with people		no longer feel exhilarated by job

cause burnout is multifaceted, programs and interventions designed to combat it can only be successful if they are designed to address all three facets of the burnout experience.

WHAT ARE THE CONSEQUENCES OF BURNOUT?

Clients Receive Low-Quality Service

Throughout the early writings on burnout there was a clear assumption that "burned out" staff members perform more poorly on the job than their counterparts who are still "fired up." Thus, it was a concern over the negative effects of burnout on clients rather than concern over the negative effects of burnout on staff members that stimulated interest in the burnout phenomenon. The assumption that job performance is affected by burnout is prevalent, but the accuracy of this assumption has been difficult to demonstrate because job performance is difficult to measure in human service organizations. Performance quantity and performance quality are likely to be inversely related to each other.

Consider, for example, an intake interviewer in a legal aid office. For the organization, the intake interview serves as a screening device through which all potential clients must pass. During the interview, specific information about the nature and details of a case must be assessed and an evaluation of the "appropriateness" of the case for the office must be made. Since as many as forty intake interviews may be conducted per day, it is important that the interviewer work as efficiently as possible. Here the major index of efficiency is the number of forms accurately filled out for further processing. Thus, the interviewer's attention must be focused on gathering information requested by the form. To the extent that time is spent talking about problems not relevant for these forms, efficiency decreases.

Now consider a client's perspective. Upon arriving for an interview, the client is likely to be fuming inside as she rehearses in her mind the injustices done to her and the retaliations she hopes for. She does not think in terms of the precise statutes encompassing her problem or the essential details that make her case worthy of attention. Rather, she is concerned with the problems now being faced by her family. Her primary concern is that her emotional and physical life return to normal—the law seems to offer a solution. For the client, the intake interview may be the first chance to explain the problems she is facing. From her perspective, good job performance is displayed by an interviewer who lends a sympathetic ear.

How will the interviewer handle this situation? Typically, the person doing the interview will be a relatively recent graduate of law school with little or no clinical experience to rely on. The only guidance received has been generalities about the professional approach to analyzing cases: socialization has emphasized the supremacy of objectivity. But clearly, adoption of an objective, analytic attitude, combined with the pressure to fill out forms efficiently, does not add up to the sympathetic ear the client is looking for. Because of these differing expectations about what should occur during the interview, both the client and the interviewer will perceive the other as a hindrance. The objective interviewer appears unconcerned and the client becomes frustrated. The emotionally involved client becomes an obstacle to detached efficiency and frustrates the interviewer. Whether or not open hostility erupts, both participants are aware of the antagonistic relationship they have formed.

One way for the interviewer to cope with this situation is to develop a limited set of case types and then focus on determining which type a client fits into. Once a case has been "typed" the unique nuances of the case can be ignored. Processing of the case then proceeds as it does for all other cases of that type. This method of coping can result in the interviewer adopting a rigid line of questioning that is governed by the papers to be filled out rather than by the clients and their concerns. Although the interviewer will probably recognize that this strategy is less than optimal, it may be the only feasible way to deal with the myriad of complexities and details offered by each client. To the client, the interviewer seems like just another example of a petty bureaucrat who is more concerned with paper than with people.

Co-workers Suffer

Another unfortunate consequence of burnout is a deterioration of one's relationship with co-workers. A study of mental health workers found that people who were experiencing calloused feelings toward their clients also complained more about their clients to their co-workers, thereby generating a negative atmosphere within the work unit. These burned out mental health workers were also absent from work more often and took more frequent work breaks (Maslach and Jackson, 1981b). Such withdrawal or "flight" behaviors are undoubtedly practiced by the worker as a way of coping with personal feelings. Withdrawing from a stressful situation can be a very effective coping technique for the individual, but it often places additional burdens on the undeserving co-workers of the burned out employee.

Job Involvement Decreases

In addition to being absent and taking frequent work breaks, a more subtle form of withdrawal behavior that burned out workers engage in is completely shutting out the job from their thoughts during off-work hours. This mental coping strategy is used more and more often as burnout progresses (Maslach and Jackson, 1981b). Reflected in this coping strategy is the staff person's decreasing involvement in, and commitment to, the job. Though difficult to assess, this decreased commitment may result in diminished quality of job performance simply because the person spends less time thinking about how to solve job-related problems. For example, instead of contemplating how best to "work the system" in order to get Mr. Smith some badly needed financial help, a burned out case worker may simply resort to telling the client that "rules are rules" and "no one can do anything to help him." Similarly, a burned out administrator may resort to making snap decisions based on surface-level information, rather than pondering an issue throughout an evening or over the weekend in order to determine whether additional information would be useful.

Turnover

From an organizational perspective, a particularly serious form of withdrawal behavior is quitting one's job altogether, a strategy commonly used by burned out workers (Barad, 1979; Jackson and Maslach, 1982). No systematic studies have been reported in which burnout workers were followed up after leaving their jobs, so little is known about the effectiveness of this solution for the individual. However, anecdotal evidence suggests that, especially among human service professionals, leaving one's job often coincides with a decision to get more education in order to "move up" to an administrative position. For these people, part of the attractiveness of an administrative position is a decrease in the amount of direct contact they have with the client population. While it is true that administrative positions in human service organizations typically do not require extensive contact with clients, they do involve a great deal of contact with people in general. If the cynical attitudes toward clients that develop as part of the burnout syndrome are carried up into the new administrative position, the negative effects of burnout on the organization will continue, and may even spread. In effect, burnout may be contagious.

Family Life Suffers

Just as burnout leads to behaviors that have a negative impact on the quality of one's work life, it leads to behaviors that cause a deterioration of the quality of one's home life. In a study of police families (Jackson and Maslach, 1982), burnout was assessed in 142 married, male police officers. Their wives were then asked, independently, to describe how these officers behaved at home when they were interacting with their families. Emotionally exhausted officers were described by their wives as coming home tense, anxious, upset, and angry, and as complaining about the problems they faced at work. These officers were also more withdrawn while at home, preferring to be left alone rather than share time with the family. The wives' reports also revealed that officers who had developed negative attitudes toward the people they dealt with also had fewer close friends.

Health May Deteriorate

Finally, burnout may eventually lead to health-related problems. In the study of police families described above, victims of burnout were more likely to suffer from insomnia and to use medications of various kinds. The officers reported using alcohol as a way of coping with their burnout, a finding that would not surprise anyone who knows that social drinking is a traditional aspect of the police subculture. Somewhat more surprising is an unpublished study of female nurses

Table 5-2.   Consequences of Burnout.

On the Job	At Home
complain to co-workers	tense and anxious with family
take frequent work breaks	comes home in irritable mood
unnecessary absences	escape from family
lowered involvement with job	prefer to be alone
decreased motivation to perform well	insomnia
quit job	alcohol abuse
seek promotion	overuse of medications

that revealed a similar link between burnout and alcohol use (Jackson and Maslach, 1983), suggesting that using alcohol to cope with burnout is not unique to the members of police departments or to males.

A summary of all these job and non-job consequences from burnout is illustrated in Table 5-2.

WHAT CAN ORGANIZATIONS DO ABOUT BURNOUT?

The question of what to do about burnout is most likely to be asked by two categories of people: those who are personally experiencing it, and those who believe it is a problem among their own staff members. When either a worker or a worker's supervisor asks, "What can I do about burnout?", the question is usually a request for information about how to help people cope with, or overcome, their present symptoms. Coping implies that the crisis has already arrived. Until recently, the question has been asked less frequently by people who are hoping to make changes now in order to prevent burnout in the future. Answers to the question differ greatly depending on whether the real question is, How can I cope with burnout? or How can I prevent burnout? Answers also differ depending on whether the question is asked by someone with the power to intervene by making organizational changes (e.g., supervisors or managers of burnout victims), or by an individual who wants to know about individual strategies for coping or burnout prevention. As they are defined here, coping strategies treat the symptoms of burnout without attacking the causes of those symptoms; they are viewed as short-term solutions that help the victim survive a crisis. From a larger perspective, it is clear that resources must be devoted to prevention strategies that involve changing work environments in order to decrease the probability of burnout. Many useful stress coping strategies have been described in other chapters of this book. Because burnout is a type of stress response, these coping strategies can be used by burnout victims.

PREVENTING BURNOUT

One of the consequences of the dearth of scientific studies on burnout is that we cannot conclusively point to particular job conditions and label them as causes of burnout. However, as Cherniss (1980) points out, organizations cannot afford to wait for definitive answers before beginning to implement prevention programs. Instead, we should use our theories about burnout, along with whatever empirical knowledge we have, to devise and test those prevention strategies that are most promising.

Expecting the Possible

In *Reality Shock*, Kramer (1974) argues that a major source of stress or burnout among members of the nursing profession is the gap that exists between the expectations nurses have when they begin their first job and the realities they discover there. Nurses and others who enter human service professions are often strongly motivated by a concern for humanity and a desire to help people. Upon beginning their first job, they anticipate being able to make visible improvements in other people's lives, and although they may not realize it yet, they also expect their contributions to be recognized as valuable. As any seasoned human service worker has discovered, the lofty expectations and goals they had as a novice were unrealistic. From the beginning they were doomed to failure if success meant achieving those naive goals.

That feelings of failure are related to stress reactions is a prominent theme in the stress literature. Studies of "learned helplessness" (Seligman, 1975) have been especially useful for advancing our understanding of the failure-stress relationship. In experimental studies of learned helplessness, subjects first go through a training phase during which they experience repeated failure on some task. After repeated failures, the person eventually learns that success on the task is impossible and failure is unavoidable. Subsequently, when these people are placed in a similar situation or asked to perform a similar task, their performance is very poor. Research on the learned helplessness phenomenon shows that repeated failures induce emotional disturbances such as anxiety, stress, and depression (Miller and Norman, 1979). These studies suggest that the feelings of disillusionment experienced by human service professionals early in their careers may result from a similar experience of repeated encounters with failure. In the early years of one's career, unrealistic expectations about what can be accomplished through one's job make the novice especially vulnerable to the feelings of helplessness. These soon translate into the burnout symptoms of emotional exhaustion, cynicism, and feelings of low accomplishment.

What can be done to prevent the devastating shock that occurs as a result of the discrepancy between naive ideals and reality? Kramer (1974) presents convincing evidence that anticipatory socialization programs can help decrease the magnitude of reality shock and its consequences. The philosophy underlying anticipatory socialization programs is that reality shock should be experienced before the human service worker begins the first full-time human service job. Furthermore, the reality shock should be experienced in a context that permits and encourages the development of constructive strategies for coping with the unexpected reality one faces. Throughout such a program, ideals are purposely challenged, and conflicts—such as the difference between the way things should be done based on professional standards and the way things actually are—are exposed. The initiates are then taught how to survive within the existing system without compromising their professional standards.

Kramer (1974) has also demonstrated that anticipatory socialization can be an effective method for decreasing the severity of the reality shock experience on the job. This, in turn, decreases turnover rates and absenteeism. Perhaps as a result of the coping skills learned during such a program, nurses who had gone through Kramer's program were more successful change agents once on the job, were more empathic toward patients, were happier, and exerted more leadership compared to other nurses. Because Kramer's anticipatory socialization program can serve as a model for any occupational group, it is outlined briefly below.

Phase 1. The purpose of the first phase of the program is to produce a mild form of the reality shock that an uninitiated worker might experience on the job. This is accomplished by presenting examples of real, on-the-job incidents that have been experienced by others. Kramer obtained tape-recorded examples of such experiences by asking relatively young nurses to describe a work situation that had been especially dissatisfying to them. One example of an incident used in Phase 1 of Kramer's program was a description of a physician who performed an open cardiac massage on an 80-year-old man "just for practice." Upon hearing about such an incident, novices were understandably upset and outraged. The role of the instructor at this time was to provide counter-arguments and defenses for the student to use in resolving the conflict between personal values and reality. (For example, if the physician doesn't practice, how will the procedure be learned? Or, if the nurse withdraws from the situation, isn't it more dangerous for the patient?) An important characteristic of the counter-arguments and defenses students were exposed to during this phase is that they were obtained from interviews with experienced nurses who had adopted them because they help them live with, or resolve, the conflicts they face.

Phase 2. By the end of Phase 1 of Kramer's program, participants had been exposed to the negative aspects of the bureaucratic practices that characterize most human service organizations. During Phase 2 participants were encouraged to think actively about alternative solutions for improving the situation. By thinking about the problems they saw and by trying to devise solutions, students came to appreciate and better understand the reasons why certain imperfect conditions exist. In conjunction with this, participants in the program were required to find and interview a position role model. The role model's attitudes and behaviors were then analyzed in order to identify the specific behaviors and traits that constituted a well-functioning professional.

Phase 3. Whereas Phases 1 and 2 focused on the participants' own expectations of how they should behave as nurses, Phase 3 of Kramer's program was aimed at teaching the participants what others expected of them. For example, the nature of the nurse-physician relationship was presented by a panel of physicians and nurses. Similarly, a panel composed of head nurses, supervisors and administrators exposed the novice to the expectations held by their immediate superiors. Another important aspect of Phase 3 was a panel discussion by recent nursing graduates who described what they were and were not able to accomplish on their jobs, thereby providing a realistic baseline against which the participants could evaluate their own future success and failure.

Phase 4. The final phase of Kramer's program taught theories and techniques of conflict resolution and negotiation. The intention of this phase was to teach skills that would aid the nurses in their role as agents for change. These skills would give them the option in the future to work toward changing those parts of a system that presented conflicts that were unacceptable to them.

There are several features of anticipatory socialization that should be apparent to the reader by this point. First of all, its major goals are to give participants a *realistic* picture of the jobs they are about to enter, and to provide skills for coping effectively with the difficulties they will face. Because the job is not idealized, some of its negative aspects are exposed. While the intent of this exposure is not to dissuade people from entering a job, it may have such an effect on some participants. Therefore, organizations may be reluctant to conduct such programs for fear of losing potential future employees. Alternatively, an organization may conduct anticipatory socialization programs but downplay the negative aspects of the organization, thereby defeating the purpose of narrowing the gap between expectations and reality. For these reasons, anticipatory socialization programs may be most beneficial when they are conducted by nonemploying groups, such as professional associations and training institutions.

A second important feature of anticipatory socialization programs is that they are aimed at burnout prevention, and are designed to be most applicable to new members of an occupational group. Exposing a 5-year veteran to such a program would probably do little to help with burnout prevention.

A third important feature of anticipatory socialization programs is that they are not designed to *change* reality, but merely to expose it in hopes that forewarning will lead to better preparation. As such, anticipatory socialization programs are likely to be useful for decreasing the frustrations that occur during the first two or three years. However, simply being prepared for the negative aspects of one's job does not guarantee that long-term exposure to that job will not lead to burnout. Changes in the job itself may also be necessary.

Increasing Participation in Decisionmaking

The importance of being able to control, or at least predict, future outcomes is well-recognized by psychologists (Averill, 1973; Miller and Norman, 1979). The opportunity to be self-determining, combined with the freedom and the ability to influence events in one's surroundings, can be intrinsically motivating and highly rewarding (Deci, 1980). When opportunities for control are absent and people feel trapped in an environment that is neither controllable nor predictable, both psychological and physical health are likely to suffer.

In most organizations, and especially in bureaucracies, employees are controlled by organizational rules, policies, and procedures. Often these rules and procedures are creations from an earlier era of the organization and are no longer as effective as they once were. Nevertheless, their enforcement continues until new rules are developed. Most often, the new rules are created by people in the highest levels of the organization and then imposed upon people at the lower levels. Sometimes the new rules are an improvement over the old rules, other times they are not. Regardless of whether or not they are an improvement, the new rules or procedures are likely to be experienced as another event in the organization over which the employees have no control.

Recent studies of burnout suggest that increasing employees' participation in the decisionmaking process, and thus increasing the amount of control they have, can be an effective way to prevent burnout from occurring. For example, in a study of hospital nurses, we found that feelings of emotional exhaustion were linked to feelings of lack of control (Maslach and Jackson, 1982). Nurses often feel unable to exercise control, either over the behavior of the physicians with whom they are closely interdependent, or over the decisions of the administrators who determine the hours and conditions of their work. Emotional exhaustion was higher for nurses who were less able to influence policies and decisions and for those who had more bureaucratic hassles. Emotional exhaustion was also higher for nurses who had fewer opportunities to be creative in carrying out their work.

In addition to increasing employees' feelings of control, participation in decisionmaking may help prevent burnout by clarifying role expectations and giving employees an opportunity to reduce some of the role conflicts they experience. The amounts of role ambiguity and role conflict people experience are strongly related to burnout. In particular, role ambiguity leads to emotional exhaustion and feelings of low accomplishment. Role conflict causes emotional exhaustion also, as well as the development of cynical attitudes toward clients (Schwab and Iwanicki, 1982).

Several studies have found that the decisionmaking processes in organizations have important implications for the amount of role conflict and ambiguity experienced by workers (Van Sell, Brief, and Schuler, 1981). Such studies suggest that an effective strategy for minimizing job-related strains and their consequences is to increase workers' opportunities to influence the decisions that they will eventually execute (participative decisionmaking), rather than isolating decisions in the higher levels of the organization.

Besides giving workers a feelings of control, participation in decisionmaking gives them the power they need to remove obstacles to effective performance, thereby reducing frustration and strain. One effective use of influence would be to persuade others to change their conflicting role expectations for one's own behavior. Through the repeated interchanges required by participative decisionmaking, members of the organization can also gain a better understanding of the demands and constraints faced by others. When the conflicts workers face become clear, perhaps for the first time, negotiation is likely to begin over which exepctations should be changed in order to reduce inherent conflicts. With participative decisionmaking people also become less isolated from their co-workers and supervisors. Through their discussions, employees learn about the formal and informal expectations held by others. They also learn about the formal and informal policies and procedures of the organization. This information can help reduce feelings of role ambiguity. It also makes it easier for the person to perform the job effectively.

In addition to reducing role conflict and ambiguity, participation in decisionmaking helps prevent burnout by encouraging the development of a social support network among co-workers. Recent studies have found that social support networks help people cope effectively with the stresses they experience on the job (see Chapter 6 of this book). Among human service professionals, one of the most important functions of a social support network is that it can assure workers that they are not the only ones experiencing difficulties on the job.

As Maslach and Jackson (1982) have noted, there is a tendency for people in human service occupations to blame themselves for any job-related failures they experience. Instead of seeing organizational constraints as the source of their problems, they are likely to conclude that "there is something wrong with me," or "I'm not cut out for this job." Human service workers come to this conclusion partly because a state of ignorance exists among them. In their efforts to maintain their professional demeanor, service providers may deny their difficulties and put on a facade that says, "I'm competent and everything is going well for me." Unfortunately, if everyone puts on their "I'm okay" facade, it intensifies the secret concerns individuals have and convinces them that they are alone with their problems. Participative decisionmaking helps build trust among the members of a unit. Gradually, as interpersonal relationships among co-workers are strengthened, people rely less on their facades; they begin to discuss their feelings openly and to build social support groups.

To summarize, allowing employees to participate in an organization's decisionmaking process can help prevent burnout by: (1) giving the workers a chance to influence how their role in the organization is defined by others, thereby preventing unnecessary role conflict; (2) providing information to employees about both formal and informal policies and procedures, thereby reducing role ambiguity and improving the employee's ability to work effectively within the constraints of the organization; and (3) encouraging the development of a supportive social network among co-workers.

While participative decisionmaking appears to be a very promising strategy for keeping burnout to a minimum, organizations that plan to use it should be aware of a number of factors that can determine whether increasing participation is likely to be effective or backfire. Among the most difficult issues an organization faces when increased participation is put into place is specifying the types of decisions in which employees will be allowed to have input. Two guidelines that should be followed when topics for discussion are chosen are: (1) an employee's input is most valuable when the decisions being made will have a direct impact on the day-to-day activities of the employee, and (2) asking employees to provide input into a decision and then ignoring their advice is worse than never asking their opinions.

Most employees recognize that there are some decisions for which they are unprepared to provide meaningful input because they do not have all of the relevant information needed to make the decision. However, most employees do consider themselves to be experts at their own particular job and the workings of their own particular unit. By necessity, people in other jobs and departments of the organization are less in tune with the factors that affect how well one is able to perform one's own job. Therefore, to have such people making decisions about procedures and policies that will affect one's own job creates frustration and a sense of lack of control. By giving employees opportunities to have input into decisions that impact them directly, supervisors and managers will find that better-quality decisions are made because the unintended, negative side effects of a particular decision are more likely to have been foreseen by the workers. In addition, employees will have more positive attitudes toward implementing decisions that they helped make.

Whereas asking employees to provide input into decisions can have very positive effects, it can also be disastrous if the employees perceive that management is "just playing games." In organizations where employees' opinions have traditionally been ignored, suddenly to ask people to devote time and energy to thinking about how to solve a difficult problem is likely to draw a response such as, "Why should I bother getting involved? They don't really care what I think anyway." Employees who doubt the sincerity of a request for their viewpoint may see the request as an attempt on the part of management to manipulate the employees. If employees can be convinced to participate in spite of their doubts, managers and supervisors should be prepared to accept fully and act on the input they receive, or risk sending their employees into a state of permanent apathy and cynicism.

In addition to carefully considering which topics employees should be asked to discuss, careful thought should also go into designing the procedure for obtaining employees' opinions. For example, Mechanic (1962) distinguished between the formal and informal power that members of an organization can have. Formal participation in decisionmaking would occur when official decisionmaking bodies, such as unions or councils, are created (Locke and Schweiger, 1979). Informal input might be obtained by holding regularly scheduled staff meetings. Locke and Schweiger (1979) identified two additional dimensions along which participation varies: forced versus voluntary participation, and direct versus indirect participation. If participation is forced, the force is likely to be applied to management by law, decree, or contract. In such cases, the attitudes of both management and nonmanagement personnel can be more antagonistic than when participation in decisionmaking is voluntary. Participation may allow for direct input from all individuals (one member, one vote), or it may occur indirectly through selected representatives. Information about how one's supervisor defines one's role is unlikely to be gained through indirect participation, so direct participation may be necessary for preventing burnout by reducing role conflict and ambiguity. Finally, workers' input might be sought for all decisions or only for a selected number of decisions. Asking employees to participate in all decisions would undoubtedly increase their workload to such an extent that any potential benefits of participation would be outweighed by the negative side effect of work overload.

Quantitative and Qualitative Changes in "Caseloads"

In almost any service organization, the major duties of the members are related to "handling the caseload," so suggestions for change often focus on this issue. Burnout seems inevitable when a professional is forced to provide care for too many people. As the ratio of clients-to-staff increases, the result is greater and greater emotional overload, until, like a wire that has too much electricity flowing through it, the worker burns out and emotionally disconnects. It is often concluded that if caseloads can be decreased (and the time pressure removed) more humane interactions would follow.

Both theory and research support the contention that decreasing the number of people for whom an employee is responsible will lower that employee's risk for burnout. In a nationwide study of 845 public contact employees, Barad (1979) found all three aspects of burnout (emotional exhaustion, depersonalization or cynicism, and feelings of low personal accomplishment) directly related to caseload size. In another study, physicians who spent a greater percentage of their total time in direct contact with patients experienced more emotional exhaustion and were more cynical (Maslach and Jackson, 1982). Finally, Pines and Maslach (1980) reported that decreasing the clients-to-staff ratio in a daycare setting reduced exhaustion levels among teachers. These and similar results reinforce a widely held belief that a major cause of burnout in human service professions is lack of human resources.

Believing that lack of resources is a primary cause of burnout, while at the same time knowing that it is extremely difficult, if not impossible, to lower caseloads in the type of economic situation that characterizes the 1980s, could be a source of stress in and of itself. Fortunately, the mere quantity of interaction that a person engages in is not the only determinant of burnout. Indeed, the tendency to assume that most problems could be solved if more resources were available is dangerous because it inhibits a search for alternative solutions that do not require additional spending.

One alternative to making quantitative changes in staff caseloads is to make qualitative changes. Maslach and Pines (1977) have suggested that burnout can be prevented by decreasing the number of clients for whom one is responsible, even if the total number of clients with whom one has contact is unchanged. In many organizations, the workload is arranged such that several staff members share responsibility for all of the clients. For example, if a daycare center has 5 staff members and 100 children to supervise, each staff member may be one-fifth responsible for 100 children. Such an arrangement is more likely to lead to staff burnout than if each staff member were given total responsibility for 20 children.

Qualitatively changing the workload to give more intensive responsibility for a smaller number of clients is an improvement for several reasons. First, it can sharply decrease the number of people with whom the staff member is expected to have high-quality relationships. It is easier to remember the details of 20 lives than the details of 100 lives. To cope effectively with 100 different people almost requires the staff member to ignore the unique characteristics of each person and lump them into categories based on their similarities, a strategy that can quickly lead to depersonalization and detachment.

Second, sharing responsibility with other staff members increases the likelihood of conflict and ambiguity concerning the specific responsibilities of each staff member. As Schward and Iwanicki (1982) have found, role conflict is strongly associated with feelings of emotional exhaustion and with the development of negative attitudes toward clients. They also found that role ambiguity, or a lack of clarity about one's job requirements, is associated with feelings of low personal accomplishment, perhaps because it is difficult to know you have done a good job when you are unsure about what the job is you are expected to do.

Finally, giving staff members total responsibility for a smaller number of clients results in jobs that are enriched. The staff member becomes responsible for engaging in a greater variety of tasks vis-à-vis each client, and when progress is made the staff member has the satisfaction of being able to claim personal credit for a job well done.

In addition to the distribution of responsibility for clients, the "mix" of clients with whom a staff member interacts may affect burnout (Cherniss, 1980). In almost every service occupation, certain types of clients are thought of as being less "desirable" than others. Their low desirability status may be because failure is almost inevitable vis-à-vis these clients (e.g., dying patients), because they require more intensive attention (e.g., handicapped students), or because their problems raise difficult moral and ethical issues (e.g., accused rapists). Often a few staff members are expected to carry a disproportionately large percentage of such clients. Such an arrangement puts excessive demands on some of the staff and sharply increases their susceptibility to burnout. A better arrangement would be to distribute the most desirable and least desirable clients across staff members to ensure that all staff have some likely sources of satisfaction and relatively few sources of inevitable difficulty or failure.

Increasing Feedback About Performance

A final job-related change that organizations concerned about burnout should consider is increasing the amount of feedback workers receive about their job performance. In many human service occupations, the job is structured such that the employee seldom hears when things went right for a client, but always hears if things went wrong. This is especially true in jobs where the main service the employee provides is advising people about how to solve their problems. For people in jobs like these, having clients never show up again may be the only form of positive feedback available. Clients who do not return have probably solved their problems, but because the practitioner's contribution to the solution is taken for granted by clients ("that's the job she's paid to do"), clients are unlikely to make a special effort to thank the practitioner. On the other hand, when things go badly for a client, the service provider is on the receiving end of complaints, threats, and verbal abuse. As a consequence, human service providers develop negative attitudes toward their clients and perceive themselves as failing in their jobs more than succeeding (Maslach and Jackson, 1982).

Because of the structure of human service organizations, there is a built-in bias that prevents employees from receiving positive feedback for a job well done. Therefore, organizations need to make a conscious effort to devise ways of obtaining such feedback for employees. One method of obtaining feedback is to ask clients to indicate how satisfied they are with the service they received using a Client Feedback Survey. When these surveys are conducted on a regular basis, they not only provide feedback about how well the service provider is currently performing, they also give the employee information about whether the performance has improved or declined.

A difficulty that sometimes arises with Client Feedback Surveys is that the typical client has contact with several members of the service organization. When this is the case, it is unreasonable to ask clients to evaluate the service they received from each person they dealt with. However, it may not be unreasonable to ask the client to evaluate the service received from each unit or department. A second problem with Client Feedback Surveys is that they may be perceived as threatening by the employees, especially if the information obtained by the survey becomes public information to be used by employees' supervisors. If an organization decides to develop a Client Feedback Survey, it should weigh carefully the costs and benefits of obtaining evaluations of departments rather than evaluations of individuals.

Co-workers are also a potential source of feedback about how well employees are doing on their jobs. Just as an organization might ask clients to complete a Client Feedback Survey, co-workers can be asked to make evaluations of each other, assuming they are able to observe each others' performance on the job. An advantage of co-worker evaluations is that they are being made by a person who is fully aware of the constraints placed on employees by the organization. Whereas clients will tend to evaluate the service they received against an ideal standard, the evaluations of co-workers will be based on an understanding of professional ethics and practices. Furthermore, the evaluation of co-workers has been shown to correlate with employees' own, self-reported burnout (Maslach and Jackson, 1981b).

CONCLUSIONS

Earlier in this chapter, it was noted that little research had been conducted to evaluate the effectiveness in preventing burnout of various interventions or changes in the job setting. Such research is badly needed in order to determine which interventions are most effective for particular situations. It is hoped that the lack of documented evidence will not completely inhibit organizations from exploring innovations designed to prevent burnout. Instead, the fact that so little evaluation research exists should prompt organizations to make changes cautiously and to monitor the effects of these changes. Rather than assume that one cure exists for all situations, we should assume that each organization is somewhat unique, and this uniqueness must be taken into account when potential burnout prevention programs are being considered. For example, if the opinions of employees are already actively solicited before most major decisions are made, increasing participation in decisionmaking is unlikely to affect future burnout levels. Similarly, if caseloads are already fairly low, or as low as they ever can be, changes in caseload quality, not quantity, should be seriously considered.

Not only is it prudent for organizations to recognize the need to be cautious in selecting an intervention strategy, it is prudent for them to accept the possibility that the particular intervention they choose may be ineffective. Therefore, organizations should evaluate the effects of any intervention they implement. Such evaluation information is usually crucial for convincing administrators to continue investing resources toward the solution of a problem. In addition to its usefulness to the particular organization implementing a change, evaluation data, if publicly available, can improve our understanding of the burnout phenomenon.

REFERENCES

Averill, J.R. 1973. "Personal Control over Aversive Stimuli and its Relationship to Stress." *Psychological Bulletin* 80, no. 4: 286–303.

Barad, C.B. 1979. "Study of Burnout Syndrome among Social Security Administrator Field Public Contact Employees." Unpublished report, Social Security Administration.

Cherniss, C. 1980. *Staff Burnout: Job Stress in the Human Services*. Beverly Hills: Sage.

Deci, E.L. 1980. *The Psychology of Self-Determination*. Lexington, Ma.: D.C. Heath.

Golembieski, R.T. 1981. "Organizational Development (OD) Interventions: Limiting Burnout through Change in Interactions, Structures, and

Policies." In *Proceedings of the First National Conference on Burnout*. Darby, Penn.: Gwynedd Mercy College/Mercy Catholic Medical Center.

Jackson, S.E., and C. Maslach. 1982. "After-Effects of Job-Related Stress: Families as Victims." *Journal of Occupational Behavior* 3: 63–77.

Jackson, S.E., and C. Maslach. 1983. "Burnout in the Medical Work Environment." Unpublished manuscript, University of California, Berkeley.

Kramer, M. 1974. *Reality Shock: Why Nurses Leave Nursing*. St. Louis: Mosby.

Locke, E.A., and D.M. Schweiger. 1979. "Participation in Decision-Making: One More Look." In *Research in Organizational Behavior*, Vol. 1, edited by B.M. Staw, pp. 265–340. Greenwich, Ct.: JAI Press.

Maslach, C., and S.E. Jackson. 1981a. *The Maslach Burnout Inventory*. Palo Alto, Ca.: Consulting Psychologists Press.

Maslach, C., and S.E. Jackson. 1981b. "The Measurement of Experienced Burnout." *Journal of Occupational Behavior* 2: 99–113.

Maslach, C., and S.E. Jackson. 1982. "Burnout in Health Professions: A Social Psychological Analysis." In *Social Psychology of Health and Illness*, edited by G. Sanders and J. Suls, pp. 227–251. Hillsdale, N.J.: Lawrence Erlbaum.

Maslach, C., and A. Pines. 1977. "The Burnout Syndrome in the Day Care Setting." *Child Care Quarterly* 6: 110–13.

Mechanic, D. 1962. "Sources of Power of Lower Participants in Complex Organizations." *Administrative Science Quarterly* 7: 349–64.

Miller, I.W., III, and W.H. Norman. 1979. "Learned Helplessness in Humans: A Review and Attribution Theory Model." *Psychological Bulletin* 86: 93–118.

Perlman, B., and E.A. Hartman. 1982. "Burnout: Summary and Future Research." *Human Relations* 35, no. 4: 283–305.

Pines, A., and C. Maslach. 1980. "Combatting Staff Burnout in a Child Care Center: A Case Study." *Child Care Quarterly* 9: 5–16.

Schwab, R.L., and E.F. Iwanicki. 1982. "Perceived Role Conflict, Role Ambiguity, and Teacher Burnout." *Educational Administration Quarterly* 18, no. 1.

Seligman, M.E.P. 1975. *Helplessness: On Depression, Development, and Death*. San Francisco: Freeman.

Van Sell, M.; A.P. Brief; and R.S. Schuler. 1981. "Role Conflict and Role Ambiguity: Integration of the Literature and Directions for Future Research." *Human Relations* 34: 43–72.

6 THE ROLE OF SOCIAL SUPPORT GROUPS IN STRESS COPING IN ORGANIZATIONAL SETTINGS

James A. Wells

The twentieth century has witnessed a profound change in the regime of diseases that account for the greater proportion of human morbidity and mortality. The shift from infectious diseases attributable to a single virulent micro-organism, to chronic diseases with unobserved onset and long-term, degenerative consequences has considerably altered how the causes of disease are both conceptualized and researched. A number of propositions may be stated concerning the study of chronic mental and physical disorders. First, the causes of disease are to be found in all levels of the personal environment, including not only biological, chemical, and nutritional factors, but also psychological and social factors. A second proposition is that chronic diseases may be influenced by multiple environmental factors drawn from diffuse sources within the several levels of the personal enviornment. Another is that these multiple factors may interact with one another in complex ways either to exacerbate or mitigate the likelihood of disease. Finally, a given environmental factor, rather than being specific to a particular disease, may be implicated in the etiology of a wide variety of diseases.

The author is indebted to Barbara C. Rowe and Becky Torstrick for suggestions and editorial assistance, to Becky Torstrick for typing the final draft, and to Opal Barbour for typing earlier portions. The writing of this paper was supported in part by NIMH Grant # MH14235.

113

The role of social support in stress management can be understood in the context of this kind of etiological model of physical and mental well-being. The growing awareness and acceptance that an adequate understanding of disease demands attention to psychosocial factors has led to considerable research, much of it in organizational contexts. Yet the thrust of this research has been largely confined to pathogenic aspects of the psychosocial environment, namely, psychosocial stress. Although psychosocial stress appears to exhibit generality, (that is, a given stressor may be implicated in the etiology of several diseases, and many diseases are related to multiple stressors), it is clear that psychosocial stress does not always lead to illness. Attention has therefore shifted to delineating those conditions of the person and environment that mitigate or exacerbate the disease-promoting effects of stress. The recent focus on social support as one such conditioning factor is a product of this shift.

Writers concerned with the phenomenon of social support have not been able to provide a clear, conceptual definition, nor, in light of this shortcoming, have researchers arrived at a single model of how social support operates to promote resistance to stress and disease. What these writers have provided is a collection of creative and enlightening reviews of social science and epidemiological studies pointing to the health-promoting character of primary social relationships (Cassel, 1976; Cobb, 1976; Gore, 1973; Gottlieb, 1981; House, 1981; Kaplan, Cassel, and Gore, 1977; McMichael, 1978; Payne, 1980; Pinneau, 1975). The scope and exhaustiveness of these reviews have perhaps militated against precise definitions and theoretical consensus, while empirical tests of primitive notions of social support have seldom been cumulative and have often been plagued with methodological problems. Still, a number of promising themes have begun to develop and be repeated in this literature. Rather than recapitulate the initiatives already taken by the rather exhaustive reviews cited above, this chapter will discuss a number of the themes that have developed out of attempts to specify the scope and nature of social support.

Most conceptualizations begin with the notion that social support represents, in its most general sense, resources for coping with stress. Defining social support therefore becomes the task of defining those qualities of social relationships that are pertinent coping resources. The major problem in defining social support specifically is the same as that in defining coping resources specifically—there is an almost unlimited repertoire of psychological and behavioral processes that may be invoked in coping with stress. Thus, the first definitional problem is in achieving scope of conceptualization. In addition, many behaviors are multiplex: they may sometimes, but not always, be invoked for the purpose of coping, for example, in the case of drinking or watching television. A second definitional problem therefore inheres in the ambiguity of psychological and behavioral processes as indicators of coping. Very closely related to this is the idea that coping is purposeful, goal-oriented behavior. The failure to recognize, or the wish to ignore, this aspect of coping has often led to tautological definitions that equate coping with results rather than with responses. Finally, there is the telic character of coping. If coping is invoked in order to manage stress, a given coping attempt may be judged as successful or unsuccessful, and one style of coping as more successful or better than another. The telic problem is especially piquant when coping attempts, such as drug use, denial, or withdrawal, carry with them burdens unrelated to their original purpose.

Most efforts to define coping and social support have reduced the scope of conceptualization to a manageable set of constructs with which to guide theory and measurement. The most common reduction concerns the domain of the coping objective. Lazarus and his colleagues (Folkman, 1982; Folkman and Lazarus, 1980; Lazarus, 1981) distinguish between coping that is problem-focused, coping aimed at altering or managing a situational stressor, and coping that is emotion-focused, coping aimed at altering or managing emotional responses to stress. Pearlin and Schooler (1978) also distinguish coping responses that help people to accommodate emotionally to existing stress. This basic distinction is also found in definitions of social support. Pinneau (1972, 1975) has argued for the existence of two distinct clusters of supportive behaviors: ". . . one in which the supportive other attempts to improve objective conditions for the person and the other cluster in which the supportive other . . . seeks to reduce the person's suffering (i.e. psychological strain)" (1972: 15–16). These two clusters are termed tangible support and psychological support respectively. House (1974) makes a similar distinction between socio-emotional and instrumental support.

Another component of coping is appraisal (Lazarus, 1966). Primary appraisal refers to the initial perception of a situation as stressful, that is, that environmental demands exceed the person's abilities or that environmental rewards do not meet the person's needs. The essence of primary appraisal is the person's assessment of the situation in terms of the individual's own personal resources, resulting in the perception of the need for coping. Secondary appraisal refers to the decision on how to cope. Folkman (1982) argues that secondary appraisal determines whether one will opt for problem-focused coping, when ameliorative action is deemed possible, or emotion-focused coping, when ameliorative action is impossible. Pearlin and Schooler (1978) do not distinguish appraisal as a separate entity, but at least include primary appraisal as an objective of coping. Thus, they argue for a category of coping responses that function to control the meaning of a problem situation. In addition, they point to the importance of psychological resources for coping that center around self-identity, for example, self-esteem, and perceived environmental mastery.

One finds these additional coping concerns often reflected in definitions of social support. Cobb (1976) distinguishes three types of information that constitute social support: (1) emotional support, leading the person to believe he is cared for; (2) esteem support, leading the person to believe he is valued; and (3) a sense of belonging to the social network of mutual obligation. Cobb sees esteem support as promoting the mobilization of resources and the others as sources of self-validation. "It would not be unreasonable to suppose that esteem support would encourage a person to cope, i.e., to go out and attempt to master a problem. Likewise emotional support and a sense of belonging might provide the climate in which self-identity changes can most readily take place" (1976: 311). Cobb's definition, therefore, seems to limit the function of social support to the mobilization of psychological resources for coping.

Others have added support for secondary appraisal to their conceptualizations of social support. Caplan and Killilea (1976), for example, define the functions of social support as the promotion of emotional mastery, feedback validating self-identity, and guidance regarding problems and methods for dealing with them. The last function clearly promotes secondary appraisal. Similarly, Kahn and Antonucci (1980) add affirmation to a list already including affect and aid. They define affirmation as the acknowledgement of the appropriateness of coping decisions. Pinneau (1975) likewise divides psychological support into an emotional component and an appraisal component. Appraisal support, for Pinneau, largely consists of information for problem-solving.

House (1981: 23), after a careful and thoughtful review of social support definitions, has constructed the most inclusive typology of support. In this typology, he has adapted each of the major elements of his predecessors' definitions into his own categories and suggested contents:

1. Emotional support (esteem, affect, trust, concern, listening).
2. Appraisal support (affirmation, feedback, social comparison).
3. Informational support (advice, suggestion, directives, information).
4. Instrumental support (aid in kind, money, labor, time, modifying environment).

House (1981: 39) further distinguishes appraisal and information support by noting that the former is information relevant to self-evaluation, while the latter is information about the environment.

In evaluating these attempts to define the scope of social support, one is struck by how closely they come to conceptualizing social support in terms fully commensurate with the elements of the coping process without explicitly doing so. House (1981: 22) has declared that an adequate conceptualization of social support requires answering the question, "*Who* gives *what* to *whom* regarding *which* problems?" The *what* to which so much attention is paid is implicitly recognized to be support for coping. It would therefore seem productive for both theory and research to make this connection explicit by categorizing social support directly in terms descriptive of the coping process. The following list of supports incorporates five elements of coping already introduced by Folkman (1982), Lazarus (1966), and Pearlin and Schooler (1978).

1. Support for primary appraisal: information pertinent to the person's subjective assessment of fit with the environment. Information about environmental rewards and demands, as well as personal needs and abilities is included. This is support for experiencing, or suppressing the experiencing, the need to cope. This corresponds to House's appraisal support and, perhaps, some elements of informational support as well.
2. Support for secondary appraisal: information offering or delimiting ways of coping with experienced stress. This includes at least those portions of House's informational support concerned with advice, suggestion, and directive.

3.   Support for environmental modification: help in enacting problem-focused coping. This coincides with House's instrumental support.
4.   Support for emotional control: help in enacting emotion-focused coping, by allaying or controlling emotional distress. This covers much of House's emotional support, especially such behaviors as concern, listening, and affective sympathy.
5.   Support for psychological resources: help in maintaining self-identity, esteem, and mastery. This also is placed under emotional support by House and is better represented in Cobb's (1976) esteem support.

With reference to House's guiding question for conceptualizing support (Who gives what to whom regarding which problems?), it was noted that most attention has been paid to types of support. Considerable attention has been paid to sources of support as well (the "who" in question). Sources of support are fairly limited in scope and tend to vary in emphasis with the type of problem or stress under study. Studies of work organizations emphasize supervisors, co-workers, and subordinates, whereas broader epidemiological studies emphasize family and friends (Udris, 1982). Studies by clinical psychologists emphasize professional sources, such as counselors and therapists (Caplan, 1974; Cottlieb, 1981). Few studies answer the question of which source provides the most support. One organizational study, Caplan et al. (1975: 122), measured support from supervisors, co-workers, and home (family and friends) on comparable scales. This study finds the means of these three sources to be 2.89, 3.08, and 3.49, respectively. Thus, the workers in their sample report considerably more support from home than from workplace sources, where support from co-workers is somewhat greater than that from supervisors.

Who gets support is also a question that is seldom asked. There is little evidence pertaining to individual differences in rates of social support. Caplan et al. (1975: 294) again provides some evidence for differences due to social background. Correlations of years of schooling, socioeconomic status, and income with co-worker support are 0.22, 0.30, and 0.28, respectively. The same correlations for supervisor support are 0.12, 0.18, and 0.13, and those for home support are 0.10, 0.08, and 0.14. Thus, support for work stress is positively related to social status. There is a double deficit for lower-status workers since they also experience greater levels of job stress (Caplan et al., 1975; Fletcher and Payne, 1979).

Little attention has likewise been paid to the behaviors of providers of social support and how the provision of social support relates to the recipient's perceptions of receiving social support. This issue is given scant attention in definitions of social support, and no attention at all in the measurement of social support, where the "who gives what to whom" question is invariably answered from the point of view of the recipeint (the "whom"). Thus, what we know of social support is confined to subjective support, the recipient's perceptions of who provides them with support, of what types, and how much. Such an approach is not completely without justification, since social support theory presumes that the acts of supporters are mediated through the perceptions of recipients (based on the Lewininan notion of a psychological life space that mediates the outer hull of social intercourse). Certain questions can only be answered with information not mediated in this manner. For example, Caplan (1972) reports in his study of NASA scientists, engineers, and administrators that social support from subordinates is a more important buffer of stress effects on the risk of coronary heart disease than is support from supervisors or co-workers. Is this due to differences in the kind or amount of supportive behaviors on the part of subordinates, or is it due to differences in how the support of subordinates is perceived by the recipient? An answer requires objective, extra-individual measures of social support. If social support is to serve as an effective tool for stress management, then its causes, as well as its consequences, will have to be explored.

A related issue also requires the measurement of objective social support. This issue revolves around the notion that a given individual may be both a source of stress and of social support. This fact is given somewhat more attention in studies concerned with families than in studies of organizations, but in most research sources of support are specified concretely while sources of stress are left quite vague. It must be remembered, however, that, even in organizations where job demands and rewards derive ultimately from the formal characteristics of the institution, these demands and rewards are communicated by individuals. Thus, for example, role conflict or responsibility pressure will be induced by the concrete actions of others in the workplace. What then are the consequences of supportive behaviors by these same individuals? In a recent paper (Wells,

1982), this author found that supervisor support is an especially effective buffer of the effects of objective job conditions on perceptions of stress. Supervisors may be a more important source of support than co-workers specifically because they are the carriers of organizational demands and rewards whose impact they are in a position to ameliorate. No study to date has incorporated either the notion of individuals as simultaneous sources of stress and support or measures of objective support.

Clearly then, the conceptualization of social support has not advanced evenly on all fronts. Most effort has been expended on taxonomies of support that more or less indicate the ways in which perceptions of social support may be implicated in the coping process. It seems that this owes in large part to the fact that conceptualization has been in response to research indicating that perceived support can mitigate the disease-inducing effects of stress. Thus, social support and its definition are derivatives of stress theory. Payne (1980) has implied that social support ought to be studied in its own right—a point that is well-taken insofar as it emphasizes the need for research into the structure and causes of social support and more specificity in both its relation to coping and its interaction with stress.

The author is aware of only one study, that of Pearlin et al. (1981), that explicitly combines measures of social support and coping in the same analysis. This study is concerned with changes in depression following job disruption (firing, lay-off, demotion, or illness leave), and how changes in perceived economic strain, changes in self-esteem, and changes in mastery intervene in the process. As one would expect, job disruption increases strain and depression and decreases self-esteem and mastery; strain increases depression and decreases self-esteem, and mastery; and self-esteem and mastery each decrease depression (all effects are statistically significant controlling for age, sex, race, occupational status, marital status, and education). Pearlin's measure of coping consists of several survey questions concerned with positive comparisons of income and standard of living and devaluation of the importance of money. This type of coping seems most consistent with the primary appraisal category (coping with person-environment fit). Unfortunately, the study's measure of social support is not oriented specifically to eliciting resources for primary appraisal, but is rather broader in scope (Pearlin et al. regard it as emotinal support). Social support consists of the sum of the following two variables:

Among your friends and relatives, including your (husband/wife), is there someone you feel you can tell just about anything to, someone you can count on for understanding and advice? (Scored 0 = nobody, 1 = one person, 2 = two or more people).

(My spouse is someone . . .) I can really talk with about things that are important to me.

Clearly, these two measures might comprise resources for a number of types of coping (with the possible exception of support for environmental modification). The rather different content of the coping and social support measures is reflected in a low correlation (0.14) between the two.

Both coping and social support are implicated in the stress process described by Pearlin et al. (1981) and, as might be expected by their different content, in quite different ways. Coping directly increases mastery and buffers the impact of job disruption on economic strain, self-esteem, and depression. (Note that primary appraisal coping buffers primary appraisal, i.e., economic strain, but its effects are not restricted to that.) Social support directly decreases economic strain and buffers the effect of job disruption on self-esteem and mastery. In other words, social support in this case functions to reduce perceived stress and buffer psychological resources (i.e., persons higher in support are not susceptible to decrements in psychological resources owing to job disruption).

HYPOTHESIZED EFFECTS OF SUPPORT

In the last example, social support exhibits two quite different types of effects. In the first type, an increase in social support leads directly to a reduction in the level of a second variable. This is known as a main effect. In the second type, an increase in social support leads to a reduction in the strength of relationship between two other variables. This is known as a buffering effect. A theme that has evolved from empirical studies of social support is a contention over which of the two types of effects of social support, main effect or buffering, is more crucial. The difference between the two types of effects is, perhaps, subtle, but it can be reduced to the question of whether it is everyone, or only those persons under stress, who can benefit from social support. If, for example, social support directly increases health (a main effect), then everyone could benefit from more social support. If social support reduces the impact of stress on health, then social support will be pertinent for only those persons under stress and will bring no benefit to those without stress. Insofar as intervention is a practical goal of such research, the "main effect" hypothesis implies universal intervention, or at least identification of those with little or no social support as a high-risk group. The "buffering" hypothesis implies identification of those with medium to high stress as a high-risk group.

The issues are not as clear-cut, however, as implied in the foregoing analysis. House (1981: 33) graphically illustrates how it is possible for both effects to be operating simultaneously, so that social support at once reduces the impact of stress on ill health (buffering), and reduces the mean level of ill health (main effect). Yet, this type of simultaneity has been ignored in the theoretical and empirical literature. For example, LaRocco, House, and French (1980: 217) report forty-nine regression equations in which they found significant buffering effects (statistical interactions). Although the authors do not report statistical significance, the magnitudes of some of the social support coefficients seem to indicate that important main effects are operating in conjunction with buffering. Indeed, most empirical reports (those of the present author being no exception) tend to concentrate on evidence of buffering, while main effects are relegated to a minor role or ignored altogether. In light of one of the usual features of these studies, this seems in retrospect to be a glaring omission. This feature is that many of the studies measure multiple indicators of stress, multiple sources of social support, and multiple outcomes, such as psychological strain or ill health. This makes many tests of social support's effects, one for each combination of stress, support, and outcome, possible. The usual procedure is to test each combination for a buffering effect (a statistical interaction of support and stress that exhibits evidence of support reducing the effect of stress on the outcome), and to report the proportion of all tests performed in which evidence of buffering appears. If this proportion exceeds a proportion attributable to statistical error, say five or ten percent, then evidence for buffering is declared. The problem is that among the tests in which no buffering is found, there may well be significant main effects of social support. The question of types of effects would be better understood if, in the future, authors were to report four proportions: (1) the proportion of tests in which there is no effect of social support whatsoever; (2) the proportion in which social support exhibits a main effect on the outcome; (3) the proportion in which support buffers stress effects on the outcome; and (4) the proportion in which both types of effects are exhibited. The resolution of the issue of main effects versus buffering is not likely to be realized in favor of one of the two alternatives, but rather in a better specification of which sources of support buffer which stresses, which sources of support have main effects, which have both types of effects, and which have few or no effects at all.

It is interesting to note that this lack of empirical specificity is not wanting in pertinent data. A number of studies provide evidence of the buffering effects of social support (e.g., Caplan, 1972; Cobb and Kasl, 1977; Eaton, 1978; Gore, 1978; House and Wells, 1978; LaRocco, House, and French, 1980; Nuckolls, Cassel, and Kaplan, 1972; Wells, 1980; Winnubst, Marcelissen, and Kleber, 1982). Yet, the urge to search for buffering effects remains strong, and in these studies, social support main effects play second fiddle, if they play at all. Indeed, those studies that promote the main effects hypothesis largely represent failures to find the expected buffering effects (e.g., Andrews et al., 1978; LaRocco and Jones, 1978; Lin et al., 1979; Pinneau, 1975, 1976). The search for buffering effects is grounded in a conceptualization of social support wherein support is viewed as a condition of individuals within whom stress-outcome relationships are occurring. Questions are phrased to ask what social support does to the stress-outcome relationship, and not what it does to the components of that relationship. Thus, the authors of the aforementioned studies cannot be faulted for testing the specified theory, but only for failing to advance it.

There are other obstacles to the advancement of theory. An unclear central concept is a distinct disadvantage to any theory, and the lack of definitional consensus regarding social support has already been discussed. When different theoretical definitions result in widely varying operational definitions, comparability of research is compromised. This is true of much of the research on social support. Likewise, comparability is sacrificed when methodologies differ. This is brought home rather forcefully in the re-analysis of Pinneau's (1975, 1976) results by LaRocco, House, and French (1980). Pinneau chose to test for buffering effects among those combinations of stress, support, and outcome in which the indicator of support had a significant correlation with both the stressor and the outcome. This procedure is entirely arbitrary since such correlations are not a necessary prerequisite for buffering. Furthermore, Pinneau divided his sample into subgroups according to level of social support and compared correlations of stress and outcome across subgroups to ascertain evidence of buffering. This again is an invalid procedure since it is statistically inappropriate to compare correlations across subsamples of observations (regression slopes should be used). As a result, Pinneau found an insubstantial proportion of buffering effects among his multiple tests and reported this as a failure of the buffering hypothesis. In their re-analysis of his data, LaRocco, House, and French (1980) eschewed Pinneau's arbitrary selection technique and employed regression analysis for testing for buffering. These authors found buffering effects in a substantial proportion of the tests.

Important as it may be to establish empirical results derived from a theory (in this case, main effects or buffering), it is equally important to replicate those results across varying populations. Conceptual confusion, variability of measurement, and methodological differences all conspire to prevent generalization of results and to promote the kind of theoretical elaboration that ensues when generality does not hold. It is regrettable that so little attention has been paid to this important issue. Fortunately, there are at least three studies of social support for which some claims to replication can be made. It is worthwhile to attempt a comparison of the results.

SOCIAL SUPPORT IN THREE STUDIES

We will be examining a study of twenty-three occupations by LaRocco, House, and French (1980), a study of rubber workers by House and Wells (1978), Wells (1980), and a study of Dutch workers by Winnubst, Marcelissen, and Kleber (1982). The first of these was a U.S. sample of 636 workers stratified into twenty-three occupations ranging from unskilled blue-collar work to highly trained professionals (see Caplan et al., 1975). The rubber study was based on 1,809 blue-collar workers from a U.S. rubber, tire, and chemicals manufacturing plant (see House et al., 1979). The Dutch sample consisted of 1,246 blue- and white-collar workers from thirteen industrial concerns in the southeastern Netherlands. These three studies are closely tied by the similarity in conceptualization and measurement of social support. The operationalization was based on asking questions concerning emotional and instrumental support about a variety of potential sources of support. The three items used in House and Wells (1978) and Wells (1980) are common to all three studies:

1. How much can each of these people be relied on when things get tough at work?
2. How much is each of the following people willing to listen to your work-related problems?
3. How much is each of the following people helpful to you in getting your job done?

One additional item was asked in the twenty-three occupations study, and two additional items were asked in the Dutch workers study that were similar in content. The twenty-three occupations study elicited responses to these items concerning supervisor, co-workers, and support at home (family and friends). The research on rubber workers elicited responses similarly for supervisors and co-workers, but separately for spouse and friends/relatives. The Dutch workers study elicited responses concerning supervisor and co-workers only. The Dutch study also reported no reliabilities of the social support measures, but those in the other studies were quite comparable (in the range of 0.73 to 0.92).

Other pertinent measures varied more widely across the studies. Although the broad categories of perceived stress, affective strain, and health outcome were adhered to in each study, the concrete instrumentation within these broad constructs was not always the same. In a few cases, the very same or quite similar measures were employed, thus allowing for direct comparisons among the studies. The following is a comparison of the rates and nature of buffering effects and main effects of social support in the three studies of work organizations.

It is the buffering effect of social support with which these studies were more concerned, and it is with rates of buffering that this comparison will begin. The rate of buffering is an important indicator for two reasons. First, because these studies employ multiple indicators of stresses, strains, and health outcomes, social support may buffer some of the relationships between stress and strain, stress and health, or strain and health but not others. Rates of buffering are observed to ensure that they exceed levels that might be owing to chance variation alone. Secondly, there is the concern, noted in the previous section, that buffering may be receiving too much attention relative to the main effects of social support. Observation of the rates indicates the magnitude of importance of buffering effects.

Table 6–1 presents a comparison of rates of social support buffering effects in the three samples of workers. An overall rate is reported, with rates broken down by type of relation buffered, by source of social support, and, where comparable measures exist, by outcome and by predictor involved in the relationship. For each of the study samples, two overall rates are given. One is the overall rate of significant statistical interactions with social support, and the other is the rate of effects in which the result is in the theoretically expected direction (i.e., social support reduces the impact of stress or strain on the outcome). The remainder are rates of buffering in the expected pattern as well.

The first line of entries in the table gives the overall rates of interaction. The rates of significant interactions are 29.2, 18.2, and 20.0 percent respectively in the twenty-three occupations sample, the Dutch workers sample, and the rubber workers sample. The rates of true buffering are 23.0, 15.3, and 13.6 percent respectively. Since all three studies employed a 10 percent level of significance, one could expect 10 percent of the tests to be significant due to chance alone. One sees that the rates of all significant tests and of tests in the expected direction exceed the level of chance variation. The rates of social support effects in the direction contrary to the theoretical hypothesis (i.e., the rate of all significant equations minus the rate of theoretically expected equations within each sample), are 6.2, 2.9, and 6.4 percent respectively. It is noteworthy that these rates are all within the bounds of chance variation.

The overall rate is broken down into the type of relation buffered in the second panel of Table 6–1. Rates are presented for relationships of perceived stress with health outcome, affective strain with health outcome, and perceived stress with affective strain. As with the overall rate, the rate of buffering of stress-health relationships is considerably higher in the twenty-three occupations sample than in either of the other two samples. Indeed the rates of buffering in the expected manner are barely at chance level in the Dutch workers and rubber workers samples (10% and 12.2% respectively). The rate of buffering of strain-health relationships is again quite high in the twenty-three occupations sample (44.4%), but the others are also

Table 6-1. Comparison of Rates of Social Support Buffering Effects in Three Samples.[a]

	Twenty-three Occupations Sample	Dutch Workers Sample	Rubber Workers Sample
Overall Rate	29.2[b]	18.2[b]	20.0[b]
	23.0[c]	15.3[c]	13.6[c]
By Relation:			
Stress-Health	30.0	10.0	12.2
Strain-Health	44.4	16.7	20.0
Stress-Strain	13.3	18.3	—
By Support:			
Supervisor	16.0	18.8	18.2
Co-worker	34.6	11.8	12.7
Spouse	(19.8)	—	20.0
Friend/Relative	( )	—	3.6
By Outcome:			
Irritation	36.1	40.0	—
Anxiety	25.0	10.0	—
Depression	38.9	10.0	—
Somatic complaints	25.0	—	22.7
Heart problems	—	22.7	13.6
By Predictor:			
Role conflict	47.6	22.7	25.0
Workload	33.3	22.7	10.0
Future ambiguity	19.0	18.2	—
Responsibility	—	9.1	10.0
Job satisfaction	27.8	—	20.0

[a]Entries are percentages indicating the proportion of tested equations in which the designated interaction between stress (or strain) and social support occurred. Sources of data as follows—23 Occupations Sample: LaRocco et al. (1980); Dutch Workers Sample: Winnubst et al. (1982); Rubber Workers Sample: House and Wells (1978), Wells (1980).

[b]The proportion of tests in which a significant interaction occurred between the predictor and social support without regard to theoretical fit.

[c]The proportion of equations in which a significant interaction occurred between the predictor and social support which also provides evidence of the buffering effect of social support. This applies to all remaining entries in the table.

above chance levels. Remarkably, there are no reversals (i.e., effects contrary to the theoretical hypothesis among these relationships). In each sample, rates of buffering of strain-health relationships are greater than rates of buffering of stress-health relationships. Buffering of stress-strain relationships is tested only in the twenty-three occupations and Dutch workers samples. In contrast to the other types of relations, buffering of stress-strain relationships is less prevalent in the twenty-three occupations sample.

The next breakdown of buffering rate is by source of social support. Supervisor and co-workers are sources of support common to all three studies. Support from spouse and support from friends or relatives are measured separately in the rubber workers study and as a composite (home support) in the twenty-three occupations study. Rates of buffering by supervisors are strikingly similar in the Dutch workers sample and the rubber workers sample, with the rates of expected buffering being 18.8 and 18.2 percent respectively. In the twenty-three occupations sample, the rate of buffering in the expected manner is somewhat lower than in the other samples. For co-worker support, the rates of theoretical buffering are also quite similar in the Dutch workers and rubber workers samples. In contrast, the rates of buffering of co-workers' support in the twenty-three occupations sample is three times the rate in either of the other two samples. Finally, the rate of buffering for home support in the twenty-three occupations sample is quite similar to the rates of spouse support buffering in the rubber workers sample. In the latter sample, the rate of theoretical buffering by friend/relative support does not exceed the level of chance variation.

In disaggregating the overall rates of buffering in the three studies by type of relation and by source of support, a number of intriguing issues are revealed. It appears that rates of buffering of relationships between affective strain and health are higher than rates of buffering of relationships between perceived stress and health (this is true for all three studies). It is possible that the particular measures of social support employed in these studies emphasize that type of support (emotional) most appropriate for buffering emotional strains. House and Wells (1978) explicitly state that their measures emphasize the emotional component. This will remain a guess until more is known as to whether support effects are general or specific to particular problems, and until more is known about the separability of measures of emotional support and affective strain (cf. Kasl, 1978). Buffering effects of social support on relationships between perceived stress and affective strain exhibit contradictory effects. Not only is the rate of this type of buffering greater in the Dutch workers sample, but stress-strain relationships are the most likely type of relationship to be buffered. Conversely, this is the least likely relationship to be buffered in the twenty-three occupations sample. It is therefore difficult to determine whether this interesting difference is due to sample differences or to the differences in modes of buffering.

The pattern of rates of buffering by sources of support is quite revealing. It seems that the excess rate of buffering in the twenty-three occupations sample is due to a threefold rate of buffering due to co-worker support. In both the Dutch workers and rubber workers samples, all workers are employed in hierarchical, industrial organizations. House and Wells (1978) have remarked that this type of vertical organization may block the kind of collegial interactions that might lead to social support among co-workers, but that supervisors, because of their strategic placement in the flow of workplace communications, may be in a position to buffer workplace stresses and strains. Unlike the other two samples, the twenty-three occupations sample includes a considerable number of professional workers who are self-employed or employed in horizontally organized workplaces. Since supervisors are a characteristic of hierarchical organization, most of these workers have no supervisor. As one would therefore expect, rates of buffering due to supervisor support in the twenty-three occupations sample are similar to the rates in the other two samples. However, the rates of co-worker support are very much higher in the twenty-three occupations group. This hypothesis should be tested by evaluating support buffering separately for hierarchical and collegial occupations. Such a test may well show that more attention should be paid to occupational and organizational structure than has been done in past studies of social support.

The final two panels of Table 6-1 illustrate buffering rates for those outcomes (health variables and strains) and predictors (stresses and strains) common to at least two of the studies considered here. Three outcomes, irritation, anxiety, and depression, are common to both the twenty-three occupations sample and the Dutch workers sample. Rates of buffering of irritation are fairly high and quite similar in the two samples. However, the rates are considerably higher in the twenty-three occupations sample for support's buffering of effects on anxiety and depression. Rates of buffering of effects on somatic complaints are quite similar in the twenty-three occupations and rubber workers samples, while the rate of buffering of effects on heart problems is nearly twice as high in the Dutch workers sample as in the rubber workers sample. Among predictors, two are common to all three samples, namely, role conflict and workload. The effects of role conflict are buffered at nearly equal rates in the Dutch workers and rubber workers samples, but at a rate twofold greater in the twenty-three occupations sample. The effects of future ambiguity, common to the twenty-three occupations and Dutch workers samples, is buffered at almost equal rates in the two samples, as is responsibility in the Dutch workers and rubber workers samples. Effects of job satisfaction are buffered at somewhat higher rates in the twenty-three occupations sample than in the rubber workers samples.

These results must be understood in light of the qualification that though the outcomes or predictors may be similar across the studies, the other elements of the buffering effects are not the same in all cases. Thus, two samples share irritation as an outcome, but the rate within each sample consists of tests of different predictors of irritation and different sources of support as buffers. Some of the results regarding outcomes and predictors may reflect little more than the higher rate of buffering (presumably due to co-worker support) in the twenty-three occupations sample. This may be the case, for example, with anxiety, depression, role conflict, and job satisfaction. However, there are other cases where this excess of buffering is not exhibited, for example, irritation, somatic complaints, and future ambiguity. In a similar way, comparisons of rates of buffering between the Dutch workers and rubber workers samples are quite similar for role conflict and resonsibility, but rates in the Dutch workers sample are greater for heart problems and workload. There is little with which to inform an interpretation of these varied patterns of results. Yet, with previous qualifications in mind, it ought to be noted that there may well be important differences in how particular predictors interact with social support to produce particular outcomes. The current mode of research which explores numerous predictors, outcomes, and social supports is not well-suited to elicit these particularities and should be superceded by more focused studies.

Although not every buffering effect is replicated across the studies, there are a few instances where the exact same relationship of predictor and outcome is tested for the buffering effect of social supports. These are presented in Table 6–2. The table is designed to make pair-

Table 6-2. Results of Social Support Buffering among Replications across Three Samples.

Outcome	Stress or Strain	Social Support	Stress or Strain	Social Support
	Twenty-three Occupations		Dutch Workers	
Irritation	Future ambiguity	Supervisor	Future ambiguity	None
	Role conflict	Supervisor Co-worker	Role conflict	Supervisor Co-worker
	Workload	Supervisor Co-worker	Role overload	Supervisor
Anxiety	Future ambiguity	Supervisor	Future ambiguity	Co-worker
	Role conflict	Co-worker	Role conflict	None
	Workload	None	Role overload	None
Depression	Future ambiguity	Co-worker	Future ambiguity	None
	Role conflict	Co-worker	Role conflict	None
	Workload	Co-worker	Role overload	Co-worker
	Rubber Workers		Twenty-three Occupations	
Somatic complaints	Role conflict	Supervisor Co-worker Spouse	Role conflict	Co-worker Home
	Workload	Spouse	Workload	Co-worker
	Job Satisfaction	Spouse	Job dissatisfaction	None
	Rubber Workers		Dutch Workers	
Heart problems	Role conflict	None	Role conflict	None
	Workload	None	Role overload	Supervisor Co-worker
	Responsibility	None	Responsibility	None

wise comparisons of the samples. An outcome is listed in the left column, and across each row one reads under the heading for each of two samples an entry for the stress or strain with a presumed effect on the outcome and an entry for those sources of support, if any, that buffer the relationship between the designated predictor and outcome. Thus, in the first row of the table, the outcome is irritation, and the stress measure replicated in both the twenty-three occupations and Dutch workers samples is future ambiguity. The relationship between future ambiguity and irritation is buffered by supervisor support in the twenty-three occupations sample, but is not buffered in the Dutch workers sample. Since the Dutch workers study measured only supervisor and co-worker support, only those two sources are considered in this comparison. In this instance, two tests are performed in each sample, one each for supervisor and co-worker support as sources of buffering for the relationship between future ambiguity and irritation. Since co-worker support had no buffering effect in either sample, this is evidence of a replication, just as if it had had a buffering effect in both. Since supervisor support had an effect in one sample but not the other, this is a failure to replicate.

In the comparison between the twenty-three occupations and Dutch workers samples, there are nine relationships (three stresses or strains on three outcomes), each tested for the buffering effects of two sources of social support, resulting in eighteen potential replications. Among these, eleven (61.1%) replications are observed. Four of the eleven are replications of observed buffering effects, while the remaining seven are replications of no buffering effect. The proportion of replications of observed buffering is over one-third and compares favorably with the overall rates of buffering reported in Table 6-1. Thus, this evidence of replication is probably not capitalizing on instances where no buffering is found in either sample. Three relationships exhibit complete replication of buffering effects: (1) the effect of role conflict on irritation is buffered by both supervisor and co-worker support in each sample; (2) the effect of workload (called role overload in the Dutch sample) on anxiety is buffered by neither source of support; and (3) the effect of workload on depression is buffered by co-worker support but not supervisor support. Of the remaining relationships, five have one replication and one failure to replicate, and a single relationship, between future ambiguity and anxiety, exhibits no replications of buffering. Finally, it is noteworthy that of the seven failures to replicate, four are cases in which a buffering effect of co-worker support is found in the twenty-three occupations sample, but not in the Dutch workers sample. Thus, half of the failures to replicate may be attributed to those differences in the occupational structure of the two samples that account for the excess buffering effects of co-workers in the twenty-three occupations study, rather than to a failure of the buffering hypothesis of social support.

The second panel of entries in Table 6-2 consists of replications between the rubber workers and twenty-three occupations samples. These studies share only one outcome (somatic complaints), but do share three stresses or strains and three sources of support. These sources of support are supervisor support, co-worker support, and a third source of support which in the twenty-three occupations study is called home support (a combination of spouse, family, and friends), and in the rubber workers study is simply spouse support. Since Table 6-1 showed that the rates of buffering by spouse support in the rubber workers sample and home support in the twenty-three occupations sample are comparable, and that in the rubber workers sample a separate measure of friend/relative support had no appreciable buffering effects, these two measures will be treated as comparable for present purposes. As a result there are nine tests with the potential for replication between samples. Among these, five (55.6%) are replications, which compares favorably with the previous example (61.1%), and two (40.0%) of the replications are replications of observed buffering, again similar to the previous results (36.4%). Observed buffering effects of co-worker support and of spouse/home support on the relationship between role conflict and somatic complaints are found in each sample. The relationship between workload and somatic complaints is similar across samples in not being buffered by supervisor support, while the relationship between job satisfaction (dissatisfaction) and somatic complaints is similar across samples in not being buffered by either supervisor or co-worker support.

The final panel of Table 6-2 compares buffering in the rubber workers and Dutch workers samples. There are six potential replications since the samples share one outcome, three stresses or strains, and two sources of social support (supervisors and co-workers). Among these six tests, four (66.7%) replications are realized. None of the replications involves observed buffering. Thus, while the rate of replication is comparable to the results above, the rate of replication of observed buffering (as opposed to replication of no buffering) is different. This should not be overly interpreted, however, since a single instance of replicated buffering would make the rate considerably more comparable.

In all, Table 6–2 provides evidence of substantial replicability of results across the three samples. Twenty replications are realized out of the thirty-three tests for a rate of 60.6 percent. Of course, since the absence of buffering in each of the two studies compared is counted a replicaton, these results may be capitalizing on this type of replication. This is not indicated, however, by the rate of replications of observed buffering among these tests. Its magnitude of 30 percent well exceeds the overall rate of buffering in any of the three studies. There is little else to credit such a large number of replications, all the more so because of three obstacles present in comparing these studies. First, there are differences in the composition of the three samples. It has been noted previously that the twenty-three occupations sample, in contrast to the others, comprises a number of workers who are self-employed or who work in collegial organizations. This may account for that study's relatively high rate of buffering due to co-worker support. In any case, nearly half (5 of 11) of the failures to replicate that involve the twenty-three occupations sample are cases where co-worker buffering effects are present in that sample, but not in the sample to which it is contrasted. A second obstacle is presented by the lack of exact comparability of measures across studies. Although most of the variable conceptualizations are the same, many of the operationalizations are different. Thus, for example, the social support measures share some similar component items across studies, but are not exactly the same in any pair of studies. In a few cases, measures are equivalent (e.g., job satisfaction); in others, items are shared but do not perfectly overlap (e.g., somatic complaints); and in still others, concepts are approached through quite different instruments (e.g., workload). A final obstacle, combining elements of the previous two, is that one of the studies was conducted in the Netherlands. Cultural differences aside, the problems of translating measurement instruments often militate against replication. (Winnubst, Marcelissen, and Kleber, 1982, do not indicate whether steps were taken to ensure the cross-national validity of their instruments.) Although buffering effects do not seem to be exceptionally frequent, they do appear to be quite strong.

A comparison of main effects among these three samples is not as straightforward as the comparison of buffering effects. One would prefer to discuss as main effects those combinations of stress, support, and outcome where there is no buffering effect and where social support significantly decreases ill health or stress. Such results are reported in none of the studies treated here. Instead, they report only simple correlations between support and stresses or strains and between support and health outcomes. These are not comparable to the buffering tests, since in some cases those tests were performed with statistical controls for potentially confounding variables. Furthermore, correlations between support and health do not control for level of stress; thus one cannot tell if support has a main effect separate from stress. Finally, as a problem restricted to this comparison, correlations are not an appropriate statistic for comparisons across samples (regression slopes are desirable).

Subject to these qualifications, Table 6-3 presents a comparison of social support main effects for those relationships common to the three samples. Stresses and outcome are listed on the left margin, and correlations are organized by study within each source of support. The organization of columns under "Home Support" differs from the others in that there is no such measure in the Dutch sample, and home support is disaggregated into two measures (spouse and friend/relative support) in the rubber workers sample. In general, the correlations in Table 6-3 are rather small in magnitude. Of the sixty-four entries, fourteen (22.2%) are not significant, these being confined largely to the home support variables in the rubber workers sample. Another twenty-eight (44%) are correlations less than 0.20 in magnitude. Of the remainder, seventeen are between 0.20 and 0.30, while five are between 0.30 and 0.42. The larger coefficients do not seem to be distributed in any way related to the samples such that comparisons would be compromised. Since support is hypothesized to decrease stress, strain, or ill health, all coefficients are theoretically expected to be negative. In only two instances this expectation is not met; supervisor support and co-worker support are positively related to responsibility in the Dutch workers sample.

In Table 6-3 there are thirty-six possible pairwise comparisons across samples of correlations between social support and stress or illness. (Eight correlations between home support and other variables in the twenty-three occupations and rubber workers samples are included for completeness but cannot be compared.) Of these comparisons, ten (27.8%) involve correlation differences less than 0.05 in magnitude. Two of these are comparisons of the nonsignificant corre-

Table 6-3. Results of Social Support Main Effects among Replication across Three Samples.[a]

	Supervisor Support			Co-worker Support			Home Support		
	23 Occ[b]	Dut Wrk[c]	Rub Wrk[d]	23 Occ[b]	Dut Wrk[c]	Rub Wrk[d]	23 Occ[b]	Dut Wrk[e]	Rub Wr.
Stresses									
Role conflict	−30	−40	−22	−14	−25	−10	−11	ns	ns
Workload	ns	−20	−12	ns	−15	−08	ns	ns	ns
Responsibility	−	08	−13	−	07	−04	−	ns	ns
Job satisfaction	29	−	38	29	−	22	11	07	14
Future ambiguity	−25	−28	−	−24	−20	−	−15	−	−
Strains/Health									
Heart problems	−	−08	−04	−	−07	ns	−	ns	ns
Somatic complaints	−15	−	−07	−15	−	ns	−13	−06	ns
Irritation	−22	−41	−	−22	−33	−	−08	−	−
Anxiety	−15	−21	−	−24	−21	−	−13	−	−
Depression	−30	−26	−	−38	−17	−	−24	−	−

[a]Entries are correlation coefficients with decimal points suppressed. Sources of data as follows: twenty-three Occupations Sample: LaRocco et al. (1980); Dutch Workers Sample: Winnubst et al. (1982); Rubber Workers Sample: House and Wells (1978), Wells (1980).

[b]Correlations from twenty-three Occupations Sample.

[c]Correlations from Dutch Workers Sample.

[d]Correlations from Rubber Workers Sample.

[e]Correlations with spouse support in Rubber Workers Sample.

[f]Correlations with friend/relative support in Rubber Workers Sample.

"ns" = Correlation not statistically significant.

lations between home support and workload in the twenty-three occupation and rubber workers samples, but the remainder are significant correlations such as those between supervisor support and future ambiguity or co-worke support and role conflict (twenty-three occupations versus rubber workers) An additional nine comparisons (25.0%) involve differences of magnitud between 0.05 and 0.10. By the difference criteria of 0.10 or less, about hal (52.7%) of the comparisons result in replications. This proportion i somewhat lower than that obtained for buffering replications, but those wer comparisons of statistical significance, not of the magnitude of coefficients In this table, replications of significant (or nonsignificant) correlations ar found in 75 percent of the cases, a proportion slightly higher than for the buffering results.

THE ROLE OF SOCIAL SUPPORT IN COPING

Reviews that attempt to highlight a few current issues, such as this one, as opposed to reviews which attempt inductive generalizations from a resume of research findings, tend to take on a negative hue. Current issues are issues indeed, precisely because they are the foci of controversy in theory or research. Given a controversial issue, one either marshals evidence for a chosen side in the debate, or attempts a synthetic resolution of the controversy. Each of these tactics has been employed here: synthesis with regard to the matter of definition, and advocacy with regard to the existence of buffering effects.

Merging the definition of social support with that of coping is important not only because it unites the efforts of two major research initiatives, but also because it asks questions and suggests research that has not previously been considered. One may quibble with the categorization of coping employed here, but the procedure of linking social support to coping remains unchanged and the implications of doing so undiluted. Simply stated, coping is what people do, either behaviorally or psychologically, to deal with stress in their lives, and social support is what others do to help people cope. It follows, therefore, that social support should be described in terms commensurate with the categories of coping. Furthermore, this commensurability produces a number of research questions that have not been specifically addressed in the social support literature. For example, which actual or perceived (by the supportee) behaviors produce which kinds of coping? Are the effects of supportive behaviors generalized, such that similar supports bolster a variety of categories of coping, or are they specific? Is support a necessary condition for some categories of coping, but not others? Is social support related to the instigation of coping, its maintenance, or both? Finally, how do the answers to these questions differ depending on the type of supporter-supportee relationship, or the type of stress involved? This list is far from exhaustive, but it illustrates a number of initiatives that would benefit the understanding of both coping and social support.

Linking social support with coping does not diminish the importance of a number of questions noted earlier. How are perceptions of received support grounded in the concrete behaviors of supporters? What situational and personal characteristics might condition such grounding? Might not some putatively supportive behaviors have adverse consequences, for example, in producing demands that are stressful in their right (reciprocity may be one) or encouraging coping attempts that are faulty or misguided? The latter question recognizes a strict differentiation of coping *attempts* from coping *results*. Consequently, support might effectively promote coping techniques that may fail to reduce stress or avoid illness. Moreover, how is support conditioned by other components of the relationship with a supporter that may be nonsupportive or stressful in themselves? Is there a halo effect of good relationships not found in poor relationships?

It is commonplace that questions are far easier to produce than answers, but linking support and coping also points to some design issues that may prove valuable. In most social support studies, measures of stress are many or broadly inclusive (e.g., measures of life events), and measures of social support are general and nonspecific with regard to a particular stress. Conversely, studies of coping have tended toward designs in which measures of coping are situation-based and specific to a particular stressor (cf. Folkman, 1982). Measurement arrangements in which elicitations of coping behaviors are linked to particular stressors and in which elicitations of social support are linked to concrete coping behaviors are more suited to the kinds of questions currently being raised in the study of social support. This scheme is more in accordance with discussions of support that allow it to be situationally variable, than most current measures that treat it as an individual trait. Research based on this kind of methodology is more likely to emphasize the varieties of supportive relationships, their relative prevalence, and their interplay with stress and coping in producing an outcome. What is more, this methodology may be used as an assessment in applied settings, thus creating a comparability of basic research and practical intervention that should promote discourse between the two.

In contrast to the more taxonomic concerns of social support definitions, social support research has had as its focus the establishment of evidence for the buffering effect of social support. Given the nature of the two pursuits it perhaps should not be surprising that their goals are somewhat at odds. Especially to the degree that social support conceptualizations have relied at least as much on educated guess and logical consistency as on induction from empirical results, they have been fairly free to be changeable. Research on social support, by comparison, has been rather plodding. For example, data for the twenty-three occupations study discussed above, was collected in 1973, the first reports of buffering tests were disseminated as a dissertation and a presented paper two and three years later (Pinneau, 1975, 1976), and the revision and re-analysis appeared in print after four more years (LaRocco, House, and French, 1980). The measures of social support employed in that study were in the field prior to the publication of any of the social support definitions discussed here. The nature of many of the early measures of social support (which account for the bulk of empirical results) precludes answering many of the questions that have subsequently arisen.

This is not to say that the research has not contributed to our understanding of support. Indeed, it might be argued that not enough has been made of what has been found. Interpretive discussions of these results suffer from what might be thought of as arrested development. Most research proceeds by hypothesizing an effect, establishing its existence, and explaining the mechanism of the effect. Social support research has gotten bogged down in determining whether the effect to be elaborated is the buffering effect or the main effect. However, most research has found that social support buffers the effect of stress, or where multiple tests are performed, that social support buffering is found in some significant proportion of those tests. It is the remainder of the tests, where evidence of buffering is not found, that gives most researchers pause. Yet few have entertained the notion that buffering and main effects are not mutually exclusive, and that the type of effect to be expected may be a function of the specific configuration of stress, support, and health that is tested.

The results in this paper of comparing three studies of social support are very instructive. Buffering effects in one study tend to be replicated (though not perfectly) in another. It is equally true, however, that the absence of buffering is also replicated; buffering and its absence are equally prevalent. Although neither the absence of buffering nor the presence of a simple correlation is, strictly speaking, a main effect, both tend to be replicated in a majority of the opportunities for comparison presented by the three studies. Thus it would seem that both types of effect are indicated. It remains to specify particular stress-health relationships with which a given source of support has a main effect or buffering effect, and to begin the process of explaining the mechanisms by which these occur.

One principle for elaborating these relationships is to explore the kinds of coping that may intervene. Indeed, certain types of coping would lead one to expect main effects, whereas others lead one to expect buffering effects. Environmental modification, changing objectively stressful conditions, or primary appraisal, changing perceived stress, are each hypothesized to lead to a reduction in stress. If support were to be related to either type of coping, one could expect to find a negative correlation between social support and stress and a positive correlation with health, but not necessarily a buffering effect. Conversely, coping that bolsters emotional control or psychological resources is hypothesized to allow perceived stress to remain high without adversely affecting health. Social support related to these types of coping would likely exhibit a buffering effect on the relationship between stress and health.

The results of the comparison of studies also indicates that triat support has effects and that these effects exhibit generality. The measures in these studies elicit reports of social support for the category of problems at work rather than for any specific problem (others employ categories such as social support for personal problems). Likewise, the types of supportive behaviors to be reported are often broad: availability of the supporter, willingness to listen, willingness to help, and so forth. While the relationship of situational (or state) support to trait support is presently unknown, it seems likely that situation-based measures of support will exhibit stronger rather than weaker effects.

All in all, the evidence for social support effects seems firm. Indeed, it appears that such effects may take either the form of main effect or buffering. What remains is to elaborate the mechanisms by which these effects operate. As is argued in this paper, this elaboration may proceed by pursuing the link between social support and coping. At a time when much is to be done in understanding social support, it seems to be the object of faddish enthusiasm. One hopes that its future is as bright as its present.

REFERENCES

Andrews, G.; C. Tennant; D.M. Hewson; and G.E. Vaillant. 1978. "Life Event Stress, Social Support, Coping Style, and Risk of Psychological Impairment." *Journal of Nervous and Mental Disease* 166: 307–16.

Caplan, G. 1974. *Support Systems and Community Mental Health.* New York: Behavioral Publications.

Caplan, G., and M. Killilea. 1976. *Support Systems and Mutual Help.* New York: Grune and Stratton.

Caplan, R.D. 1972. "Organizational Stress and Individual Strain: A Social-Psychological Study of Risk Factors in Coronary Heart Disease Among Administrators, Engineers and Scientists." Ph.D. dissertation, University of Michigan.

Caplan, R.D.; S. Cobb; J.R.P. French, Jr.; R.V. Harrison; and S.R. Pinneau. 1975. *Job Demands and Worker Health.* HEW(NIOSH) publication no. 75-160. Washington, D.C.: U.S. Government Printing Office.

Cassel, J.C. 1976. "The Contribution of the Social Environment to Host Resistance." *American Journal of Epidemiology* 104: 107-23.

Cobb, S. 1976. "Social Support as a Moderator of Life Stress." *Psychosomatic Medicine* 38: 300-14.

Cobb, S., and S.V. Kasl. 1977. *Termination: The Consequences of Job Loss.* HEW(NIOSH) publication no. 77-224. Washington, D.C.: U.S. Government Printing Office.

Eaton, W.W. 1978. "Life Events, Social Supports, and Psychiatric Symptoms: A Reanalysis of the New Haven Data." *Journal of Health and Social Behavior* 19: 230-34.

Fletcher, B., and R.L. Payne. 1979. "Stress—How Big a Problem is it?" Paper presented at Annual Conference Occupational Psychology Section, British Psychological Society, Sheffield, UK, January.

Folkman, S. 1982. "An Approach to the Measurement of Coping." *Journal of Occupational Behaviour* 3: 95-107.

Folkman, S., and R.S. Lazarus. 1980. "An Analysis of Coping in a Middle-Aged Community Sample." *Journal of Health and Social Behavior* 21: 219-39.

Gore, S. 1973. "The Influence of Social Support in Ameliorating the Consequences of Unemployment." Ph.D. dissertation, University of Pennsylvania.

Gore, S. 1978. "The Effect of Social Support in Moderating the Health Consequences of Unemployment." *Journal of Health and Social Behavior* 19: 157-65.

Gottlieb, B.H. 1981. "Social Networks and Social Support in Community Mental Health." In *Social Networks and Social Support,* edited by B.H. Gottlieb, pp. 11-42. Beverly Hills, Ca.: Sage Publications.

House, J.S. 1974. "Occupational Stress and Coronary Heart Disease: A Review and Theoretical Integration." *Journal of Health and Social Behavior* 15: 12-17.

House, J.S. 1981. *Work Stress and Social Support.* Reading, Ma.: Addison Wesley.

House, J.S.; A.J. McMichael; J.A. Wells; B.N. Kaplan; and L.R. Lander-Man. 1979. "Occupational Stress and Health Among Factory Workers." *Journal of Health and Social Behavior* 20: 139–60.

House, J.S., and J.A. Wells. 1978. "Occupational Stress, Social Support and Health." In *Reducing Occupational Stress: Proceedings of a Conference,* edited by A. McLean, G. Black, and M. Colligan, pp. 8–29. HEW(NIOSH) publication no. 78–140. Washington, D.C.: U.S. Government Printing Office.

Kahn, R.L., and T. Antonucci. 1980. "Convoys Over the Life Course: Attachment, Roles and Social Support." In *Life Span Development and Behavior, Vol. 3,* edited by P.B. Baltes and O. Brim, pp. 475–82. Boston: Lexington Press.

Kaplan, B.H.; J.C. Cassel; and S. Gore. 1977. "Social Support and Health." *Medical Care* 25(Supplement): 47–58.

Kasl, S.V. 1978. "Epidemiological Contributions to the Study of Work Stress." In *Stress at Work,* edited by C.L. Cooper and R. Payne, pp. 3–48. New York: John Wiley and Sons.

Lazarus, R.S. 1966. *Psychological Stress and the Coping Process.* New York: McGraw-Hill.

Lazarus, R.S. 1981. "The Stress and Coping Paradigm." In *Theoretical Bases for Psychopathology,* edited by C. Eisdorfer, D. Cohen, A. Kleinman, and P. Maxim, pp. 173–209. New York: Spectrum.

LaRocco, J.M.; J.S. House; and J.R.P. French, Jr. 1980. "Social Support, Occupational Stress, and Health." *Journal of Health and Social Behavior* 21: 202–18.

LaRocco, J.M., and A.P. Jones. 1978. "Co-worker and Leader Support as Moderators of Stress-Strain Relationships in Work Situations." *Journal of Applied Psychology* 63: 629–34.

Lin, N.; R.S. Simeone; W.M. Ensel; and W. Kuo. 1979. "Social Support, Stressful Life Events, and Illness: A Model and an Empirical Test." *Journal of Health and Social Behavior* 20: 108–19.

McMichael, A.J. 1978. "Personality, Behavioural, and Situational Modifiers of Work Stressors." In *Stress at Work,* edited by C.L. Cooper and R. Payne, pp. 127–47. New York: John Wiley and Sons.

Nuckolls, K.B.; J.C. Cassel; and B.H. Kaplan. 1972. "Psychosocial Assets, Life Crisis and the Prognosis of Pregnancy." *American Journal of Epidemiology* 95: 431–41.

Payne, R. 1980. "Organizational Stress and Social Support." In *Current Concerns in Occupational Stress,* edited by C.L. Cooper and R. Payne, pp. 269–98. New York: John Wiley and Sons.

Pearlin, L.I.; M.A. Lieberman; E.G. Menaghan; and J.T. Mullen. 1981. "The Stress Process." *Journal of Health and Social Behavior* 22: 337–56.

Pearlin, L.I. and C. Schooler. 1978. "The Structure of Coping." *Journal of Health and Social Behavior* 19: 2–21.

Pinneau, S.R. 1972. "Complimentarity and Social Support." Unpublished paper, University of Michigan.

Pinneau, S.R. 1975. "Effects of Social Support on Psychological and Physiological Strains." Ph.D. dissertation, University of Michigan.

Pinneau, S.R. 1976. "Effects of Social Support on Occupational Stresses and Strains." Paper presented at Annual Meeting of the American Psychological Association, Washington, D.C.

Udris, I. 1982. "Soziale Unterstutzung: Hilfe gegen Stress?" ("Social Support: Help Against Stress?"). *Psychosozial* 5: 78–91.

Wells, J.A. 1980. "Social Support as a Buffer of Stressful Job Conditions." Ph.D. dissertation, Duke University.

Wells, J.A. 1982. "Objective Job Conditions, Social Support and Perceived Stress Among Blue Collar Workers." *Journal of Occupational Behaviour* 3: 79–94.

Winnubst, J.A.M.; F.H.G. Marcelissen; and R.J. Kleber. 1982. "Effects of Social Support in the Stressor-Strain Relationship: A Dutch Sample." *Social Science and Medicine* 16: 1–17.

7 MEDITATION FOR COPING WITH ORGANIZATIONAL STRESS

Amarjit S. Sethi

INTRODUCTION

In this chapter we will describe the importance of meditation in the context of recent psychoneuroendocrine research on stress and health. Various systems of meditation are described and then followed by a diagnostic method of meditation. This method emphasizes that meditation should not be used in isolation, but in combination with other stress coping strategies such as biofeedback, fitness, time management, and burnout prevention.

Meditation is defined here as a noncalculating mood. This mood, which may occur spontaneously or with the aid of a technique, indicates an altered state of consciousness (Tart, 1975) that is free of anxiety, tension, or distress. It is a contemplative, as opposed to a calculating or analytical, state of mind in which the individual is relaxed. All the individual's desires and ruminations are quieted as one enters the meditative mood (Carrington, 1977). The person's sense of separateness is transformed into a unitary form of consciousness in which the individual no longer perceives the self as a separate ego but as part of the universal concern (Watts, 1973).

IMPORTANCE OF MEDITATION

We believe that meditation as a coping resource may help the individual at both the psychological and physiological level. Stress is a transaction between the person and his psychosocial environment, and is characterized by coping resources, opportunities, constraints, and demands (Beehr and Schuler, 1982). It is a transaction precisely because stress arises from the person's cognitive appraisal of the severity of the situational demand on the one hand, and the individual's personal coping resources on the other (Frankenhaeuser, 1979a). According to Frankenhaeuser, the neuroendocrine responses to the psychosocial environment reflect the emotional impact of this environment on the individual. "Diverse environmental conditions may evoke the same neuroendocrine responses because they have a common psychological denominator" (Frankenhaeuser 1975a: 2). Meditation assumes that the mind manufactures stress. Brown (1980: 59) has explained that stress is not 'out there', and mind creates stress because the mind's problem solving activities lack information necessary to solve problems it detects.

The transactional definition of stress is in accord with Lazarus's (1977) theory of stress and coping as dynamic, transactional processes, and Mason's (1971) "specificity" concept, emphasizing the susceptibility of several neuroendocrine systems to the varying demands, constraints, and opportunities of the environment.

One of the key questions in relating meditation to stress is the hypothesis that meditation helps the individual to gain personal control in stress and coping. Based on experimental studies, Frankenhaeuser (1975a: 8) has indicated "that lack of personal control, when accompanied by feelings of fear and helplessness, will generally activate both pituitary-adrenal system (e.g., Sachar, 1975) and the sympathetic adrenal system." In one experiment, "the high controllability of the task was the chief reason why the effort that the subjects invested in their performance was associated with positive feelings only" (Frankenhaeuser, 1975a: 9). The conclusion is that "challenging but controllable tasks are likely to induce effort without distress" (Frankenhaeuser, 1975a:9). On the coping level this means that the individual can use a strategy (e.g., meditation) to gain a perspective that helps maintain control of the situation, despite constraints or demands of the situation or lack of information. In other words, meditation can help the person to see each environmental demand as an avenue for present or future opportunity, thus turning even the negative situation to his or her positive advantage. This strategy probably is more effective in the long run, as meditation will allow the individual to visualize and understand the dynamics of the psychosocial environment.

MEDITATION AND TYPE A PERSONS

Some of the recent applications of meditation strategies have proved successful in modifying Type A behavior in post-infarction cases (Friedman, 1982). Research supports the view that Type A behavior constitutes a major independent risk factor for coronary heart disease (Rosenman et al., 1976). Time urgency (Friedman and Rosenman, 1974) and fear of losing control (Glass, 1977) are the two key features of Type A persons, and high catecholemine levels associated with their achievement orientation are generally assumed to play a significant part. The key point to note is that Type A persons are distressed not because of heavy workload as such, but because of lack of strategies for coping with non-work conditions (Frankenhaeuser, 1979b; Lundberg and Forsman, 1978). Frankenhaeuser (1975a: 12–13 explains the results of recent research:

> We interpret our results as showing that the Type A person, when in control of the situation, sets his or her standards high, copes effectively with the self-selected heavy load, and does so without mobilizing excessive physiological resources. There is an interesting parallel between this experimental illustration of how Type A cope with an acute work load and epidemiological data (Jenkins, Zyzanski, and Rosenman, 1971; Kenigsberg et al., 1974) showing that persons high in "job involvement," i.e., one of the major components of Type A behavior, had a relatively lower incidence of coronary heart disease then those high in the "hard-driving" and the "speed and impatience" factors (cf. review by Lundberg, 1979). This suggests that conditions calling for effort may be less threatening to health. Our data point to controllability as a major key to coping without distress. Support for this view comes both from the laboratory studies reviewed above and from studies of people exposed to job stress in real life.
>
> . . . We found that Type B subjects were consistently less aroused (according to self-reports and physiological indices) when asked to remain unoccupied in the laboratory than when asked to do arithmetic under noise exposure. In contrast, Type A persons tended to be equally aroused or more aroused when deprived of work than when given work to do. In line with this general tendency to rebel against passivity Type A secreted significantly more cortisol than Type B during a prolonged vigilance task, but not during rapid information processing.

As an intervention coping strategy, meditation may help the person to unwind from activity more easily, thus moderating the stress-prone behavior. Frankenhaeuser (1975a) summarizes results of some recent research on the relationship between psychoendocrine stress responses and health:

> Our results show that a healthy person, who deals with acute environmental demands by "raising the thermostat," may have to pay a price in terms of increased psychological involvement and physiological arousal. . . . Comparisons between persons classified as rapid and slow "adrenaline decreasers" support the assumption that a quick return to physiological baselines after energy mobilization induced by a short-term exposure to a heavy mental load, implies an "economic mode of response." Conversely, a slow return to baseline indicates poor adjustment in the sense that the person "over-responds" by spending resources that are no longer called for. In agreement with this reasoning, results from a laboratory study (Johansson & Frankenhaeuser, 1973) showed that "rapid decreasers" tended to be psychologically better balanced and more efficient in achievement situations than "slow decreasers." There is also some indication (Frankenhaeuser, Lundberg and Forsman, 1978) that the coronary-prone behavior pattern A (see e.g., Glass, 1977; Rosenman, Brand, Sholtz, and Friedman, 1976) may be characterized by low flexibility in physiological arousal relative to situational demands.

> An equally important finding is that the time for "unwinding" varies predictably with the individual's state of general well-being. Thus, in a group of industrial workers, the proportion of "rapid decreasers" was significantly higher after than before a vacation period, which had improved the workers' physical and psychological condition (Johansson, 1976).

If the individual's state of general well-being is a critical factor in coping with stress, then meditation can play a positive role in moderating that aspect of Type A behavior that is more susceptible to distress.

RESEARCH ON MEDITATION

During the 1960s and 1970s, research on meditation grew out of studies on altered states of consciousness in the United States, a growing popularity of meditation as a coping skill with the general public, and through reports by psychophysiologists that humans and animals alike can learn to control their autonomic functions through biofeedback (Brown, 1977). Another major reason for scientific interest in meditation is the ability of meditation techniques to bring relaxation. In systematic desensitization psychologists are also interested in examining meditation as a relaxation-inducing technique.

The scientific investigation of meditation during the last two decades has emphasized the somatic effects of meditation (Anand, Chhina, and Singh, 1961a, 1961b; Benson, Rosner, and Mazretta, 1973; Brown, 1975; Kasamatsu and Hirai, 1969; Ornstein, 1972; Pope and Singer, 1978). This research suggests that persons in meditation experiments reveal "reductions in oxygen consumption, carbon dioxide elimination, and the rate and volume of respiration; a slight increase in the acidity of arterial blood; a marked decrease in the blood-lactate level; a slowing of the heartbeat; a considerable increase in skin resistance; and an electroencephalogram pattern of intensification of slow alpha waves with occasional theta-wave activity" (Wallace and Benson, 1972: 86–87). Wallace and Benson (1972), in a landmark in meditation research, provided the first laboratory proof that meditation can lower metabolism in a profound manner. Summarizing the various tests, Wallace and Benson (1972: 86–87) concluded that meditation may

> produce the effects through control of an 'involuntary' mechanism in the body, presumably the autonomic nervous system. The reduction of carbon dioxide elimination might have been accounted for by a recognizable voluntary action of the subject—slowing the breathing—but such an action should not markedly affect the uptake of oxygen by the body tissues. Consequently, it was a reasonable supposition that the drop in oxygen consumption, reflecting a decrease in the need for inhaled oxygen, must be due to modification of a process not subject to manipulation in the usual sense.

The overall conclusion on meditation is summed up by Raymond Van Over (1978: 114) as follows:

> Regarding the physiological effects of meditation, the conclusion appears to be that traditional learning is limited to producing specific responses and depends on a stimulus and feedback, while meditation is independent of such conditions and produces not a single response, but a complex of responses that mark a highly relaxed state beneficial to the body overall. Further, the pattern of physiological changes suggests that meditation generates an integrated response, or reflex, that is mediated by the central nervous system.

A study of a yogi who meditated inside a sealed, airtight box for ten hours showed that the subject consumed oxygen at a rate 30 percent below the amount required for human sustenance (Anand,

Chhina, and Singh, 1961a). In another physiological study of forty-five meditators, the researchers found that these subjects showed an increase in the electrical resistance of the skin, heart rates slowed down by 6 to 9 percent (although they never went below sixty-two beats per minute) during meditation, and that respiration rates decreased by an average of 23 percent (Bagchi and Wenger, 1957). In a study of a profound state of meditation (*samadhi*) in selected meditators, it was found that they showed persistent alpha waves, and were able to stay in that state despite deliberate introduction of intense stimuli such as lights, sounds, burning rods, and freezing temperature (Anand, Chhina, and Singh, 1961a). These results were confirmed in a study of Zen monks who were exposed to a repeated click as a source of distraction while meditating in a soundproof room. They showed no habituation to the clicks while they were meditating (Kasamatsu and Hirai, 1969). This experiment has an important implication for coping with stress since, during meditation, it is possible to notice things and events, and yet not be affected by them.

The documented and publicized research on Transcendental Meditation (TM), which uses a standardized technique, claims beneficial effects of meditation (Bloomfield, Cain, and Jaffe, 1975; Denniston and McWilliams, 1975; Orme-Johnson and Farrow, 1977), but not all of the studies depicted by TM advocates are reliable (Carrington, 1977). Despite this caution, some of the recent research on meditation has confirmed the finding that meditation relaxes people and reduces tension and stress (Benson, 1975). Banquet (1972), in his study of TM meditators, found that brain activity showed an unusual evenness and that the recordings from a number of different areas of the brain were synchronized, which Banquet (1972: 449) called an "outstanding EEG characteristic of meditation". Using galvanic skin response as a measure of stress, Wallace (1970) found that within minutes after starting meditation, his subjects' skin resistance increased on the average of 160 percent. Other studies have reported a rise of at least 30 to 40 percent (Schwartz, 1973; Glueck and Stroebel, 1975). In an experimental study of nine patients diagnosed as anxiety neurotic, Girodo (1974) found that meditation was beneficial for patients with a short history of illness and that "flooding" was effective in those with a long history. The results suggest that "transcendental meditation may be of benefit in reducing anxiety symptoms in those patients who are still attempting to master anxiety" (Girodo, 1974).

In assessing meditation as a coping tool, the critical question is to examine if meditation can be used as a strategy for handling stress. Meditators should in general be able to recover from stress more easily than nonmeditators. To test this question, David Orme-Johnson performed a comparative study of a group of meditators and nonmeditators to assess galvanic skin response (GSR) to intermittent noise which was as loud as a pneumatic hammer drilling pavement. He found that the meditators stopped reacting to the loud sound after about eleven repetitions, whereas the nonmeditators kept on reacting the same way for 30 or 40 repetitions (Orme-Johnson, 1973). This finding was repeated in another study conducted by the same researcher. Goleman and Schwartz (1976) found that the meditators recovered from stress more rapidly than nonmeditators. In this case the subjects, who meditated before seeing a stress-producing film, showed greater alertness, but at the same time, they were able to impersonalize the stress. Studies have also shown that meditation helps hypertensive patients to reduce their blood pressure over time (Benson, Rosner, and Mazretta, 1973).

Research indicates that meditation is a low-stress state (Carrington, 1977) and provides the individual with a strategy that will in the long run prove beneficial for stress management. But no one form of meditation can claim any exclusive benefit. Benson has shown that by using his own method of meditation he found equally impressive reductions in body metabolism as in his original TM studies (Benson, 1975). Meditation increases the sense of having control over one's life (Hjelle, 1974; Orme-Johnson and Farrow, 1977), and, as Frankenhaeuser (1979a,b) has found in her studies in Sweden, that controllability is a critical variable in moderating Type A behavior in stress management.

Fenwick (1974) has stated that many of the reported drops in metabolism during meditation, as originally found by Wallace and Benson (1972), are due to a "contrast effect." Subjects who were already relaxed before meditation could not produce any further metabolic changes during meditation. This does not negate the value of meditation as a coping strategy; however, it does imply that future meditation studies will have to prove that metabolic changes during meditation "are not simply the result of muscle movement preceding meditation vs. muscle stillness during it, but due, to some unique quality of the meditative state itself" (Carrington, 1977: 57). Other areas of concern for future research are the awareness of the experimenter's effect on one's own research, greater attention to appropriate research design, the development of criteria for comparability between mediators and nonmeditators, and the refinement of measurement techniques in detecting the effects of the meditative mood on clearly defined concepts of stress and stress management.

TECHNIQUES OF MEDITATION

There are a variety of approaches to meditation in different religions that prescribe a particular lifestyle. We are interested in focusing on those techniques that are practical and can be used in modern society as tools for stress management. These tools or centering devices are not in themselves true meditation, but they are means that lead to a meditative state. Meditation is basically an inner experience—the techniques described below are easy to learn and can be used as centering devices.

Transcendental Meditation (TM)

The student repeats a Sanskrit word (or *mantra*) for twenty minutes, twice daily, while sitting quietly in a chair with eyes closed. If the mind wanders from the mantra, the student is instructed not to fight it but "normalize" it, that is keep repeating the mantra in a passive manner by "favoring" the mantra over other thoughts. Although TM is not a religion, the practitioner has a chance to learn certain Hindu metaphysical assumptions such as *prana* (universal energy) and *Brahaman* ("the irreducible essence of all creation") (Carrington, 1977). The technique is taught by TM instructors in four lessons over a period of four days, and does not require a particular lifestyle for meditators, though it may pose some lifestyle requirements for TM instructors.

Clinically Standardized Meditation (CSM)

Carrington (1977) developed a standardized set of instructions as a relaxation technique. The student selects his own mantra, unlike TM, out of a list of sixteen Sanskrit mantras. The length of the meditation session varies for each individual. No belief system (such as transcendence or cosmic unity) is necessary, and CSM can be taught in two lessons. No chanting is involved, though there is a short ceremony of selecting and transmitting the mantra. CSM, like TM, is a passive form of meditation as opposed to other techniques, such as yoga and Zen, that require discipline and concentration.

Benson's Method or Relaxation Response

Benson's technique is a form of breathing meditation in which a person thinks the word "one" (or any other sound of the individual's choice) on every out breath. In practice, one needs a quiet environment, a passive attitude, and a comfortable position. One is urged to repeat the exercise for ten to twenty minutes, once or twice daily. "A passive attitude appears to be the most essential factor in eliciting the Relaxation Response" (Benson, 1975: 111). The object is to dwell upon a word or sound repetition, to gaze at a symbol, or concentrate on a particular feeling. When distractions occur one can return to the repetition of the syllable to help eliminate other thoughts. According to Benson, the Relaxation Response is a "universal human capacity," and to manage stress we can modify our behavior by regularly evoking the relaxation response that effectively counters life stress. He concludes that unlike the flight or fight response, "which is repeatedly brought forth as a response to our difficult everyday situations and is elicited without conscious effort, the Relaxation Response can be evoked only if time is set aside and a conscious effort is made" (Benson, 1975: 178). For example, Benson recommends Relaxation Response breaks instead of coffee breaks, thus utilizing an "innate asset for combating stress" (1974: 49).

Zen Meditation

The word "Zen"is derived from the Chinese word "Ch'an," which in turn is derived from the Pali Buddhist term "Jhana," a derivative of the Sanskrit word "dyana" meaning meditation. In order to manage stress, Zen suggests a way of intuitive experience that releases all stress. It entails a change in attitude and is therefore a dynamic strategy.

In Zen meditation, one perceives that stress results from socialized conditions, and that the way out of stress is to understand that this very experience of stress is part of the "eternal fitness of things." In the words of the Zen master Gensha: "If you understand, things are such as they are. If you do not understand, things are such as they are" (Watts, 1973: 25). The release from stress occurs when one is "willing to be as imperfect as one is—perfectly imperfect" (Watts, 1973: 25). The release from stress lies through and not away from the problem—and the problem is born, and has its sole existence, in the mind (Humphreys, 1971). Through insight meditation, one realizes this by becoming constantly aware of the immediate present, as distinct from ruminations either about the past or the future. You don't "try to live in the present" because we are "always completely in the present" (Watts, 1973: 30), even when we are ruminating. Being stressful is also OK because each experience in its "inescapable nowness" is precisely what it should be. Coping then is not a negative means for solving specific problems, but rather a meditative state in which the person regards coping itself as "more playful than purposeful" (Watts, 1973: 32). Coping, according to Zen, is an art, and like the art of music and dance, successful coping reveals and celebrates the background of personal and social environment. The meditative state is a release from self-consciousness, from the fixed belief and feeling that one's organism is an absolute and separate thing as distinct from a convenient unit of perception (Watts, 1973). The meditation experience realizes the relatedness of things, events, persons, and the universe—the relationship between the person and the environment is inseparable. As Humphreys (1971: 159) says: "For you and the problem are not two things in opposition but one thing; you are one, though still two . . . You are the problem and the problem is you. Where, then is the problem?". Zen is a way of stopping all worry about the problem.

The highest goal of Zen is to attain *satori* (selflessness), an intuition that there is no little man or "I" in us who controls or owns consciousness. "What is troubling us", said Wittgenstein "is the tendency to believe that the mind is like a little man within" (quoted in Watts, 1973: 56). Watts (1973: 57) puts it dramatically: "When I can no more identify myself with that little man inside, there is nothing left to identify with—except everything! There is no longer the slightest contradiction between feeling like a leaf on a stream and throwing one's whole energy into responsible action, for the push is pull."

As an exercise, Humphreys (1971: 168–170) outlines the following steps in Zen meditation. As preparation, a few preliminary steps are helpful. These include: laugh; be serious; and undress your thoughts. Now the exercise begins:

1. Form the habit of synthesis of thought. Concentrate on similarities rather than analyze differences.
2. Learn to objectivize. Examine all stressors whether at home or at work and face them.
3. Meditate. Focus all attention on an object for five to ten minutes daily. The purpose is to be silent, and listen to yourself.
4. Encourage the intuitive factor in mind.
5. Expand your understanding till it hurts. Move through space and come back with a renewed look at problems.
6. Stop rushing about.
7. Relax. "Just drop it, whatever it is that is worrying you, and go on dropping it." Laugh and laugh still more; if you cannot, find out why.
8. Walk on!

Sikh Meditation or *Nam Simran*

Nam Simran literally means constant remembrance and awareness of Nam, the Universal Spirit. This technique is close to Zen, yoga, and CSM. It was pioneered by Guru Nanak and is drawn from Sikhism. The goal is, as in Zen, to go beyond ego and be in a "Wah state"—the meditative state characterized by peace, wonder, and joy. The exercise begins by realizing that the ego or "I-ness" is the cause of all distress. Repeat the word "Wahguru" for ten to twenty minutes daily. This can be done either while sitting or walking. The time can also be changed subject to need. This is the preliminary step in this exercise. In an advanced state the student repeats inwardly or silently the mantra Wahguru during all his waking hours. This stage is called "Liv." Wahguru is pre-selected for all persons and is open for anyone to practice. Wahguru literally means Wonderful Light and meditation produces a feeling of wonder or "Vismad." The goal of Simran is to free the mind from all mental constructions by dissolving ego. Freedom from passions and attachments is achieved. If any thoughts disturb the learner, breath awareness can be practiced by repeating the word "Wah" while inhaling and the word "Guru" while exhaling. An alternate word for repetition is "Ekonkar," which is derived from the Sikh scripture, Guru Granth.

Nam Simran differs from TM in that meditation is considered a constant and natural state and should be practiced while doing another activity. Although one can sit and repeat the word Wahguru for ten to twenty minutes, there is no prescribed rule. The goal is to put oneself in a meditative state while working or doing any acton. Nam Simran also does require certain ethical behavior, the most important being truthfulness, congruence, and selflessness. Unlike Transcendental Meditation, there is no secret word in Nam Simran and the same mantra should be repeated by everyone.

Nam Simran is more than mere utterings of the mantra. Like Zen, Nam Simran emphasizes self-awakening, equipoise, and harmony.

Diagnostic Meditation (DM)

Diagnostic Meditation (DM) combines selected aspects of several meditational systems, and draws upon the works of Watts (1972), Krishnamurti (1973), Rajneesh (1976), Ram Dass (1973), and Brown (1980). We have integrated various meditation traditions with strategies such as biofeedack, time management, and problem-solving. It is our hypothesis that one should select a set of techniques suited to one's needs depending upon the nature of the stressful situation and one's own capacity; it is therefore diagnostic. The individual diagnoses the situation according to the problem-solving strategy, learns to manage time, and uses meditation to achieve relaxation and one's goals through strategically planned actions.

Key Processes in Diagnostic Meditation.   Diagnostic Meditation is a method of direct perception that bridges the gap between the present stressful situation and the future goal. As preparation, the individual is encouraged to meditate on the following aspects of the situation:

(1) Meditation on Inner Power.   To solve problems creatively you must tap your inner resources and learn to appreciate the value of the present moment and its reality, because it is during these moments that a new source of intelligence and inner power is experienced. Internal freedom occurs when you come to grips with your present reality. This is not withdrawal, nor avoidance of problems,

nor aimless wandering; rather, it is using your creative self for effective problem-solving.

(2) Meditation on Organizational Problem-Solving. Problem-solving involves perception of the problem and its relation to various goals. When solving a difficult problem it helps to relate the problem to goals, but it does not help if you cannot perceive the gap that exists between "what is" and "what should be."

You must become problem-free by emptying your mind from all sorts of corrupting data. Without this internal weapon, approach to problem-solving remains at best a ritual. You cannot find any innovation, spark, or creativity if you try to grasp the problem without grasping yourself. A paralyzed approach to problem-solving results from not using your real self; the strength already resides within you. If you stick to the old ways you will approach problems without freshness or spontaneity—too systematized for creativity.

(3) Meditation on Organizational Decisions. Decisionmaking is central to stress coping. In order to make decisions, thinking and action should be integrated. Decisions are distorted when you try to act with a split mind: one part thinking and standing aside from the other. Improvement in the quality of the decisionmaking process results from deep reflection in a detached way.

(4) Meditation on Self. It takes time to diagnose yourself. It may take several months or even years to arrive at an adequate and positive level of stress coping. But the process must be followed systematically, objectively, and precisely. You can analyze your behavior to determine stress and coping, with modifications to suit your needs, strengths, and goals.

Self-analysis should be objective, though this cannot be completely so because it involves perception of conscious and subconscious levels. Objectivity will be affected by goals sought through meditational analysis. If the goal is to cope with stress, then analysis will achieve that and no more. If you wish to proceed further and gain some spiritual insights, then meditation may become a bit more objective, because in the higher stages of contemplation one must become completely relaxed, neutral, and universal (Sethi and Daya, 1978: Sethi, 1983).

To make self-analysis an effective coping strategy, you must be precise to perceive your worth and your state of mind about relationships with other people. It is essential to be aware of all the defense mechanisms, your desires and cravings and instincts. Meditation is a good strategy for the person to prevent stress. "Meditation is a 'centering' technique by which you can get out stereotyped responses, and substitute repetitive urgency for creative energy" (Friedman and Rosenman, 1974).

How to Practice Diagnostic Meditation.   How do you meditate? First, sit cross-legged on the floor, keeping your back straight. (Alternatively, you may select any comfortable position.) Close your eyes, not too tightly, and look upwards in the center of your eyes. next, let go of your thoughts and muscle tensions by repeating numbers. Number 4 lets go of bodily tension: visualize each part of your body and let it go. Number 3 lets go of your emotional tensions: let them go as they come to your mind. Number 2 lets go of your conceptual ruminations arising out of past events or future anticipations. Number 1 lets go of your goals or purposes in life. Number 2 and Number 1 will require some training in order to accomplish the "letting go." All purposes and goals are abandoned, even the goals of doing this meditation for avoiding stress. You do not feel any sense or time urgency or goal achievement. You meditate for fun and relaxation and are not even bothered about the superiority of your technique. Number 0 relaxes you without guilt, purpose, or any agitation. You are no longer impatient and are at peace with yourself. As you practice meditation, you will realize that both the voluntary and involuntary aspects of your experience are a happening. Thoughts are a happening and so is your breathing. As Watts (1976: 33) puts it: "Everything is happening to you and you are doing everything. For example, your eyes are turning the sun into light, it's the nerve ends in your skin turning electric vibrations in the air to heat and temperature, it's your eardrums that are turning vibrations in the air into sound. This is the way you are creating the world. But when we're not talking about it . . . then there is just the happening." Don't worry about the past or the future, and don't be concerned about the efficiency of your meditation technique.

To assist you in attaining the zero stage, you may use a mantra, a word that you repeat to yourself, first loudly as a chant and then slowly within your mind. Repeat the word "Wahguru," or, substitute the word "Om" (drawn from the *Upanishads*), or "One" (as recommended by Benson). There are, of course, a variety of mantras and the choice is left to the practitioner. It is important to use the mantra as a technique to alter your consciousness from a tense, hurried, goal-oriented state to a relaxed, goal-less, playful, energetic, blissful, and peaceful state. Initially your attention will be focused on the meaning of the mantra, but gradually it will shift to the sound and the vibration created by the meditator. "You will become completely absorbed in the sound [of your mantra] and find yourself living in an eternal now in which there is no past and there is no future, and there is no difference between what you are as knower and what you are as the known, between yourself and the world of nature outside you. It all becomes one doing, one happening" (Watts, 1976: 39). When you come to a zero state, you should enjoy that warm cozy feeling. As you hear thoughts coming into your head, simply listen to them without evaluating them. Look at your thoughts as just noises, and soon the inside noise will be united with outside noises (whatever they may be in the environment).

Another technique that can be used to arrive at a zero state is to breathe naturally and watch the inflow and outflow of air. Breath awareness is known to be helpful in stress management. Count your breaths, beginning with the next exhalation as 1. Count the next inhalation as 2, the next exhalation as 3, and so on up to 10. Then go back to 1. If any thoughts come to mind, just let them pass over and through you, without either holding on to them or rejecting them. Just let them come and go without condemnation, justification, or evaluation. If you lose your focus of attention, relax your breathing and go back to 1. You can do this breath counting for five to fifteen minutes depending upon your need.

It should take about thirty minutes for you to complete diagnostic meditation. The time, however, will vary with each individual. It can be done by yourself at any time and at any place. It can be done while walking, for it is not essential for you to sit or close your eyes. Gradually you will be able to reach the zero state through a mini-meditation lasting one to five minutes. With training and practice you will understand the state of your consciousness, and will be able to realize the ego-less or zero state in no time.

Just as one cannot try to sleep, you should not try to meditate. Let it become a happening of which you are a part. Meditation will help you to realize the fact that you do not exist as a separate entity but are one pattern in the whole scheme of things.

MEDITATION AND OTHER RELATED COPING TECHNIQUES

Although meditation as a coping technique is closely related to self-hypnosis, autogenic training, free association, progressive relaxation, and biofeedback, it is different from all of the above. All of these techniques require special conditions, such as lowering of external stimulation or the presence of monotonous stimulation, and sometimes evoke a meditative mood "with the possible exception of self-hypnosis, which only does this if the specific directions which the person gives her or himself are to 'relax' " (Carrington, 1977: 36). None of the techniques mentioned, however, create what meditation does, that is, a noncalculating or nonstriving mood. It is possible, though, to combine meditation with one or more of the other techniques; for example, gestalt, time management, or problem-solving strategies.

Meditation and Biofeedback

Certain physiologic functions, such as the flow of nerve impulses, can be controlled with biofeedback training. When the brain responds under pressure, it signals beta frequencies (alpha reflects a more relaxed and contemplative mood; theta is associated with creative thinking; and delta, the lowest frequency, with sleep). An EEG is used to monitor the activity within the brain or an EMG is used in muscle control. In diagnostic meditation, for example, we use a biofeedback exercise to let go of various tensions to arrive at an ego-less state. For more details on particular uses of biofeedback the reader is referred to Chapter 9 of this book.

Meditation and Gestalt

In self-diagnosis you must be prepared to face all the positive and negative aspects of your feelings and thoughts, and both the "figure" and "ground" aspects of the situation (Perls, Hefferline, and Goodman, 1977). In this respect, the process resembles a gestalt approach in which both negative and positive feelings are expressed. You should not only diagnose yourself but make others more aware of mutual problems. In any organization everyone should have the opportunity to understand and share one's role to reach agreement about duties and performance.

The gestalt approach is different from either a "participative manager" or MacGregor's "Theory Y" manager approach, since with these one tends to show the better side of one's personality, but suppresses the so-called "bad" feelings within oneself that, of course, burst out at some point.

Like meditation, the gestalt approach emphasizes the exploration of both good and bad feelings about people and the situation. According to Perls, Hefferline, and Goodman (1977), one should not back away from impulsive behavior, but go further into it until it reaches its natural conclusion. Like meditation, you go into instincts and impulses, and recognize the true nature of your being and behavior.

To express yourself fully, as in a gestalt approach, you should be guided into a process of understanding, through meditative approaches, to know and experience "where you are." Do not jump into solutions without first understanding where you stand in relation to your positive and negative feelings. Dramatize and even exaggerate your behavior in order to become fully aware of what you are doing and how you are doing it. Become attentive so that you are able to listen to your inner ruminations. Meditation can assist in this process of listening or paying attention to variables that prevent awareness and understanding.

Meditation and Time Management

Stress results from an interaction between the person and the environment, and one of the key tasks in this interaction is selection and use of your resources (e.g., time) to manage opportunities and demands more constructively. To do so, time management can help the person to conserve and control time. The individual can learn to make time through meditation and relaxation. During meditation one could use one of the key time management techniques: reviewing the situation in order to create priorities among competing tasks. Stress is multifaceted and requires strategic planning. Time management and meditation can be combined to set goals and establish strategies for specific problems. This kind of meditation can be done by sitting in a chair or in a traditional yogic posture. The focus is not on a specific mantra, but on the multiple stressors themselves and analysis of them in relation to specific needs and values (Schuler, 1979).

CONCLUSION

Without an effective diagnostic approach to coping, individuals may fail to realize some of their own developmental goals, because at some point they have not come to grips with their conflicting selves. They can do this by meditative coping combined with other strategies of adaptation to stress. The overall conclusion of research on meditation is that it is an effective mode for producing relaxation. To deal with organizational stress and job burnout, meditation can be an effective tool by sharpening one's perceptions about one's environment (e.g., job situations), letting go of pressures, listening to one's body, lowering one's expectations, and gaining greater control over one's situation. We recommend that one of the best methods available is that of diagnostic meditation since it combines meditation with other stress coping strategies. In effect, the person should moderate any Type A propensities and pay attention to the joys of *being* instead of promoting ambition and competitiveness.

REFERENCES

Anand, B.K.: G.S. Chhina; and B. Singh. 1961a. "Studies on Sri Ramananda Yogi During His Stay in an Air-Tight Box." *Indian Journal of Medical Research* 49: 82–89.

Anand, B.K.: G.S. Chhina; and B. Singh. 1961b. "Some Aspects of Electroencephalographic Studies in Yogis." *Journal of Electroencephalography and Clinical Neurophysiology* 13: 452–456.

Bagchi, and M.A. Wenger. 1957. "Electrophysiological Correlates of Some Yogi Exercises." *Journal of Electroencephalography and Clinical Neurophysiology* 132–49.

Banquet, J.P. 1972. "EEG and Meditation." *Journal of Electroencephalography and Clinical Neurophysiology* 33: 449–58.

Beehr, T.A., and R.S. Schuler. 1982. "Stress in Organizations." In *Personnel Management,* edited by K.M. Rowland and G.R. Ferris, pp. 390–420. Boston: Allyn and Bacon.

Benson, H. 1974. "Your Innate Asset for Combating Stress." *Harvard Business Review:* (July-Aug.): 49–60.

Benson, H. 1975. *The Relaxation Response.* New York: Avon.

Benson, H.; B.A. Rosner; and B.R. Mazretta. 1973. "Decreased Systalic Blood Pressure in Hypertensive Subjects who Practice Meditation." *Journal of Clinical Investigation* 52: 80.

Bloomfield; M. Cain; and D. Jaffe. 1975. *TM: Discovering Inner Energy and Overcoming Stress.* New York: Delacorte Press.

Brown, B. 1975. *New Mind, New Body.* New York: Harper and Row.

Brown, B. 1977. *Stress and the Act of Biofeedback.* New York: Harper and Row.

Brown, B. 1980. "Stress: The Role of Information and Intellectual Mechanisms." *Journal of Comparative Sociology and Religion* 6 and 7: 38–77.

Carrington, P. 1977. *Freedom in Meditation.* New York: Anchor Press.

Dennston, D., and P. McWilliams. 1975. *The TM Book.* Allen Park, Mi.: Versemonger Press.

Fenwick, P.B.C. 1974. "Metabolic and EEG Changes During Transcendental Meditation." Paper presented at a conference entitled "TM: Research and Applications." sponsored by the Institute of Science and Technology, University of Wales, Cardiff.

Frankenhaeuser, M. 1975a. "Sympathetic-adrenomedullary Activity, Behaviour and the Psychosocial Environment." In *Research in Psychophysiology,* edited by P.H. Venables and M.J. Christie. New York: Wiley and Sons.

Frankenhaeuser, M. 1975. "Experimental Approaches to the Study of Catecholamines and Emotion. In *Emotions—Their Parameters and Measurement,* edited by L. Levi. New York: Raven Press.

Frankenhaeuser, M.; Lundberg, U.; and Forsman, L., 1978. "Dissociation between sympathetic-adrenal and pituitary-adrenal responses to an achievement situation characterized by high controllability: Comparison between Type A and Type B males and females", Department of Psychology, University of Stockholm, no. 540.

Frankenhaeuser, M. 1979a. "Psychololgical Aspects of Life Stress." University of Stockholm and Karolinska Institute, Sweden. Mimeo.

Frankenhaeuser, M. 1979b. Psychoneuroendocrine Approaches to the Study of Stressful Person-Environment Transactions. In *Selye's Guide to Stress Research,* edited by H. Selye. New York: Van Nostrand Reinhold.

Friedman, M. 1982. "The Modification of Type A Behavior in Post-Infraction Patients: A Feasible Process." Paper presented at the Workshop on Occupational Stress Research, York University, Toronto, April 21, 1982.

Friedman, M., and R.H. Rosenman. 1974. *Type A Behavior and Your Heart.* New York: Fawcett Crest.

Girodo, M. 1974. "Yoga Meditation and Flooding in the Treatment of Anxiety Neurosis." *Journal of Behavior Therapy and Experimental Psychiatry* 5: 157–160.

Glass, D.C. 1977. *Behavior Patterns, Stress, and Coronary Disease.* Hillsdale, N.J.: Lawrence Erlbaum Associates.

Glueck, B.C., and C.F. Stroebel. 1975. "Biofeedback and Meditation in the Treatment of Psychiatric Illness." *Comprehensive Psychiatry* 16: 303–21.

Goleman, D.J., and G.E. Schwartz. 1976. "Meditation as an Intervention in Stress Reactivity." *Journal of Consulting and Clinical Psychology* 44: 456–66.

Hjelle, L.A. 1974. "Transcendental Meditation and Psychological Health." *Perceptual and Motor Skills* 39: 623–28.

Humphreys, C. 1971. *Zen Buddhism.* London: Unwin Books.

Jenkins. C.D., S.J. Zyzanski; and R.H. Rosenman. 1971. "Progress Toward Validation of a Computer Scored Test for the Type A Coronary-prone Behavior Pattern." *Psychomatic Medicine* 33: 193.

Johansson, G. 1976. "Subjective Wellbeing and Temporal Patterns of Sympathetic-Adrenal Medullary Activity." *Biological Psychology* 4: 157.

Johansson, G., and M. Frankenhaeuser. 1973. "Temporal Factors in Sympatho-Ardrenomedullary Activity Following Acute Behavioral Activation." *Biological Psychology* 1: 63.

Kasamatsu, A., and T. Hirai. 1969. "An Electro-encephalographic Study on the Zen Meditation (Zazen)." In *Altered States of Consciousness,* edited by C.T. Tart, pp. 489–501. New York: Wiley and Sons.

Kenigsberg, D.; S.J. Zyzanski; C.D. Jenkins; W.I. Wardell; and A.T. Licciardello. 1974. "The Coronary-prone Behavior Pattern in Hospitalized Patients with and without Coronary Heart Disease." *Psychosomatic Medicine* 36: 344.

Krishnamurti, J. 1973. *The Awakening of Intelligence.* New York: Avon.

Lazarus, R.S. 1977. "Psychological Stress and Coping in Adaptation and Illness." In *Psychosomatic Medicine: Current Trends and Clinical Applications,* edited by Z.J. Lipowski, D.R. Lipsitt, and P.C. Whybrow. New York: Oxford University Press.

Lundberg, U. Forthcoming. "Psychophysiological Aspects of Performance and Adjustment to Stress." In *Achievement, Stress and Anxiety,* edited by H.W. Krohene and L. Laux. Washington: Hemisphere.

Lundberg, U., and L. Forsman. 1978. "Adrenal-medullary and Adrenal-cortical Responses to Understimulation and Overstimulation: Comparison between Type A and Type B Persons." Department of Psychology, University of Stockholm, no. 541.

Mason, J.W. 1971. "A Re-evaluation of the Concept of 'Non-Specificity' in Stress Theory." *Journal Psychiatric Research* 8: 323.

Orme-Johnson, D. 1973. "Autonomic Stability and Transcendental Meditation." *Psychosomatic Medicine* 35: 341–49.

Orme-Johnson D., and J.T. Farrow, eds. 1977. *Scientific Research on the Transcendental Meditation Program: Collected Papers,* Vol. 1. New York: Mahowski International University Press.

Ornstein, R.E. 1972. *The Psychology of Consciousness.* San Francisco: W.H. Freeman.

Perls, F.; R.F. Hefferline; and P. Goodman. 1977. *Gestalt Therapy.* New York: Bantam.

Pope, K.S., and J.L. Singer. 1978. *The Stream of Consciousness.* New York: Plenum Press.

Rajneesh, B.S. 1976. *Meditation: The Art of Ecstasy.* New York: Harper and Row.

Ram Dass. *The Only Dance There Is.* 1973. New York: Anchor Books.

Rosenman, R.H.: R.J. Brand; R.I. Sholtz; and M. Friedman. 1976. "Multivariate Prediction of Coronary Heart Disease during 85 Year Follow-up in the Western Collaborative Group Study." *American Journal of Cardiology* 37: 903.

Sachar, E.J. 1975. "Neuroendocrine Abnormalities in Depressive Illness." In *Topics in Psychoendoctrinology,* edited by E.J. Sachar. New York: Grune and Stratton.

Schuler, R.S. 1979. "Managing Stress Means Managing Time." *Personnel Journal* (December): 851–854.

Schwartz, G.E. 1973. "Pros and Cons of Meditation: Current Findings on Physiology and Anxiety, Self-Control, Drug Abuse and Creativity." Paper presented before the 81st Annual Convention of the American Psychological Association, Montreal, 1973.

Sethi, A.S. 1983. "Stress Coping Strategies: The Role of Meditation." In *Selye's Guide to Stress Research,* Vol. 3, edited by H. Selye. New York: Van Nostrand Reinhold.

Sethi, A.S., and A. Daya. 1978. "Management and Meditation." *Dimensions in Health Services* 55, no. 7: 32–33.

Tart, C.T. 1975. *States of Consciousness.* New York: E.P. Dutton.

Van Over, R. 1978. *Total Meditation.* London: Collier MacMillan.

Wallace, R. 1970. "Physiological Effects of Transcendental Meditation." *Science* (March): 1751–54.

Wallace, R., and H. Benson. 1972. "The Physiology of Meditation." *Scientific American* (February): 84–90.

Watts, Alan. 1972. *The Supreme Identity.* New York: Vintage.

Watts, Alan. 1973. *This is It.* New York: Vintage.

Watts, Alan. 1976. *Meditation.* New York: Pyramid Books.

8 YOGA FOR COPING WITH ORGANIZATIONAL STRESS

Amarjit S. Sethi

During the last two decades the West has developed a growing interest in yoga as a stress coping strategy. Yoga is a vast field of knowledge, and there are a number of approaches and techniques. Although interest in yoga (and meditation) has grown rapidly, there are some difficulties in the scientific study of either yoga or various meditative states. The methodologies remain largely undeveloped. Because a common language is not yet available, various methods, tools, and techniques used in yoga and meditation are defined variously by different researchers. Further difficulty is met in trying to assess the objectivity of states of consciousness, although the field of consciousness research is making its transition to a new importance and validity.

YOGA AND ORGANIZATIONAL COPING: A DEFINITION

For purposes of this chapter, we define yoga as a system of stress coping that develops awareness and control of the physical body, emotions, mind, and interpersonal relations. Yoga, as defined by Master Patanjali one thousand years ago, is an "art of mental modification" (Bahm, 1967)[1] and is concerned with freedom from mental

---

[1] This definition of yoga is from Patanjali, *Yoga Sutras*, first section, 2nd sutra, quoted in Bahm, 1967.

disturbances. Yoga is intended for coping with current or future stress by imparting information, conditioning attitudes, or increasing skills of self-realization. This definition implies that the results of yoga must be defined in terms of measurable change in either learner states or learner performance. Yoga development requires primarily a change of attitude, understanding, or awareness as a preventive measure for promoting mental health.

Organizational stress is a dynamic condition in which an individual is faced with an opportunity to achieve what he desires. In this process of wanting and acting to achieve a desired state, the individual must face certain constraints and demands that may result in unfavorable outcomes (Beehr and Schuler, 1982).

According to this definition, stress may be positive (an opportunity) or negative (a constraint or demand). As Beehr and Schuler (1982: 394–95) explain:

> The environment presents dynamic conditions (potential stressors) that can be perceived as opportunities, constraints, or demands, and that have perceived levels of uncertainty of resolution, as well as important outcomes. Stress and the desire for resolution are precipitated by events that cause a disrupton of homeostasis, either physiological or psychological. . . . Unfortunately, with the opportunity or constraint stress associated with sociophysiological stress conditions, the body also responds involuntarily, as with the physical stress conditions, with similar physiological reactions. In this case, however, it is less likely that the increased blood sugar, adrenaline, and nonadrenaline will be utilized through any physical exertion to restore the sociopsychological disequilibrium caused by the situation of opportunity or constraint. If other strategies for dealing with the stress are not utilized, long-run wear and tear on the body will occur as the body fights to restore physiological homeostasis, resulting in diseases of adaptation.

The word "yoga" means union. In essence it implies union with the ultimate where the process of desiring has come to an end, and where stress is non-existent. The purpose of yoga is thus to stop all stress, positive and negative, and arrive at a state of self-realization where the goals of life has been fully achieved. Such union may be experienced at different levels. There is the union of forces in body and mind which are often in conflict with each other and need to be brought into a state of harmony. There is the union of body and mind with the individual's spirit or self. And, finally, there is the ultimate union of that individual spirit with the Infinite or the Universe. Union with the Infinite is the highest goal of yoga, and all the different systems are designed to reach eventually to that supreme union.

A variety of yogas have been developed: some display different beliefs or conceptions about the nature of the ultimate and advocate different methods of achieving union or a stress-less state. We will focus on the *techniques* or tools of yoga, as the discussion of different metaphysical systems falls more in the province of philosophy and religion. A brief explanation of the fundamental philosophical beliefs of yoga, however, is in order. One of the popular metaphysical beliefs is that ultimate reality is a pure, bare, complete, perfect unity. This is a Vedantic view. As all plurality is illusory, the purpose of yoga is to achieve union with this ultimate unity. As the reality is, in effect, perfect unity, the stresses that the individual experiences are illusory, and the yogic effort is to understand and overcome illusion. Another way of conceptualizing yogic effort is to separate real unity (*purusha*) from unfortunate association with material plurality (*prakriti*). The term yoga is used, not only for unifying processes, but also for separating material processes, as a means of attaining ultimate purity or pure consciousness. In this second view the goal of yogic practice is to get rid of the impurities of the material world, along with its stresses and strains, and to be in a stress-less or peaceful state. Patanjali's view is included in this interpretation (Bahm, 1967).

Approaches to Yoga

Karma Yoga.   According to this type of yoga, it is assumed that actions (*karma*) result from our willing or desiring, and this may lead to positive or negative stress. According to Karma Yoga, each good deed will lead to a good reward, and each bad deed will result in a bad or negative reward. The appropriate attitude in doing any good deed is as important in Karma Yoga as the deed itself. As Bahm (1967: 17) explains: "The willingness with which one does his duties, no matter they be particular duties . . . or universal duties, determines his future rewards and progress toward ultimate union. . . . Each thought and each deed which brings one nearer to his goal is . . . yogic since it brings its degree of union. Thus ordinary ethical practices constitute an aspect or phrase of yoga."

Gnana or Philosophical Yoga.   This path provides techniques of discernment through which one may comprehend the stresses that prevent the individual from attaining ultimate unity. One begins to realize the real worth of each stress and stressor and why it is obscuring the ultimate reality. As the ultimate reality in yoga is freedom from all distinctness, the goal of Gnana Yoga is to realize the "illusoriness of all perceptive and discursive knowledge" (Bahm, 1967: 18). As a person realizes that things one desires lack permanence, one withdraws attention from them. Gnana Yoga thus goes beyond analytical knowledge to a yogic intuition in which awareness and being are identical. Knowledge involves a distinction between knower and known, but in yogic intuition knower and known are one, not two (Bahm 1967: 19). It is this realization that frees the individual from life's stresses.

Bhakti or Devotional Yoga.   As the term implies, this approach uses devotion as a means of achieving yoga's goal through union between lover and beloved. This union is achieved through surrender to the ultimate value one cherishes. This surrender is accomplished by submitting one's ego, that is, giving up of oneself. All actions and thoughts are performed for the sake of the beloved (which may be one of the gods or God), or any one of the incarnations (*avatars*). All stresses are thus interpreted as gifts of the Lord, and suffering is used as a means for freedom. All happiness and bliss are equally considered as means for freedom as long as one remembers one's object of love. One does one's duty without any hope for reward or any fear of punishment, because the devotee is performing them not for any ulterior motive but for the sake of the beloved. All stresses dissolve in this total devotion. "The supreme value loved is so great that any willful withholding of any lesser values from it amounts to a defilement of it, and of one's self as united with it" (Bahm, 1967: 20). As one surrenders, one realizes one's real worth and is able to put all stress in perspective. "One loses his life in order to find it, and the more fully he loses himself through devotion the more completely he finds himself realized in the object of his devotion" (Bahm, 1967: 20).

Yoga thus involves not only regulation of the body through physical exercise, right breathing, and control of the emotional nature, but also the practice of meditation, devotion, and spiritual evolution. One of the techniques used in Bhakti Yoga is the repetition of a word or *mantra*, as in transcendental meditation. The aim of the devotee is to calm the mind and re-orient one's awareness to a unitary level of consciousness, thus transcending the stress of material reality.

Stress is desire or wanting to achieve certain values and needs. Stress becomes distress when one is unable to find or be or become what one wants. Such desiring leads one away from one's real self. In Bhakti Yoga, in order to overcome desire, one must become desireless or be in a state of no-desire. The goal of Bhakti Yoga is to overcome all life stress through intuition.

Tantric Yoga.   As an offshoot of Bhakti Yoga, Tantric Yoga focuses on the cosmic orgasm as a means of achieving unity. Through sexual orgasm one attains a cosmic (self-less) quality. "The goal of Tantric Yoga is a kind of eternal orgasm, bereft of degrees or variations and of awareness of self versus otherness, or loved and beloved" (Bahm, 1967: 21).

Kundalini Yoga.   The aim of Kundalini Yoga is to release repressed energy and bring it into the realm of awareness. The assumption is that a great deal of energy is tied up in keeping repressed material outside awarness.

> Work is involved in holding a memory or impulse away from the conscious mind. This energy can be released and made once more accessible when the unconscious material is brought into consciousness. The patient in psychotherapy who is able to bring repressed material into consciousness is usually found to have more energy available. This reduces chronic fatigue and makes work more effective and dynamic (Swami Rama, Ballentine, and Swami Ajaya, 1979: 138).

In Kundalini Yoga, one can increase energy, symbolized by a rising serpent called *kundalini.* "Kunda" means a bowl or basin, and the kundalini serpent is said to be coiled up in the basin formed by the pelvis where it is traditionally and metaphorically said to be sleeping, "intoxicated on the energy it is sapping from one's potential supply" (Rama et al., 1979: 138). The kundalini rises, through certain centers known as *chakras,* and the energy it has absorbed is released. Although it may lead to strain in the beginning, it can help the person to overcome his stress in the long run by providing him with a "new channel of communication, a higher sense" (Krishna, 1971: 232). Khalsa and Khalsa (1979) conducted a scientific survey of physiological, psychological, and performance studies of Kundalini Yoga and concluded that, although most of the experiments are preliminary, the initial data indicates that Kundalini Yoga is capable of producing significant changes in psychological, physiological and bioenergetic systems. The tests also showed that Kundalini Yoga can be related to positive changes in self-esteem, openness to experience, cognitive perception, and attitude and may be able to stimulate healing or psychic capacities (Khalsa and Khalsa, 1979).

Raja Yoga.   Raja Yoga or the Royal Path was codified by the sage Patanjali who wrote the Yoga Sutras. This is also called *Ashtanga Yoga,* or eight-rung ladder, because it describes eight steps leading to ultimate freedom from stress. In this yoga one combines body regulation and mental functioning. The part that deals with physical education is known as *Hatha Yoga.* By using certain postures known as *asanas* the learner is able to relax his stressed muscles. This is considered preliminary work for mental and deeper Raja Yoga. As Swami Rama (1979: 3) explains: "Although the body (in Hatha Yoga) is worked with intensively, actually the goal is to become less bound up in the body and to gain some distance from it and perspective on its functioning." The eight steps of Raja Yoga are illustrated in Figure 8-1.

Figure 8-1.   Eight Limbs of Yoga.

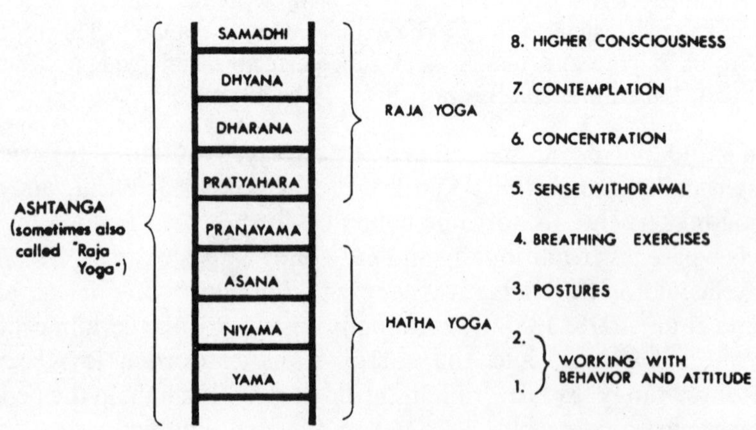

Source: Reprinted, by permission, from *Yoga and Psychotherapy* by Swami Rama, Rudolph Ballentine, M.D., and Swami Ajaya, Ph.D. © 1976 by the Himalayan International Institute.

The aim of Raja Yoga, according to its Master Patanjali, is to disentangle oneself from one's thoughts. The underlying assumption is that we are in essence different from our thoughts, and are able to observe them (Rama et al., 1979: 74). Pantanjali outlines a systematic and detailed path for overcoming stress completely through self-mastery. The first two steps in this stress coping strategy relate to lifestyle and habits known as *Yamas* (discipline) and *Niyamas* (restraint). Yamas include purity, contentment, austerity, self-study, and devotion. Niyamas includes non-hurting, truthfulness, non-stealing, chastity, and non-coveting. By regulating everyday behavior, one is able to be freed of tension, worry, and anxiety, and this allows the student to practice Hatha Yoga, that is, various physical postures or asanas. Another step involves focusing on breathing practices. In the next stage, the student learns to regulate sensory input (*pratyahara*) so that impacts from the sensory organs are cut off (Rama et al., 1979: 76) and do not distract the mind from its observations of itself. All stages work together in an integrated or synergistic way. In the final three steps the student learns to practice concentration. The primary work here is the control of thoughts. (Note that in the previous steps the student's effort was directed toward controlling behavior stress, body stress, energy stress, and stress stemming from the senses.) In the final state mental stress is to be controlled in *dharana* (concentration), *dhyana* (contemplation), and *samadhi* (which is the highest state of consciousness and can be termed a stress-less state).

YOGA TRAINING PROGRAMS AS STRESS COPING TOOLS

Stress coping has to be viewed within the framework of yoga psychology which recognizes five different levels (or sheaths) of consciousness. These include physical body, energy body, mind, unconscious, and pure or higher consciousness. The various systems of yoga described in the previous section refer to these various states. A classification of these systems along consciousness streams can be made as follows:

Yoga System	*Level of Consciousness*
Hatha	regulating physical body
Pranayama	regulating energy body through breathing exercises

Gnana and/or
Bhakti   control of mind and ego transcendence
Raja   intuitive wisdom
Samadhi   pure consciousness: in yoga this means that
                          in the individual, *purusha* (pure conscious-
                          ness) has been separated from *prakriti*
                          (material principle)

Systems of yoga, although classified separately, complement each other
so that a practitioner of Hatha Yoga can succeed in the goal of coping
with life stress by using Gnana or Raja Yoga or other methods of yoga.

Yoga recognizes that there are levels beyond reason (or *buddhi*),
but these levels are difficult to measure. We have to examine these
levels according to the philosophical perspectives of yoga in order to
understand the functions of higher levels of consciousness and their
role in coping. Figure 8-2 illustrates the layers of self along five
sheaths in yoga.

At each of the levels of consciousness (physical body, energy body,
mental body, higher buddhi, and so forth), the individual has increasing access to higher consciousness, thus giving him greater energy to
deal with life's problems. Eventually all life stresses are gone and the
material principle (prakriti) is no longer predominant. At that transcendental level, there is no need for coping because the individual
subsists in a conflict-less state. In yogic terms it is a state of purusha
or purity of consciousness. At earlier stages of development, the individual's awareness and orientation are in terms of coping, the self,
and the world. Attention is focused on material coping in which the
individual seeks release from stresses and strains of everyday life. As
the individual gains in yogic effort, the necessity for coping becomes
less important because the individual's real or pure consciousness is
awakened. The individual has become detached from the "I."

At each level the individual uses coping mechanisms that provide
certain benefits in overcoming problems and stresses. These vehicles
are increasingly more subtle and refined as the individual evolves
toward higher consciousness. In the highest achievement in yoga the
individual abandons all coping mechanisms. "In yoga psychology the
ego is only one of these possible vehicles of consciousness, whereas in
Western psychology the ego is primary and consciousness is a property
of it" (Rama et al., 1979: 69) (see Figure 8-3). Yoga as a coping
mechanism thus represents a strategy of wholly different dimension,

Figure 8-2.   Layers of Self along Five Sheaths in Yoga.

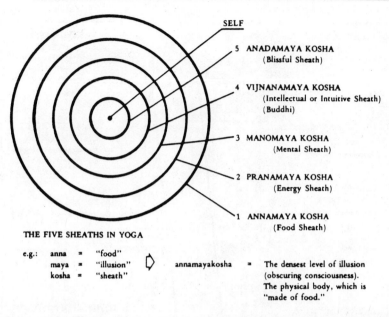

THE FIVE SHEATHS IN YOGA

e.g.:
anna	=	"food"
maya	=	"illusion"
kosha	=	"sheath"

annamayakosha = The densest level of illusion (obscuring consciousness). The physical body, which is "made of food."

Source: Reprinted, by permission, from *Yoga and Psychotherapy* by Swami Rama, Rudolph Ballentine, M.D., and Swami Ajaya, Ph.D. © 1976 by the Himalayan International Institute.

and provides a movement away from an egocentric strategy of stress coping. The ultimate aim in any yoga effort is to arrive at a level of consciousness that is beyond analytical thought (known as supramental level) "unimpaired by the distractions of sense impressions or the preoccupations of a narrow personal egoism" (Swami Rama, Ballentine, and Swami Ajaya, 1979: 98).

In yoga psychology the mind is conceptualized as "lower mind" and is in direct contact with incoming information through the senses. It collects sense impressions and coordinates them with motor responses, thus taking the form of perceptions. This lower mind (known as *manas*) is constantly changing. Two other functions of the mind are I-ness (*ahankara*) and wisdom (*buddhi*). When sensory impressions enter via the sensory-motor mind, ahankara transforms them into a personal experience by relating them to the individual's identity as a person, thus laying the foundation for separateness from the universe. It is a subjective experience. When the sensory-motor

Figure 8-3.   Concepts of Self: Yogic and Western.

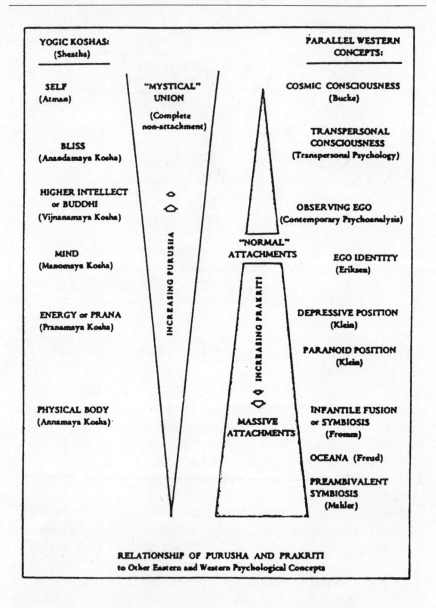

Source: Reprinted, by permission, from *Yoga and Psychotherapy* by Swami Rama, Rudolph Ballentine, M.D., and Swami Ajaya, Ph.D. © 1976 by the Himalayan International Institute.

mind functions, "stress is experienced." But when ahankara adds its influence, "I experience a stress." The third major mental function is that of evaluating or sifting the information intake and deciding on a course of action. This judgmental function is performmed by buddhi through a process of discrimination in conjunction with intelligence. These three functions are collectively known as "internal instruments" (Rama et al., 1979: 70–71) and function as a whole. Figure 8–4 illustrates this yogic conception of mind.

Preparing for Yoga

Proper breathing and the physical postures in Hatha Yoga help the individual overcome muscular tensions and nervousness. According to Swami Rama, the practice of Hatha Yoga strengthens muscles and tendons that may have become contracted due to mental tensions and faulty postures. Muscle groups that have become weak from disuse are also gradually strengthened (Rama et al., 1979: 7). When the voluntary muscles are relaxed, one becomes more attuned to internal states, and a linkage is formed between physical well-being and mental awareness.

Figure 8-4. The Yogic (Vedantic) Conception of Mind.

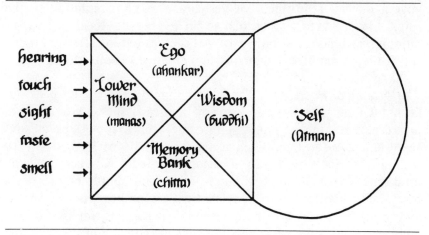

Source: Reprinted, by permission, from *Yoga and Psychotherapy* by Swami Rama, Rudolph Ballentine, M.D., and Swami Ajaya, Ph.D. © 1976 by the Himalayan International Institute.

Breathing Techniques.   In yoga "right breathing" is of utmost importance. Preliminary studies show that over 75 percent of those who suffer heart attacks breathe through their mouths instead of their noses (Nurenberger, 1981: 190). The first step then is to learn to inhale and exhale through the nose without using the mouth at all. First, bring the air all the way down to the diaphragm, and push the abdomen out with each intake of air. Pull the stomach in tightly, but gradually breath out. While breathing, focus all attention or awareness on the in-flow and out-flow process of breathing. The word "hatha" itself comes from the Sanskrit root "ha" (meaning sun) and "tha" (meaning moon), and refers to the incoming and outgoing breaths in breathing.

According to yoga, the physiological effects associated with air flow through the two nostrils are different. As Nurenberger (1981) explains, the right nostril should be made voluntarily active when one is doing active work, whereas the left nostril should be activated in nonactive or less active situations. This conscious effort helps to regain control over thoughts, and, basically a closed loop mental operation that recycles the same old information, the same problems, the same uncertainties and the same images.

Pre-conditioning Techniques.   Pre-conditioning or warm-up techniques cover good postural habits, and selected asanas are used that govern normal adjustment of vertebrae, supply circulation to the spinal cord, and relieve muscular strain and nervous tension. Preconditioning techniques include exercises such as tensing, flexing, lubricating the extremities, balancing, and creative visualization.

The Asanas or Postures.   The asanas should, technically speaking, be nondynamic, static, passive, and non-resistant to gravitational pressure. Patanjali emphasizes that the asanas should be steady, easy, and comfortable. Each asana should be performed for 10 seconds the first week, with 30 seconds added each week until the total time is brought to 15 minutes. Each asana should be measured by stability (motionlessness), relaxation, endurance, concentration, and control of body, breath, and mind. The asana is employed to acquire a perfect state of health through increasing flexibility of the skeletal structure. This, in turn, stimulates the central nervous system, the nerve endings, and the various organs associated with them. Employed over time, the asanas will stimulate and massage the muscular system and the various glands within the body. The asanas and their sequence should be selected with the needs of the learner kept in mind. For a good description of these asanas, the reader is referred to basic yoga postures illustrated by Stearn (1965: 262–325).

The asana routine should provide for the health and care of the skeleton and especially the spine. Considering the range of motion employed in every direction, increased spinal mobility, flexion, and extension, can be expected. An increased range of motion for the pelvis, the shoulders, hip joints, legs, arms, head, neck, and an improved central nervous sytem and muscular system can also be achieved (Tulloch, 1977).[2]

Remaining Techniques. In addition to breathing exercises and asanas, one can use advanced techniques such as *bandhas* or muscular locks applied during breath retention. As Stearn (1965): 322–323) explains:

> The tensing of certain inner muscles, . . . stimulate the three vital plexuses—in the throat, abdomen, and base of spine. These deliberate contractions assertedly increase muscular tone and coordination and galvanize the whole nervous system. They are said to produce an electric current or force called Kundalini Shakti (the Serpent Power) which rises through a subtle central channel of the spine, Sushmna Nadi. . . . When locks are properly applied, . . . this vital pranic energy or kundalini mounts toward the higher chakras, unfolding ever expanding levels of consciousness as it rises. Students often experience a sensation of heat which shows that the dormant energies have begun to stir.''

Two other techniques may be mentioned: yoga *mudra* and *tratakam*. Mudra involves concentration on a particular sound (usually the word *aum*) during suspension of breath; tratakam involves concentrating on a particular object or point of focus, for example, the moon, a flower, a star, or a candle. It is recommended that one gaze for as long as one is comfortable without blinking. Afterward give rest to the eyes. The tratakam exercise may then be repeated (Stearn, 1965: 327).

According to yoga experts, the overriding principle in training is to practice techniques gently and patiently and to proceed only when the

---

[2]Results obtained over a period of one year in a geriatric sample indicated a favorable change, as a pilot project correlating yoga exercises and the change in range of joint motion (Tulloch, 1977).

Table 8-1.   Suggested Timetable for Daily Yoga.

Morning

5 minutes diaphragmatic breathing (this can be done immediately upon awakening)
Shower or bath to loosen up the muscles and clear the mind
5 minutes of stretching exercises
5-10 minutes of meditation

During the Day

5 minutes of breathing exercises
A 10 minutes relaxation break in the morning and afternoon to clarify things

After Work

Yoga exercise: an excellent time to clear the mind of work-related tensions (variable time depending on one's capacity and training period
Breathing exercises: 10 minutes, gradually increasing to 15 minutes

Evening

5 minutes of diaphragmatic breathing
10-20 minutes of meditation can be done in bed right before going to sleep

Note: Use breathing exercises combined with meditation as often as one can as they will gradually help increase one's ability to overcome daily work and non-work stress.

Source: Reprinted, by permission, from *Freedom from Stress* by Phil Nuernberger, Ph.D. © 1981 by The Himalayan International Institute.

practice begin with diaphragmatic breathing, followed by warm-up or relaxation exercises, asanas, and then meditation. Table 8-1 suggests a daily schedule for relaxation and outlines only the techniques mentioned above.

CONCLUSION

Yoga provides a training program to deal with modern-day organizational stress and scientific studies, limited as they are, point to its positive psychophysiological effects (Funderburk, 1977). Further research is needed, however, to determine the precise effects of specific yogic programs and techniques, such as Hatha Yoga, on stress and coping (Sethi, 1979). We recommend a combination of yogic techniques based on personal needs and capacity. The ultimate goal of yoga, the isolation of *purusha* from *prakriti* and the transcendence of all *karma,* may lead practitioners to a complete mastery over stress.

REFERENCES

Bahm, A.J. 1967. *Yoga Union With The Ultimate: A New Version of the Ancient Yoga Sutras of Patanjali.* New York: Frederick Ungar Publishing Co.

Beehr, T.A., and R.S. Schuler. 1982. "Stress in Organizations." In *Personnel Management,* edited by K.M. Rowland and G.R. Ferris, pp. 390–419. Boston: Allyn and Bacon.

Brown, B. 1979–1980. "Stress: The Role of Information and Intellectual Mechanisms." *Journal of Comparative Sociology and Religion* nos. 6 and 7: 38–77.

Funderburk, James. 1977. *Science Studies Yoga.* Honesdale, Penn.: Himalayan International Institute of Yoga Science and Philosophy.

Khalsa, G.S., and S.S. Khalsa. 1979. "Yoga: A Scientific Survey." In *Comparative Religion,* edited by A.S. Sethi and R. Pummer, pp. 61–92. New Delhi: Vikas Publishing House.

Krishna, Gopi. 1971. *Kundalini: The Evolutionary Energy in Man.* Boulder, Co.: Shambala.

Nurenberger, P. 1981. *Freedom From Stress.* Honesdale, Penn.: Himalayan International Institute of Yoga Science and Philosophy.

Rama, Swami; R. Ballentine; and Swami Ajaya. 1979. *Yoga and Psychotherapy.* Honesdale, Penn.: Himalayan International Institute of Yoga Science and Philosophy.

Sethi, A.S. 1979. "Yoga—A Research Framework." In *Comparative Religion,* edited by A.S. Sethi and R. Pummer, pp. 93–101. New Delhi: Vikas Publishing House.

Stearn, J. 1965. *Yoga, Youth and Reincarnation.* New York: Bantam.

Tulloch, Ronda. 1977. "Biomechanics of Yoga." Toronto: Stress Consultation Centre. Mimeo.

9 STRESS COPING THROUGH BIOFEEDBACK

Barbara B. Brown

INTRODUCTION

While there is no standard definition of biofeedback, it is generally considered as the process of learning to control a selected physiologic[1] activity. Biofeedback is implemented by making representative information about the physiologic function available to the organism generating that physiologic activity. As the definition stands, it could easily encompass biological control induced by yogic practices, hypnosis, or autosuggestion; or, in fact, by all homeostatic regulating mechanisms.

Because biofeedback has so many origins and so many variations in procedure, it is difficult to arrive at definitions and concepts that are acceptable to both researchers and practitioners of biofeedback. These problems can be most easily seen by taking an example. Suppose we record an electrocardiogram (EKG) from an individual, but in place of the conventional EKG machine, we substitute a device that is constructed so that three consecutive interbeat intervals are

· Reprinted by permission of the publisher from B.B. Brown, "Biofeedback," in *Controversy in Psychiatry,* edited by J.P. Brady and A.K.H. Brodie (Philadelphia, Pa.: N.B. Saunders Company, 1978).

[1]Where appropriate, the -ic suffix is used throughout. It implies a closer relationship to the substantive being qualified than does the -ical suffix. (Webster's Collegiate Dictionary).

averaged and displayed by a meter calibrated in beats per minute. In the biofeedback context, the subject watches the meter and is asked either to increase or decrease heart rate "by some mental means." Often within a matter of minutes, and certainly in less than thirty, the average individual executes the instructions significantly and reliably.

The relationship between the individual and the individual's biological information is obviously one of feedback, and given this unembellished situation and its prompt result, definition should be a simple matter. The problems arise when we try to reconcile past knowledge about learning processes with the peculiar features of biofeedback. These features involve three exceptional elements: the new experience of perceiving the dynamics of unfelt physiologic activity; a manipulation of automatic regulating mechanisms; and the use of mental activity to affect physiologic activity. For the biomedical physiologist, these new elements are in sharp conflict with the dogma that activity of the autonomic nervous system is largely autonomous and beyond voluntary control (i.e., beyond direction by higher mental processes). For the psychological theorist, on the other hand, the difficulties in characterizing feedback lie in reconciling traditional learning concepts, such as reinforcement, and the shaping of responses with the effect of continuously available information, and the difficulty of the apparent duplexity of stimulus and response (i.e., does the change in meter reading reinforce a spontaneous change in heart rate and so shape direction and degree of change, or does the meter reading confirm the result of a mental effort, or both?).

Further, if virtually every physiologic system can be brought under control by techniques analogous to the heart rate example, what then can be generalized under the rubric of biofeedback? It is first, of course, a new procedural tool, in which "private," internal physiologic activity is not only revealed to the patient, but is essentially made his responsibility. The consequences of this break with the custom of withholding biological information from patients has far-reaching implications. It is as new to most people as requiring a senior citizen to learn hoola-hooping to qualify for medicare. The new experience is, moreover, tinged with uncertain emotions about a changing doctor-patient relationship in which the patient is an active participant in his own treatment. The role reversal during actual biofeedback training also means that the patient has little option but to direct attention to subjective states, both definitive and non-specific, a limiting circumstance that fosters changing awareness.

These are, perhaps, only a few of the subjective events that exert greater or lesser influences during biofeedback learning.

Although biofeedback is a new medical technique, the many elements involved suggest that biofeedback can also be characterized as a distinctive, new therapeutic approach. And since learning is essential to its effectiveness, biofeedback is also a learning process. Finally, biofeedback appears to be a fundamental psychophysiologic phenomenon in which complex cerebral (mental) events supervene, by intentional self-direction, in the automatic feedback regulating mechanisms of the body, including those of the brain.

THE ROOTS OF BIOFEEDBACK

It has taken some time to put biofeedback into perspective. The reasons are as diverse and as fascinating as biofeedback itself. Biofeedback sprang from psychology, neurophysiology, muscle rehabilitation procedures, and the application of cybernetics theory in physiology. Each discipline, in turn, has claimed the "discovery." Probably the most striking observation about the evolution of biofeedback is that it *did* arise from quite different sources and roughly at the same time.

The most proprietary voice claiming discovery of biofeedback has been that of experimental psychology, and particularly of researchers in conditioned learning theory. Operant conditioning employs a methodology in which changes of behavior in a desired direction are reinforced or rewarded. When researchers began to speak of changes in physiologic activity (or some signal indicating that physiologic activity had changed) as the reinforcement, it was concluded that the resulting learning met the criteria of operant conditioning. I argue that the biofeedback process is quite different. The work of DiCara and Miller (1968, 1969) has been publicized as the biofeedback breakthrough. Historically, however, it was more a prelude to the operant conditioning mode of biofeedback since information about changes in the physiologic system selected for learning were not used either as the reinforcement or as a biofeedback signal. Rather, rats were rewarded for changing heart rate (or other autonomically innervated functions) in the desired direction by applying an electrical stimulation of the brain previously determined to be effective for the rats to work at lever pressing. The important departure from operant theory was the demonstration that physiologic systems innervated by the autonomic nervous system could be so conditioned, popularly interpreted as "learning." Miller (1969) interpreted this and similar research as indicating the inherent potential of involuntary systems to come under voluntary control. The deficiencies in logic of the Miller argument are discussed below.

A significant number of research reports more directly relevant to biofeedback appeared either prior to or concurrently with the DiCara and Miller reports, beginning with Shearn (1962), and including Kamiya (1962), Brener and Hothersall (1966), Hnatiow and Lang (1965), Lang, Straufe, and Hasting (1967), and Headrick, Feather, and Wells (1970). Each of these investigations used operant techniques to demonstrate the conditionability of autonomically innervated systems. But more significantly, all the studies, except that of Kamiya, used some index of actual cardiovascular activity as the reinforcement signal, and used human beings as the experimental subjects. The general result of these studies was to establish the operant conditioning form of biofeedback.

As it ultimately evolved in clinical practice, the biofeedback principle was most closely approximated by the research of Green, Walters, Green and Murphy (1969) using biofeedback of muscle activity as a relaxation technique, by the work of Brown (1970a) who used continuous monitors of EEG alpha activity for learning voluntary control over alpha, and by Budzynski, Stoyva, and Adler (1970) who used a combination of muscle biofeedback information and operant conditioning reinforcement to reduce muscle tension. Brown's experiments most clearly differed from other methodologies and concepts in that the selected physiologic activity (EEG alpha) was displayed continuously to the subjects; no external constraints were placed upon the participants.

Surprisingly unnoticed in the genesis of biofeedback has been the contribution of clinical neurophysiology. Many muscle rehabilitation specialists have long used biofeedback techniques. To recover function in paralyzed muscles, for example, residual muscle potentials are displayed on an oscilloscope. At the same time the voltage of each potential is used to activate any auditory biofeedback information available about muscle activity that can be neither felt nor recruited for movement. Induced activity in the paralyzed muscle (with the aid of a therapist) easily establishes the goals to be achieved in muscle reeducation. The technique has been employed since the mid-1950s, but the underlying biofeedback principle was not recognized for general therapeutic application until the extensive work of Basmajian and his colleagues (1963, 1967, 1972) and others. Their research has firmly established the neurophysiologic validity of the inherent ability for learning to control not only isolated motor units, but for groups of motor units selected on either a spatial or temporal basis. The experimental technique is identical to the muscle rehabilitation technique and requires little except feedback of motor unit activity, instructions, and encouragement.

Although the impact of the experimental cybernetics approach on applied biofeedback has been small, the systems attack of Mulholland that relates biofeedback to internal control systems has supplied important insights into the underlying mechanisms of biofeedback. Mulholland (1968) and Mulholland and Evans (1966) described biofeedback technology early by employing lights activated or inactivated by the presence or disappearance of alpha activity in the EEG pattern, and used the technique to explore relationships between alpha activity and visual accommodation.

THE DIFFERENT METHODOLOGIES
OF BIOFEEDBACK

The diverse origins of biofeedback, along with its fundamental ability to affect all physiologic systems, has resulted in many different methodologic approaches and in different modalities for each system. The profusion of scientific reports, has made it difficult to agree upon or standardize biofeedback procedures, and the therapist interested in developing an understanding of biofeedback is confronted with a flood of confusing literature.

For the purpose of understanding the majority of biofeedback procedures, most research and clinical data can be generalized into two major categories of methods and four modalities.

The two methods are operant conditioning and augmented biofeedback. The conditioning method, as described earlier, uses the biological (biofeedback) information chiefly as a reinforcement of a desired physiologic change, although it often additionally employs verbal encouragement as a secondary reinforcement. This technique is employed most frequently in research studies designed to isolate influential variables, but it has also been incorporated into existing behavior modification programs by adding biofeedback information about selected physiologic activities as additional reinforcement.

When the purpose of operant conditioning biofeedback is principally to affect the functioning of psychiologic activity, effects are limited. Results of most research studies require rather elegant statistics to demonstrate changes, and, in fact, few of the studies have been controlled for biological variation, adaptation, or reliability. More often than not research studies are conducted over short time periods, such as fifteen minutes, and can scarcely be considered comparable to clinical biofeedback training. Nonetheless, because of the great bulk of psychological reports, concepts stemming from such inadequate studies have been widely popularized and accepted; when the operant technique has been used in clinical applications as biofeedback, results have generally been disappointing.

The second technique, augmented biofeedback, is widely used clinically and is significantly different from the conditioning technique. In augmented biofeedback, the biological information is provided as continuously and in as real a period of time as is feasible (i.e., given a convenient integration time for electrical muscle activity, for heart rate, or for specific EEG waveforms; some physiologic studies, such as blood pressure feedback, are however limited by the mechanics of measurement.) Secondly, the desired changes in physiologic activity are suggested to the patient rather than controlled externally, hence responsibilty for change is given to the patient rather than retained by the therapist. And finally, in contrast to the conditioning technique, many facilitating procedures are employed. Clinical research confirms the markedly superior effectiveness of augmented biofeedback, and the technique is successful even if only the first two conditions are fulfilled (biofeedback information and instructions).

Briefly, additional procedures most frequently used in general clinical practice of biofeedback include at least several of the following: Progressive Relaxation (P.R.), Autogenic Training (A.T.), guided imagery exercises, home practice with instruments, home relaxation exercises, record keeping by the patient, psychotherapy or counselling, and desensitization procedures.

The most frequently used biofeedback modalities are: (1) voltage-integrated EMG (muscle) activity and skin temperature (both used largely for relaxation and stress reduction effects) (2) skin temperature and specific cardiovascular parameters such as blood flow, pulse volume, heart rate and blood pressure (used for cardiovascular effects); (3) motor unit activity (used in muscle rehabilitation); and (4) EEG components such as alpha, theta, 12–16 Hz rhythm (used to reverse clinical conditions that are accompanied by excesses or deficiencies of specific EEG components, such as anxiety, insomnia, chronic pain, epilepsy, or learning problems in children).

There are two important theoretical and practical differences between conditioning and augmented biofeedback procedures. The first is the difference in efficiency of learning. In conditioning, when the biofeedback information is used as a reinforcement (signal), changes in physiologic activity (e.g., in heart rate or muscle tension or EEG alpha) are usually accumulated and averaged over a period of time, say two minutes. This means that the exact time of acceptable performance (i.e., changing the physiologic activity in the desired direction), is unknown, and a significant time interval may elapse before information about successful performance, given as the reinforcement, is actually presented to the patient. When dealing with continuously dynamic physiologic activity behavior, this can amount to a time interval exceeding that which would allow percept formation: the associations between the unfelt physiologic activity and the meaning of the reinforcement are thus difficult to make. In heart rate or EEG alpha biofeedback, for example, signalling patients that they have successfully changed their heart rate of alpha at some unidentified time during the previous two minutes means that the patients are apprised of appropriate performance only after that performance has been completed. If perceptual appreciation of associations (conscious or unconscious awareness) is necessary to the learning process, then giving the crucial biofeedback information *after* performance has been completed suggests that additional cerebral mechanisms are required to consolidate associations between goal-directed performance and the reinforcement. The instrumentation used also often contributes to distorting both the temporal and informational elements of the biofeedback signal since many biofeedback instruments, particularly EMG instruments, simply add muscle potential voltages.

On the other hand, when biofeedback information is continuously provided, and particularly when other relevant information is available to facilitate disposition of the biological information, the patient has the option of integrating the information and subjective associations on a continuous basis. While this mode of biofeedback also reinforces performance, it has the advantage of operating on a time scale more closely matching the physiologic dynamics. Results of both research and clinical studies bear out the importance of this temporal difference. Operant techniques lead to small and poorly sustained changes, while continuous, augmented biofeedback leads to large and well-sustained changes.

The second conceptual and practical difference between the two methods is in the interpretation and verification of "control" over physiologic activities. According to the operant tradition, control means that the organism develops differential responses to conditioning stimuli affecting the same physiologic system.[2] The "control" remains external to the organism since all conditions for providing the reinforcement are maintained by the experimenter or therapist. The reinforcement is integral for eliciting the response since failure to provide reinforcement generally results in disappearance of the response (extinction). For the patient to sustain control over the physiologic activity, frequent reinforcement is required to "remind" the physiologic system how to perform.

With continuous biofeedback, practice leads to the development of internally generated, *voluntary* control. This can be demonstrated by revising the biofeedback signal and requesting the patient to perform the task he has learned. Such voluntary control rarely occurs with operant methods.

For patients whose symptoms do not require behavior control, achieving voluntary control over physiologic functions would seem to be more appropriate; patients who do require behavior control are not likely candidates for voluntary physiologic control.

DIVERSITY OF BIOFEEDBACK APPLICATIONS

The most frustrating problem one encounters when collecting information about biofeedback in order to judge its legitimacy is the extraordinary number of scientific avenues where research and clinical reports can be found. Biofeedback research is reported in as many as twenty different speciality journals of psychology,[3] and in all the jour-

---

[2]The concept that changes in *both* directions of a physiologic activity are necessary to claim control is an important criterion; however, the impetus for "control" can be either externally determined as in conditioning, or internally determined as can be developed with augmented biofeedback.

[3]For example, a report on the management of migraine by trained control of vasoconstriction recently appeared in the *Journal of Consulting and Clinical Psychology,* a source little used in the field of medicine.

nals of psychosomatic medicine, psychiatry, electroencephalography, and even music. In addition, oral reports are abundant at meetings of all the various scientific disciplines and at the Biofeedback Society. Since these reports and studies cover diverse disciples, and since no comprehensive compendium of clinical biofeedback is as yet in the scientific literature,[4] it may come as some surprise to most clinicians that biofeedback applications are to be found in virtually every field of medicine, as well as in psychology, sociology, and education.

Beneficial effects of biofeedback have been reported for a variety of emotional and behavioral problems such as anxiety, depression, phobias, certain psychoses, insomnia, tension headache, drug abuse, alcoholism, bruxism, learning and perceptual problems, and the hyperkinetic syndrome.

In the closely related category of psychosomatic disorders, biofeedback has been effective in the treatment of asthma, ulcers, colitis, functional diarrhea, certain types of cardiac arrhythmias, essential hypertension, Raynaud's syndrome, and migrain headache. Biofeedback muscle retraining has also been used successfully in the paralysis of stroke, hemiplegia, cerebral palsy, spasticity, spasmodic torticollis, other dykinesias, as well as in chronic pulmonary insufficiency. Disorders difficult to categorize but which have been positively affected by biofeedback treatment procedures include epilepsy, low back pain, and other types of chronic pain.

It seems quite clear that however more or less effective it may ultimately prove to be in the treatment of any of the above disorders, biofeedback is capable of evoking fundamental normalizing mechanisms of the body. Considering its effects, there appear to be two common denominators that may account for the desirable remedial effects of biofeedback in such a diversity of psychological and physical disorders, although only one of these may be the basic mechanism.

From the clinical standpoint, this common denominator appears to be the ability of individuals to learn to reduce tension in all three of the body's major systems: cerebral, muscular, and visceral. EMG and temperature biofeedback are the primary modalities employed to induce tension reduction, and their use accounts for the majority of

[4]Extensive documentation and comprehensive review of both the basic research and clinical applications of biofeedback are, however, reported in the popular books *New Mind, New Body* (Brown, 1974) and *Stress and the Art of Biofeedback* (Brown, 1977). (see references)

beneficial effects in the emotional and psychomatic disorders listed above, although EEG alpha and theta biofeedback have also been reported to be effective. With biofeedback training aimed toward reducing muscle tension (through EMG biofeedback), or muscle and visceral tension reduction (through EMG, temperature, or specific cardiovascular biofeedback modalities), neural overactivity of both the motor and autonomic nervous systems can be brought back to within normal range with a disappearance of tension symptoms.

The second common denominator concerns muscle retraining, perhaps epilepsy, and possibly the relief and prevention of migraine headache (when voluntary vasomotor regulation of the anterior temporal arteries is used). The underlying mechanism in these instances appears to be the inherent ability of neural structures to accommodate to specific circumstances. This characteristic of neural tissue, known as plasticity, means that neural activity can undergo various shifts in direction and degrees of activity that are reversible. In one sense, this capacity can be thought of in terms of the ability of neural structures to be shaped into new behavioral modes with appropriate stimuli or needs, a phenomenon similar to that generally conceived of as learning. Indeed, the biofeedback shaping of overactive muscle and visceral systems may be exclusively a manifestation of neural plasticity, since it reverses an accommodation to a specific circumstance, namely, emotional tension and social pressure.

It seems to be relatively comforting to theorists to be able to relate the biofeedback phenomenon to mechanical electrochemical events, or to the roteness of operant conditioning, but, whatever mechanism implements the effector phase of biofeedback, the question still remains, how are the changes initiated and activated?

The question of how biofeedback procedures elicit learned control over physiologic functions is most dramatically delineated by motor unit learning. As noted earlier, the average individual can learn to control a single motor unit, or even a complex series of units. The learning, moreover, can occur in an exceedingly short period of time with nothing more than the visual/auditory feedback and instructions. This is a learning experiment that can easily be repeated in any physiology laboratory.[5]

[5]Basmajian recalls a demonstration for television during which the interviewer insisted upon being the experimental subject learning motor unit control while at the same time conducting the interview. Within a few minutes the interviewer was controlling motor units voluntarily while continuing his discussion with Dr. Basmajian. Learning not only takes place quickly, but voluntary activity is integral to the performance since it involves firing motor units at will.

The sole observable elements in this learning situation are the visual and auditory perception of the visual and auditory representations of motor unit activity, the cognitively perceived instructions, and the resulting performance. It can only be deduced that cerebral processes assimilate, integrate, and associate the input information in such a way as to select and activate effector mechanisms compatible with the projected objective (control of specific units). The primacy of cognitive mechanisms in biofeedback learning are amply supported by studies demonstrating the importance of the surrounding milieu and the accuracy of the supplied information. Inferences about the cognitive, albeit subconscious, mechanisms involved in the biofeedback learning process have been described, and they further indicate that biofeedback and related techniques can be used to isolate and characterize subconscious aspects of the learning process (Brown, 1975a, 1975b).

There are thus two components involved in the effect of biofeedback on physiologic activity. The first is composed of those complex cerebral processes concerned with the processing of perceptual and cognitive information; and the second is the role that the product of this processing plays in supervening in the body's physiologic, automatic feedback regulating (control) systems. Support for this contention also comes from an analysis of the normalizing action of disturbed physiologic activity through biofeedback learning in the many stress-related (i.e., emotional and psychosomatic) problems reported to be benefited.

AUGMENTED BIOFEEDBACK IN STRESS-RELATED ILLNESS

The therapeutic benefits of biofeedback in all varieties of stress-related problems creates certain difficulties for determining its primary mode of action. Neither clinical procedures nor experimental clinical research is "clean"; almost invariably, biofeedback per se is augmented by other potentially therapeutic techniques. Results with this shotgun, eclectic approach are reported to be high and diverse enough that scientific papers are rarely prepared. Moreover, due to the variety of biofeedback procedures no systematic investigation of the effects of the multiple variables has yet been completed. When a number of similar studies are compared, there is however adequate evidence to draw reasonably valid conclusions about the therapeutic effectiveness of biofeedback and its probable mechanisms of action.

As emphasized in this discussion, there is a significant conceptual and methodological gap between research studies of biofeedback and its actual clinical application. The use of augmented biofeedback to improve learned regulation of physiologic activities for clinical application can be traced to two principal studies: those of Green, Walters, Green, and Murphy (1969) and Budzynski, Stoyva, and Adler (1970), both of which used different augmenting techniques.

In retrospect, augmenting procedures might have been included because, when biofeedback began to be used clinically, it posed quite different problems for the patient-doctor relationship. Here was a therapeutic procedure in which the patient was supplied with a medical device and was literally told to do something useful with it for his own well-being. The situation was clearly one in which the therapeutic benefits could be best achieved only with "cognitive" attention and learning on the part of the patient. Thus, in addition to the usual tasks of diagnosis, treatment supervision, and recovery evaluation, the therapist was faced with the additional task of facilitating the learning process. Considerable direction for this task came from the Budzynski, Stoyva, and Adler (1970) report, and because augmented biofeedback has achieved significant success in clinical practice, the procedure has been little changed.[6]

Justification for the elaborate augmented approach appears to be empirical. It works, on the other hand, if biofeedback is considered as a learning process. If an analysis is made of the conditions necessary to promote effective and efficient learning, it is not difficult to understand the role of various augmenting procedures in the learning process. The patient has little, if any, educational background on how to manipulate internal physiology, and, in general, tends to be hesitant about taking over any part of the traditional role of the physician. In this very new situation, to achieve optimal learning it would be reasonable to supply the kinds and amounts of information that would facilitate learning. And since the learning is strictly an internal process, poorly benefited by external interventions (and, in fact, often inhibited by them), the patient also needs information,

---

[6]Details of the Budzynski procedure along with an expanded prototype clinical procedure synthesized from other clinical and from personal experience are given in the book *Stress and the Art of Biofeedback* (Brown, 1977).

coaching, and support in his task of assuming responsibility for changing his own physiologic functioning.

The essential components of the clinical procedure can, therefore, be classified according to the kinds of information and support they supply to the patient. First, of course, is the *biofeedback information*. This information is usually supplied by the biofeedback instrument which provides the crucial information about the ongoing activity of the selected phyisologic function. For the average patient this information may be meaningless and have little connection to the individual's educational background. If, however, the patient is given a briefing about the physiology involved, about the mechanics of the disease process, about the instrument, and about the objective of the training, the patient then has some background structure and organization into which the biofeedback information can be integrated. This kind of relevant background information could be called *cognitively useful information* since its use in the learning process is peripheral rather than primary. Although equipped with some preparation for the biofeedback learning experience, the patient is still unprepared for the instructions to change the patient's physiology "by some mental means." To learn with any efficiency the patient now needs *strategy information,* that is, clues about mental techniques that can alter physiologic function. The mental exercises usually employed, such as Progressive Relaxation, Autogenic Training, imagery, and meditation, are designed primarily to focus attention on internal processes and subjective states of feeling so as to foster their association with different levels of previously unfelt physiologic activity. Manipulating one's own internal, unfelt physiologic activity is, however, a new experience to most patients, and, as with all learning experiences, requires encouragement and reinforcement to consolidate and verify the learning and the changing subjective sensations. Confirmation and verification can be classified as *psychologically supporting information.* Such support also serves to ease the shift in traditional responsibility for illness and wellness from a largely external dependence to some degree of internal dependence.

The rationale behind these diverse auxiliary techniques can be deduced from the motor unit learning situation in which the patient is given only the biological information about motor unit activity and instructions to change it in a certain way. It is reasonable to deduce that complex cerebral processes of associating, integrating, and evaluating both externally and internally perceived information, and selecting and activating the required implementing mechanisms, would be enhanced by useful and appropriate information. This appears to be what the augmented biofeedback procedure does.

The supplementary procedures are also related to another important aspect of biofeedback learning: the subtle effect of general attitudes. There are strong cultural and sociopsychological determinants of emotional reactions to stressful situations that undergo gradual shifts as biofeedback treatment programs proceed. If the objective of biofeedback training is to put the control and responsibility for physiologic normality and well-being into the hands of the patient, then the shifting concepts and attitudes about the responsibility for illness and treatment that biofeedback demands must be dealt with as well as the biological learning process.

THE COMPLEXITY OF THE "RELAXATION RESPONSE"

The usefulness of biofeedback in stress-related problems lies predominantly, but certainly not exclusively, in its ability to evoke learned relaxation of tensions. Actually, the physiology of tension and relaxation states is not well known. Much of our scientific information about relaxation has come from the clinical research of Jacobson (1958) and Luthe (1963) and more recently from studies on meditation, but the available information applies mainly to muscle relaxation. It has generally been assumed in relaxation techniques, including EMG biofeedback, that a learned awareness of muscle tension directly affects the muscle-CNS feedback control loop. This leads to decreased muscle tension and hence to decreased emotional tension, and presumably to the general reduction of visceral tension as well (e.g., as in essential hypertension or ulcers).

New clinical research, however, suggests that muscle, visceral, and central (mental and emotional?) tension states can occur not only in various degress of association, but can be independently manifest or peculiarly disassociated from each other as well. The unknown relationships of tension among the major physiologic systems may account for the success of augmented biofeedback treatment programs in stress illnesses, since they generally combine EMG biofeedback with Progressive Relaxation, Autogenic Training, imagery, meditation, or desensitization. In Progressive Relaxation, where the individual alternatively tenses and relaxes muscle groups progressively around the body, the objective is to develop an awareness of the sensation of muscle relaxation. With Autogenic Training, in contrast, the self-suggestion phrases to induce relaxation are directed toward feelings of heaviness and warmth (more visceral aspects of tension than P.R.), and toward neutralizing "central" tensions via a self-hypnotic action. The effects of imagery and of desensitization procedures presumably can be directed toward any single source or group of tension symptoms, including the perceptual aspects of tension. Meditation, such as Transcendental Meditation, is directed toward the consciousness and awareness of tension, and so affects muscle and visceral tension only secondarily.

(One of the most useful consequences of augmented biofeedback use has been the streamlining of both P.R. and A.T. relaxation techniques. It has been found that short courses of either technique, lasting 20 to 40 minutes, and repeated at each biofeedback training session, are as effective as the 6 to 18 month programs previously employed.)

Although observations of the differential effects of various relaxation techniques on muscle, visceral, or central tensions, or the effect on subjective feelings of tensions, have not been reported, comparison of the results of hundreds of research studies tends to confirm the implication that the techniques do produce differential effects on the major physiologic systems. Certainly it seems logical that P.R., with its emphasis on all muscles of the body, would primarily affect muscle tension. Similarly, EMG biofeedback relaxation would be expected to affect principally those muscles involved in the relaxation training. Neither might be expected to be directly specific for visceral or central tension. On the other hand, when temperature or pulse pressure biofeedback is used, tension reduction is directed toward the cardiovascular system, and effects on muscle tension are probably both secondary and relatively less efficient. Subjective reports for imagery, A.T., and meditation indicate that either visceral tension or the subjective appreciation of tension is changed more often than muscle tension. Completing the system relaxation analysis, anecdotal material from psychiatric use suggests that with EEG slow wave biofeedback, symptomatic relief can be obtained with rather unremarkable changes in physiologic activity, although similar "disassociations" between subjective and physiologic change are also occasionally reported for EMG biofeedback.

Many research studies have compared the relaxation effectiveness between or among P.R., A.T., and EMG biofeedback without realizing the crucial differences among the techniques. It is perhaps a symptom of the "publish or perish" society that sees so many researchers delight in demonstrating the inferiority of EMG biofeedback to P.R., A.T., or meditation for reducing levels of muscle tension. And shockingly, many researchers still apparently fail to realize the inappropriateness of comparing relaxation techniques aimed at the whole body (P.R.) to EMG biofeedback relaxation aimed primarily at relaxing a single muscle (such as the frontalis). If a chief characteristic of muscles is their ability for individual specialization, then it might be expected that a learned relaxation might be individual to the trained muscle, and that if a general relaxation extends to other muscles, it occurs because of a transfer of learning and awareness of tension, or through the effective use of auxiliary procedures. It would be amusing if it were not so sad to see published reports confirming the nongeneralization effect of EMG biofeedback relaxation documented by using the meter readings of the biofeedback instrument. It appears to be generally unknown that such voltage integration readings contain multiple errors, particularly at either end of the curves for activity versus meter reading.

Even with these errors in assumptions and quantification techniques, it is curious that only fairly intensive P.R. training is generally found to be superior to EMG biofeedback relaxation training, and that even in these instances the biofeedback training was concentrated on one muscle only while P.R. was concentrated on all muscles of the body. Moreover, while muscle tension may be reduced even more by P.R., often the subjective changes in anxiety and tension may or may not be relieved by EMG biofeedback. Obviously there are important unknown factors remaining in the relaxation picture.

It cannot be emphasized too strongly that successful biofeedback treatment of stress-related illnesses incorporates multiple procedures all aimed toward tension reduction and self-responsibility. The second important aspect is that different biofeedback modalities may be employed, meaning that multiple factors are involved in the clinical stress-reduction effect.

BIOFEEDBACK MENTAL ACTIVITY AND APPLICATIONS TO ORGANIZATIONAL STRESS REACTIONS

Probably the major obstacle to developing a cogent concept of biofeedback is the long neglect of cognitive factors in health and illness. Both biomedical and psychological research efforts have concentrated on concepts of internal mechanisms that could be validated by provoking responses to external manipulations and then measuring the physiologic changes. The biofeedback phenomenon has abruptly forced consideration of "cognitive" factors.[7] One of the greatest contributions biofeedback may make is to contribute to elucidating the mechanisms of stress illness.

It is commonly held that stress illnesses arise from disturbed emotions that evoke rather primitive physical defense mechanisms. Although there are some twenty current theories of emotion, none fits more easily into the explanation of biofeedback effects than the arousal theory. The arousal theory is popular among psychophysiologists who have contributed considerable laboratory data indicating that strong emotion does indeed activate endocrine and ANS activity in a manner similar to that long ago proposed by Cannon in the flight or fight concept. It seems fairly clear that emotions that excite defense mechanisms do tend to cause a rapid pulse, increased blood pressure, decreased secretions, and a striking increase in muscle tension, as if prepared to take physical action.

The problem remains, however, that if the tensions and pressures of modern life, including organizational life, that cause stress-related illnesses are rarely so cataclysmic that they directly evoke physical defense mechanisms, how, in fact, is this *nonphysical* stress translated into arousal-activating stimuli?

It was not long ago that biomedical dogma stated that the physiologic activity of systems innervated by the autonomic nervous system were automatically regulated and beyond voluntary control. The conclusion was poorly supported experimentally, but it was buttressed by psychologic research that concluded that ANS-innervated

---

[7]It is unfortunate that it seems preferable to use quotes around the word cognitive. Because of the biomedical preoccupation with factors for explanations of human functioning, there are no satisfactory terms that connote cerebral activities subserving mental functions, or for logic sequences of subconscious information processing.

systems could not be brought under control by operant conditioning. A significant corollary of the biofeedback discovery that voluntary control can indeed be learned is an inference about the *cause* of emotional and psychosomatic disorders. There is little question that varieties of relevant information are "cognitively" used in biofeedback to develop control over selected physiologic systems, and that the "cognitive" mechanisms operate chiefly in the subconscious mode. If such subconscious events can be directed toward normalizing physiologic activity, a reciprocal complex of subconscious events might be expected to lead to disordered and impaired physiologic activity.

Few professional therapists doubt that emotional and psychosomatic disorders arise from emotional reactions to difficult social situations, yet precisely how the social milieu activates physiologic change is virtually unknown. In attempting to account for the effectiveness of biofeedback (the augmented regime) in stress problems, it became apparent that certain mental (cerebral) activities could be postulated to advantage. The following description represents a new conjecture about the mental mechanisms that can account for the development of stress disorders, as well as for the ability of biofeedback to normalize stress-disordered physiologic functions.

One of the problems in discussing stress is the lack of exact definitions. While most of us agree about what is stressful to human beings, biomedical confirmation of the effects of stress is always related to the effects of *physical* stressors (smog, chemicals, bacteria, injury). But in psychology and psychosomatic medicine what we are really talking about as stress for human beings is *social* stress. If we separate out physical stress as that which directly mobilizes defense mechanisms, nonphysical stress, because it does not directly activate physiologic defense mechanisms, is almost exclusively social stress. Social stress then can be defined as the way in which one's social environment and dynamics are perceived. Nearly all stress-related illnesses develop out of the way in which social situations are perceived or interpreted.

The effects of social stress are not always so obvious as when they are manifest as emotional or psychosomatic illness. The effects of social stress are often damaging as secondary effects in the physically ill. The stress of being ill and unable to cope both aggravates the illness and impedes recovery. Biofeedback, as an anti-stress technique, should find an important role as a supporting therapy in most kinds of illness. Similarly, the effect of social stress may be so incidious in relatively normally functioning individuals that its effects are not seen until a susceptible physiologic system succumbs, such as in essential hypertension. The usefulness of biofeedback and related techniques in stress reduction should be an important tool in preventive medicine.

The difficulty in tracing the origins of responses to social stress is that the mental activities subserving perception and interpretation of the social environment are many and complex. In order to "perceive" a social situation (e.g., in an organization), a number of interacting social events must be observed, associated, and analyzed. Since the social environment and its dynamics are displays of complex human communication and behavior involving motivation, social appearance, and custom, as well as a wide range of emotions, any perception of a social situation requires a multidimensional reconstruction. The mental reconstruction is not usually of a single situation. It is more likely to be based on a number of repeated situations or variants of a situation that entails some kind of customary, logical, or desirable mental appreciation of events, the interpretation of motivations, and the interpretation of the many modes of communication used by human beings. Thus, the appreciation of social situations is an interpretation and a mental construction of social events and their significance. It also invariably includes a mental projection of the future of the situation or relationship.

There are at least four consequences of social perceptual activity: (1) the "filling in" of data where data is missing (this is a process that introduces errors in logic and judgment about the social situation); (2) the generation of mental images as part of the reconstruction; (3) rumination, or the process of repeatedly analyzing the mental construction in an attempt to reconcile the perceived information with best guesses about missing information; and (4) perceptual modulation, the process of preferentially perceiving information prejudged to fit particular mental constructions.

At least two of these mental processes can directly affect physiologic activity. Jacobson (1955) has amply demonstrated the potency of mental images for evoking actual physiologic change. In one experiment, for example, Jacobson (1955) recorded activity of the muscles of both forearms. When his subjects were competely relaxed, he asked them to imagine a telegraph key under the middle finger of the right hand, and then, in imagination only and without moving any muscles, to send a message in Morse Code. He found that only those muscles involving the middle finger of the right hand became active (subliminal to movement). Jacobson concluded from this and many similar experiments that imagery itself can activate the specific physiologic activity imagined and, moreover, that it involves a considerable expenditure of physical energy.

If a mental construction of a problematic social situation contains uncertainty, as it usually does, then the uncertainty and the insecurity of a poorly documented mental construction may represent a product of mental activity that is accompanied by a relative excess of neurohumoral substances. These substances can directly excite the endocrine and neural structures mediating the arousal response. Where there is imprecision in defining problems, as in the inadequacy of perceptions of certain social situations, solutions are difficult. That is, uncertainty about the social problem means uncertainty also about appropriate coping mechanisms. The popular excuse for inadequate coping mechanisms may, in fact, lie more in the inability to *define* the social problem because of inadequate information, and the resulting skewing effect of rumination and perceptual modulation that leads to a self-deception. The uncertainty of coping devices, along with the uncertainty about the social situation, represents still other products of mental activities that can also directly activate arousal mechanisms. Depending upon associations, prior experience, learned emotional sensitivities, specific situations, genetic disposition, and the severity or duration of the social stress, physiologic arousal (defense) may be manifest as muscular, visceral, cerebral, or any combination of these.

BIOFEEDBACK AS A COGNITIVE THERAPY

If the kinds of cognitive factors described above are the primary agents responsible for the diverse symptoms of stress responses, then cognitive therapies would be the treatments of choice. Their disadvantage lies in the time needed for learning, which may be inefficient for acute conditions; their advantage lies in their specificity of effect and the relative permanence of the learned voluntary control.

The critical defect in the development of stress disorders may well be the deficiency of relevant and useful information. Cognitive therapies are specific for such defects. Psychotherapy provides information for a more definitive understanding of the social reality, for coping with one's environment, and for realizing and correcting inappropriate emotional responses. Biofeedback provides information for developing awareness of body responses, for realizing and correcting inappropriate physiologic responses, and for learning to discriminate productive from nonproductive physiologic states. In actual clinical practice, biofeedback treatment programs tend to combine psychotherapy with biofeedback training.

EMG biofeedback relaxation training, for example, provides information about muscle tension. When the instructions call for mental activity to reduce tension, two different streams of cognitive activity are initiated. First, the attention is directed toward the muscle tension, resulting in awareness of the muscle stress response along with an association between the instrument reading of muscle tension level and the internal feeling state. The attention and association facilitate learning to decrease muscle tension. This decreases the information about peripheral muscle tension conducted centrally as part of the muscle feedback control system, and this in turn relieves the sensation of tension. The decreased internal muscle tension feedback information decreases the cortical alerting effect on lower muscle control centers, bringing about relaxation. At the same time, attention to the internal state relieves preoccupation with the mental reconstruction-rumination—perceptual modulation process (well documented in ruminating obsessives with alpha biofeedback training), with a consequence reduction of the uncertainty-anxiety effect and a shift in the activity of neuronal circuitry toward more internally-generated associations between the peripheral and central correlates of relaxation. The result is a shift in interpretation and in emotional tone. The shifts in attention and awareness are, in effect, the catalysts that relieve the cortical inhibitory effect on general awareness. Cortical inhibitory effects are likely two-fold: the alerting action on lower muscle control centers (i.e., the alerting inhibits the normal homeostatic mechanisms that reduce tension), and the alerting effect on cognitive mechanisms which narrows the focus and concentrates attention on the alerting social stimuli, thus inhibiting perception of the physiologic reactions. While both psychotherapy and biofeedback can effectively relieve both inhibitory effects, the combination of both would seem to be an effective therapeutic effort.

The apparent widespread usefulness of slow wave EEG biofeedback in emotional and psychosomatic problems cannot be adequately explained with the data available. There are perhaps ten or more reports describing the beneficial effects of alpha, alpha-theta, or theta EEG biofeedback in everything from chronic pain to anxiety to severe behavior problems to drug abuse. Most investigators tend to relate clinical improvement to the psychophysiologic correlate that slow wave EEG activity is absent (deficient) in anxiety and tension, or that directing the attention internally tends to block the effect of external stimuli. While these changes may occur, no explanation is currently available for why the presence of EEG slow wave activity prevents or inhibits stress reactions.

The importance of cognitive factors is also indirectly suggested by the relative failure of biofeedback in schizophrenia and severe neuroses, even though biofeedback has been reported to be beneficial in severe behavior disorders.

NEURAL RE-EDUCATION

The massive experimental and clinical evidence that demonstrates the ability of biofeedback to evoke quite specific changes in neural activity also may account for the fundamental physical effector mechanisms of the biofeedback learning effect. Although the learning period to normalize disordered nerve-muscle function is lengthy and roughly proportional to the severity of the disorder, it is nonetheless striking to see normalization of muscle dysfunction, such as in torticollis, or cerebral palsy, or recovery of muscle function after the paralysis of stroke. The fact that biofeedback learning not only appears to stimulate nerve-budding processes and nerve regeneration, but is further useful in guiding the regenerated neural activity toward voluntary control, makes for tempting speculation. With only the biofeedback information and instructions at hand, the setting in motion of neural re-education processes would also seem to reside in the capabilities of higher mental processes.

The effectiveness of EEG biofeedback in the treatment of epilepsy is also richly thought-provoking. If biofeedback learning can suppress the occurrence of seizure-producing central neural activity, what are the brain mechanisms that occur between the perception of the biological information and the instructions and other supporting information? It seems to me that it is not enough to say that neural tissue has the characteristic of plasticity and that repeated associations with the desired behavior of neurons or groups of neurons is the mechanism that leads to normalization of activity. It should be obvious that "normal" neural activity must be capable of responding appropriately to a variety of conditions, since there are perhaps ten million neurons, subserving complex mental functions, that participate in the total learning process.

ROLE OF BIOFEEDBACK IN PATIENT-THERPIST COMMUNICATION

Owing to differences in informational backgrounds, emotional states, logic frames, lifestyles, and perspectives, the communications gap between therapist and patient can often be large and difficult to bridge. New research, much of it unreported, is exploring the use of biofeedback as a communications medium and tool.

There are, in fact, several ways in which biofeedback techniques can be used either directly or indirectly to improve communications. EMG biofeedback, augmented by other relaxation procedures, is an efficient means for reducing stress, anxiety, and arousal level either before or during therapy or counselling. A second technique is the use of EEG slow wave biofeedback for the purpose of shifting the patient's attention toward an awareness of internal states generally, and particularly toward an awareness of subjective activity. This amounts to shifting the general state of consciousness toward a broader awareness and a greater ability to associate perceptions and impressions more widely, and toward a broader use of imagery. Essentially, slow wave EEG biofeedback tends to focus attention away from social stress.

The newest and potentially most specific employment of biofeedback in psychotherapy is the use of physiological responses to emotional stimuli via the biofeedback instrument. Any one of several physiologic indices can be used, such as GSR, heart rate, EEG, or EMG activity, since each reflects both emotional and cognitive reactions. When the physiologic monitor is displayed to both patient and therapist during a therapy session, the monitor represents reactions that may be verbally or behaviorally repressed, or even unrecognized consciously by the patient. The biological information is, moreover, accurate and contains other information, such as the intensity, duration, and reliabilty of the emotional response. The monitor, taken in conjunction with verbal material, can provide the basis for agreement about subjective-objective interpretations, and also provides reference points for evaluating therapeutic effects.

The role of such biological communications can be extended in psychotherapy by a number of variations. The therapist might withhold the biofeedback information from the patient, for example, at certain times, or reverse the procedure. Or it might be desirable simply to observe the physiologic changes without comment; at other times comments may be important to the therapeutic process.

RISKS AND CONTRA-INDICATIONS

To date, few precise contra-indications have been detected in biofeedback use. From the standpoint of method, the greatest hazard for the patient can stem from either inaccurate instruments or improper procedures, such as failing to provide the important supporting, augmenting procedures.

Probably the most serious potential hazard occurs when endocrine disorders are treated with biofeedback stress-education techniques. It should be remembered that certain endocrine problems involve the same endocrine structures that are excited in arousal and stress reactions. When stress-reduction techniques are used, there is a high probability that endocrine imbalances may be concomitantly relieved to the extent that endocrine medication may become excessive. It has been sporadically reported, for example, that the insulin requirement of diabetics can be dramatically reduced during and after biofeedback relaxation training, and several cases of insulin shock have occurred. Similarly, in one case, the biofeedback training appeared to result in a synergistic action with thyroid function, with the result that thyroid medication became excessive.

Changing awareness during biofeedback training may pose a more subtly harmful effect. It has been reported that some patients become so involved with the biofeedback training and its subjective effects that they felt they had found all the answers and solved their problems, and so left therapy, although the patient had not actually effected a positive change.

WHY BIOFEEDBACK IS A NEW STRESS COPING APPROACH

The rush to biofeedback salvation has seen a profound neglect of serious analysis into what actually constitutes biofeedback and what elements of it may account for such widespread beneficial effects. In my view a part of the success of biofeedback, perhaps a very large part of its success, is the changing attitude about the patient-therapist relationship, the new therapeutic responsibility of the patient, and the sudden sharing of special knowledge about the functioning of human beings. What we actually do in biofeedback procedures is all directed toward providing the individual with the information necessary to shift responsibility for illness or health toward the individual. The following list indicates the new features that distinguish biofeedback from older approaches:

1. Reliable information about a selected physiologic activity is "fed back" to the individual generating that activity.
2. The physiologic information is provided in the form of signals that are easily perceived and understood.
3. The physiologic information is continuously or almost continuously available, providing information about biological variation and the dynamics of physiologic function.
4. Conceptual information useful to the learning process is provided in some detail.
5. The procedure allows the individual to interact with and to experience internal states.
6. Complex mental events are evoked to exert action on physiologic activities.
7. The individual develops voluntary control over a physiologic activity that otherwise functions by automatic regulating mechanisms.
8. Once learned, the identity and control of the self is largely shifted from external to an internal dependence.
9. Performing control over a physiologic function communicates information about internal states and events that is otherwise inexpressible.

These factors constitute a new experience for the person, and with experience, confidence is fostered and a new authority, the self, is developed. When, in the future, such experiences and controls are shared, new belief systems will evolve.

With its new therapeutic approach, and with its seeming multitude of uses, the biofeedback principle is rapidly expanding the therapeutic resources of mental health professionals.

REFERENCES

Alexander, A.B.; C.A. French; and N.J. Goodman. 1975. "A Comparison of Auditory and Visual Feedback in Biofeedback Assisted Muscular Relaxation Training." *Psychophysiology* 12: 119–123.

Alexander, A.B. 1975. "An Experimental Test of Assumptions Relating to the Use of Electromyographic Biofeedback as a General Relaxation Training Technique." *Psychophysiology* 12: 656–662.

Basmajian, J.V. 1963. "Control and Training of Individual Motor Units." Science 141: 440–441.

Basmajian, J.V. 1967. "Control of Individual Motor Units." *American Journal of Physical Medicine* 46: 1427–1440.

Basmajian, J.V. 1972. "Electromyography Comes of Age. The Conscious Control of Individual Motor Units in Man may be Used to Improve his Physical Performance." *Science* 176: 603–609.

Beaty, E.T. 1976. "Feedback Assisted Relaxation Training as a Treatment for Gastric Ulcers." *Biofeedback Research Society Meeting Abstracts* Colorado Spring.

Benson, H.; D. Shapiro; B. Tursky; and G. Schwartz. 1971. "Decreased Systolic Blood Pressure Through Operant Conditioning Techniques in Patients with Essential Hypertension." *Science* 173: 740–742.

Biofeedback and Self-Control. 1970–1976. *An Aldine Annual on the Regulation of Bodily Processes and Consciousness*. Chicago: Aldine.

Bleecker, E.R., and B.T. Engel. 1973. "Learned Control of Ventricular Rate in Patients with Atrial Fibrillation." *Sematic Psychiatry* 5: 461–474.

Booker, H.; R.T. Robow; and P.J. Coleman. 1969. "Simplified Feedback in Neuromuscular Retraining: An Automated Approach Using Electromyographic Signals." *Archives of Physical Medicine* 50: 621–625.

Braud, Lendell W.; Mimi N. Lupin; and W.G. Braud. 1975. "The Use of Electromyographic Biofeedback in the Control of Hyperactivity." *Journal of Learning Disabilities* 8: 21–26.

Brener, J., and D. Hothersall. 1966. "Heart Rate Control Under Conditions of Augmented Sensory Feedback." *Psychophysiology* 3: 23–28.

Brener, J., and R.A. Kleinman. 1979. "Learned Control of Decreases in Systolic Blood Pressure." *Nature* 226: 1063–1064.

Brown, B.B. 1970a. "Awareness of EEG-Subjective Activity Relationships Detected Within a Closed Feedback System." *Psychophysiology* 7: 451–464.

Brown, B.B. 1970b. "Recognition of Aspects of Consciousness Through Association with EEG Alpha Activity Represented by a Light Signal." *Psychophysiology* 6: 442–452.

Brown, B.B. 1975a. "Biological Awareness as a State of Consciousness." *Journal Alt. Consc.* 2: 1.

Brown, B.B. 1975b. Talk given to American Association of the Advancement of Science, Boston, December.

Brown, B.B., and J.W. Klug. 1974. "Exploration of EEG Alpha Biofeedback as a Technique to Enhance Rapport." *Biofeedback Research Society Meeting Abstracts*. Colorado Springs.

Brown, B.B. 1975c. *The Biofeedback Syllabus*. Springfield, Ill.: Charles C. Thomas.

Brown, B.B. 1974. *New Mind New Body*. New York: Harper & Row.

Brown, B.B. 1977. *Stress and the Art of Biofeedback*. New York: Harper & Row.

Brown, B.B. and J.W. Klug. 1974. *The Alpha Syllabus*. Springfield, Ill.: Charles C. Thomas.

Brudny, J.; B.B. Grynobaum; and J. Korein 1974. "Spasmodic Torticollis: Treatment by Feedback Display of the EMG." *Archives of Physical Medicine* 55: 403–408.

Brudny, J.; Korein, J.; L. Leavidow; B.B. Grynbaum; A. Lieberman; and L.W. Friedman. 1974. "Sensory Feedback Therapy as a Modality of Treatment in Central Nervous System Disorders of Voluntary Movement." *Neurology* 24: 925–932.

Budzynski, T. 1973. "Biofeedback Procedures in the Clinic." *Semantic Psychiatary* 5: 537–547.

Budzynski, T.; Stoyva, J.; and Adler, C. 1970 "Feedback induced muscle relaxation: Applications to tension headache" *Journal Behav. Ther. Exp. Psychiatry* 1: 205–211.

Budzynski, T.; J. Stoyva; C.S. Adler; and D.J. Mullaney. 1973. "ENG Biofeedback and Tension Headache: A Controlled Outcome Study." *Psychosomatic Medicine* 35: 484–496.

Childers, C.A. 1975. "Modification of Social Behavior Problems by Alpha Biofeedback Training." *Biofeedback Research Society Meeting Abstracts*. Monterey.

Coger, R., and M. Werbach. 1975. "Attention, Anxiety, and the Effects of Learned Enhancement of EEG Alpha in Chronic Pain: A Pilot Study in Biofeedback." *In Pain Research and Treatment*, edited by B.L. Drue, Jr. New York, N.Y.: Academic Press.

Cox, D.J.; A. Freundlich; and R.G. Meyer. 1975. "Differential Effectiveness of Electromyograph Feedback, Verbal Relaxation Instructions, and Medication Placebo with Tension Headaches." *Journal Consulting and Clinical Psychology* 43: 893–898.

Datey, K.K. 1976. "Temperature Regulation in the Management of Hypertension." *Biofeedback Research Society Meeting Abstracts*. Colorado Springs.

Davis, M.H.; D.R. Saunders; T.L. Creer; and A. Chai. 1973. "Relaxation Training Facilitated by Biofeedback Apparatus as a Supplemental Treatment in Bronchial Asthma." *Journal of Psychosomatic Research* 17: 121–128.

DiCara, L.V., and N.E. Miller. 1968. "Long Term Retention of Instrumentally Learned Heart-Rate Changes in the Curarized Rat." *Comparative Behavioral Biology* 2: 19–23.

DiCara, L.V., and N.E. Miller. 1969. "Changes in Heart Rate Instrumentally Learned by Curarized Rats as Avoidance Responses." *Journal of Comparative Physiology* 65: 8–12.

DiCara, L.V., and N.E. Miller. 1969. "Changes in Heart Rate Instrumentally Learned by Curarized Rats as Avoidance Responses." *Journal of Comparative Physiology* 65: 8–12.

Elder, S.T.; Z.R. Ruiz; H.L. Deabler; and R.L. Dillenkoffer. 1973. "Instrumental Conditioning of Diastolic Blood Pressure in Essential Hypertensive Patients." *J Appl Behav Anal Journal of Applied Behavioral Analysis* 6: 377–382.

Engel, B.T. 1973. "Clinical Applications of Operant Conditioning Techniques in the Control of Cardiac Arrhythmias." *Semantic Psychiatry* 5: 433–438.

Engel, B.T., and S.P. Hansen. 1966. "Operant Conditioning of Heart Rate Slowing." *Psychophysiology* 3: 176–187.

Fenwick, P.B.C.; S. Donaldson; J. Bushman; L. Gillis; and C.W. Fenton. 1975. "EEG and Metabolic Changes During Transcendental Meditation." *Electroencephalography and Clinical Neurophysiology* 39: 220–221.

Finley, W., and H. Smith. 1975. "Sensorimotor EEG biofeedback training of epileptics: A Replication Study." *Electroencephalography and Clinical Neurophysiology* 38: 336 (abstract).

Fruhling, M; J.V. Bashmajian; and T.C. Simard. 1969. "A note on the conscious controls of motor units by children under six." *Journal of Motor Behavior* 1: 65–68.

Furman, S. 1973. "Intestinal Biofeedback in Functional Diarrhea: A Preliminary Report." *Journal of Behavioral Therapy and Experimental Psychiatry* 4: 317–321.

Cannon, L., and R. Sternbach, 1971. "Alpha Enhancement as a treatment for pain: A Case Study." *Journal of Behavioral Therapy and Experimental Psychiatry* 2: 209–213.

Graham, C.; S. Fotopoulos; H. Cohen; and M. Cook. 1976. "The Use of Biofeedback During Acute Opiate Withdrawal." *Biofeedback Research Society Meeting Abstracts*. Colorado Springs.

Green, E.E.; Walters, E.D.; Green, A.M.; and G. Murphy. 1969. "Feedback Technique for Deep Relaxation." *Psychophysiology* 6: 371-377.

Haynes, S. 1974. "Assessment of the Comparative Effectiveness of Electromyographic Biofeedback and Relaxation Training in Laboratory and Clinical Settings." *Biofeedback Research Society Meeting Abstracts.* Colorado Springs.

Headrick, M.W.; B.W. Feather; and D.T. Wells. 1970. *Psychophysiology* 6: 636.

Headrick, M.W.; B.W. Feather; and D.T. Wells. 1971. "Undirectional and large magnitude heart rate changes with augmented sensory feedback." *Psychophysiology* 8: 132-142.

Hnatiow, M., and P.J. Lang, 1965. "Learned Stabilization of Cardiac Rate." *Psychophysiology* 1: 330-336.

Hauri, P.; P. Phelps; and J. Jordan. 1976. "Biofeedback as a Treatment for Insomnia." *Biofeedback Research Society Meeting Abstracts.* Colorado Springs.

Haynes, S.N.; P. Criffin; D. Mooney; and M. Parise. 1975. "Electromyographic Biofeedback and Relaxation Instructions in the Treatment of Muscle Contraction Headaches." *Behavioral Therapy* 6: 672-678.

Jacobs, A., and G. Felton. 1969. "Visual Feedback of Myoelectric Output to Facilitate Muscle Relaxation in Normal Persons and Patients with Neck Injuries." *Archives of Physical Medicine* 50: 34-39.

Jacobson, E. 1955. "Neuromuscular Controls in Man: Methods of Self Direction in Health and Disease." *American Journal of Psychology* 68: 549-561.

Jacobson, E. 1958. *Progressive Relaxation.* Chicago: University of Chicago Press.

Kamiya, J. 1962. "Conditioned Discrimination of the EEG Alpha Rhythm in Humans." Paper Presented Western Psychol Assoc.

Kleinman, K.M.; H. Goldman; M.Y. Snow; and B. Korol. 1976. "Effects of Stress and Motivation on Effectiveness of Biofeedback Training in Essential Hypertensives." *Biofeedback Research Society Meeting Abstracts.* Colorado Springs.

Kristt, D.A., and B.T. Engel. 1975. "Learned Control of Blood Pressure in Patients with High Blood Pressure." *Circulation* 51: 370-378.

Lang, P.J.; L.A. Straufe; and J.E. Hasting. 1967. "Effects of Feedback and Instructional Set on the Control of Cardiac-Rate Variability." *Journal of Experimental Psychology* 75: 425-431.

Le Boeuf, Alan. 1974. "The Importance of Individual Differences in the Treatment of Chronic Anxiety by E.M.G. Feedback Techniques." *Biofeedback Research Society Meeting Abstracts*: Colorado Springs.

Luthe, W. 1963. "Autogenic Training: Method, Research and Application in Medicine." *American Journal of Psychotherapy* 17: 174–195.

May, D.S., and C.A. Weber. "Temperature Feedback Training for Symptom Reduction in Raynaud's Disease: A Controlled Study." *Biofeedback Research Society Meeting Abstracts.* Colorado Springs.

McFarland, R.A., and J.A. Herrmann. 1974. "Precise Voluntary Heart Control in Human." *Psychological Representation* 35: 925–926.

Miller, N.E. 1969. "Learning of Visceral and Glandular Responses." Science 163: 434–445.

Miller, N.E. and A. Banuazizi. 1968. "Instrumental Learning by Curarized Rats of a Specific Visceral Response, Intestinal or Cardia." *Journal of Comparative Physiology and Psychology* 65: 1–7.

Mills, C.K., and L. Solyom. 1974. "Biofeedback of EEG Alpha in the Treatment of Obsessive Ruminations: An Exploration." *Journal of Behavioral Therapy and Experimental Psychiatry* 5: 37–41.

Miller, N.E., and L. DiCara. 1967. "Instrumental Learning of Heart Rate Changes in Curarized Rats." *Journal of Comparative Physiology and Psychology* 63: 12–19.

Montgomery, D., and H. Besner. 1975. "Reduction of Chronic Onset Insomnia Through Electromyographic Relaxation Training." *Biofeedback Research Society* Meeting Abstracts: Monterey.

Montgomery, D.; W.A. Love Jr.; and T. Moeller. 1974. "Effects of Electromyographic Feedback and Relaxation Training on Blood Pressure in Essential Hypertensives." *Biofeedback Research Society Meeting Abstracts.* Colorado Springs.

Mulholland, T.B. 1968. "Feedback Electroencephalography." *Active Nerve Supplement* (Praha), 10: 410.

Mulholland, T., and C.R. Evans. 1966. "Oculomotor Function and the Alpha Activation Cycle." *Nature* (London), 211: 1278–1279.

Patel, C. 1975. "Yoga and Biofeedback in the Management of Stress in Hypertensive Patients." *Clinical Scientific Molecular Medicine* 48: 171s–174s.

Patel, C., and K.K. Datey. 1976. "Relaxation and Biofeedback Technique in the Management of Hypertension." *Biofeedback Research Society Meeting Abstracts.* Colorado Springs.

Paul, G. 1969. "Inhibition of Physiological Response to Stressful Imagery by Relaxation Training and Hypnotically Suggested Relaxation." *Behavioral Research Therapy* 7: 249–256.

Raskin, M.; G. Johnson; and J. Rondestvedt. 1973. "Chronic Anxiety Treated by Feedback-Induced Muscle Relaxation." *Archives of General Psychiatry* 23: 263–267.

Sedlacek, K. 1976. "Combination of EMG, GSR and Peripheral Temperature Training for Treatment of Hypertension." *Biofeedback Research Society Meeting Abstracts.* Colorado Springs.

Selye, H. 1956. *The Stress of Life.* New York: McGraw-Hill.

Shearn, D.W. 1962. "Operant Conditioning of Heart Rate." *Science* 137: 530–531.

Sheridan, C.L.; M.B. Boehm; L.B. Ward; and D.R. Justesen. 1976. "Autogenic Biofeedback, Autogenic Phrases, and Biofeedback Compared." *Biofeedback Research Society Meeting Abstracts.* Colorado Springs.

Simard, T.G., and J.V. Basmajian. 1967. "Methods in Training the Conscious Control of Motor Units." *Archives of Physical Medicine* 48: 12–19.

Staples, R., and R. Coursey. 1975. "Comparison of EMG Feedback with two Other Relaxation Techniques." *Biofeedback Research Society Abstracts.* Monterey.

Steffen, J. 1975. "Electromyographically Induced Relaxation in the Treatment of Chronic Alcohol Abuse." *Journal of Consulting and Clinical Psychology* 43: 275.

Sterman, N.B., and L. Friar. 1972. "Suppression of Seizures in an Epileptic Following Sensorimotor EEG Feedback Training." *Electroencephalography and Clinical Heurophysiology* 33: 89–95.

Sterman, M.B.; L.R. Macdonald; and R. Stone. 1974. "Biofeedback Training of the Sensorimotor EEG Rhythm in Man: Effects on Epilepsy." *Epilepsia* 1, no. 5: 395–416.

Stoudenmire, J. 1972. "Effects of Muscle Relaxation Training on State and Trait Anxiety in Introverts and Extroverts." *Journal of Personality and Social Psychology* 273–275.

Strauss, N. 1976. "Electromyographic Biofeedback Versus Suggestion in Inducing Muscle Relaxation—A Test for Placebo Effects." *Biofeedback Research Society Abstracts.* Colorado Springs.

Surwit, Richard S., and David Shapiro. 1975. "Digital Temperature Autoregulation and Associated Cardiovascular Changes." *Biofeedback Research Society Meeting Abstracts.* Monterey.

Taylor, L.P. 1975. "Muscle Reduction of the Post CVA Victim Using the Electromyometer with Audio Feedback." *Biofeedback Research Society Meeting Abstracts.* Monterey.

Townsend, R., and D. Addario. 1975. "Treatment of Chronic Anxiety with Biofeedback Mediated Electromyographic Relaxation: A Comparison Study." *Biofeedback Research Society Meeting Abstracts.* Monterey.

Townsend, R.E.; J.F. House; and D. Addario. 1975. "A comparison of Biofeedback-Mediated Relaxation and Group Therapy in the Treatment of Chronic Anxiety." *American Journal of Psychiatry* 132: 598–601.

Wallace, R.K. 1970. "Physiological Effects of Transcendental Meditation." *Science* 167: 1751–1754.

Weber, E.S., and L.G. Fehmi. 1974. "The Therapeutic Use of EEG Biofeedback." *Biofeedback Research Society Meeting Abstracts.* Colorado Springs.

Welgan, P. 1974. "Learned Control of Gastric Acid Secretion in Ulcer Patients." *Psychosomatic Medicine* 36: 411–419.

Werbach, M.R. 1974. "Psychiatric Applications of Biofeedback." *Psychiatry Digest*, April: 23–27.

Whitehead, W.E. P.F. Renault; and I. Goldiamond. 1975. "Modification of Human Gastric Acid Secretion with Operant-Conditioning Procedures." *Journal of Applied Behavioral Analysis* 8: 147–156.

Wickramasekera, I. 1974. "Heart Rate Feedback and the Management of Cardiac Neurosis." *Journal of Abnormal Psychology* 83: 578–580.

10 STRESS COPING THROUGH PHYSICAL ACTIVITY

Maurice Jetté

Although vast amounts of time and money have been invested in search of the pathogenesis of coronary heart disease (CHD) and malignancies, most theories remain incomplete and conjectural. In spite of all the knowledge generated and the vast improvements in medical treatment, the morbidity of these diseases continues unabated (Dawber, 1981).

With respect to CHD, three risk factors, elevated serum cholesterol, hypertension, and cigarette smoking, long highly associated with the incidence of the disease, have now been shown to be absent in half of the encountered clinical cases (Jenkins, 1971). Furthermore, attempts to modify the course of CHD through alteration of these risk factors have met with limited success (Eliot and Buel, 1981). Hence, there is a resurgence of interest in the possible association of emotional and behavioral factors to CHD and the role of excessive sympatho-adrenal medullary response in promoting or accelerating coronary lesions in susceptible individuals (Russek and Russek, 1972). With respect to viral and neoplastic disease, there is also accumulating experimental evidence that stress can compromise the efficacy of the immunologic system by destroying circulating T-cell lymphocytes and by influencing associated organs, thus increasing an individual's susceptibility to these diseases (Riley, 1981).

Another surge of interest, though, has captured the "hearts" of North Americans in the past decade and with no indication of waning: the fitness movement. Exercise, and the lifestyle surrounding it, has become the nation's own prescription for health and the antidote par excellence to cope with anxiety and stress. The fitness boom has had such an impact it is estimated that half the adult population of the United States involve themselves daily in some form of physical activity.

Results of the Canada Fitness Survey, the largest and most comprehensive study of physical activity ever undertaken in the Western world, indicate that 77 percent of its citizens aged 14 years and over reported participating in some sport over the last twelve months, while 66 percent took part in exercise (including walking, jogging, cycling, calisthenics, exercise classes, and the like) in the month previous to the survey. The results of the survey indicate a substantial increase in the perceived role of physical activity in achieving well-being (Table 10–1). Whereas exercise in the early 1970s was viewed as being secondary to well-being (Haut-Commissariat, 1976) and far down

Table 10–1. Relative Importance of Factors Contributing to Well-being (Canada Fitness Survey).

	Proportion Age 10+ Rating as Important
1. Adequate rest and sleep	95%
2. Good diet	92
3. Adequate medical and dental care	88
4. Maintenance of proper weight	85
5. Regular physical activity such as exercise, sport, or games	78
6. Control of stress	77
7. Being a non-smoker	77
8. Positive thinking/meditation	76
9. Using alcohol moderately or being a non-drinker	74
10. Participation in social and cultural activities	66
11. Low calorie snacks between meals	56

on the list of the table, 78 percent of those questioned in the Canada Fitness Survey now consider regular exercise "very important" or "of some importance" in promoting health (Canada Fitness Survey, 1982).

This mass concern for physical activity and its ability to counteract the harmful effects of anxiety and stress is understandable in view of the well-appreciated value of exercise as an outlet for pent-up energy. Emotional tension arouses the organism by providing it with an over-abundant supply of energy substrates (free fatty acids, cholesterol, triglycerides, glucose) and an admirable cardiovascular response (increased heart rate and blood pressure, blood flow redistribution, decreased coagulation time, etc.) that prepares the individual for physical action.

Since the majority of contemporary stressors are primarily emotional, however, the physiological preparation of the organism, essential for reaction to a physical threat, is no longer required or desirable. The absence of a physical reaction maintains the organism in a state of readiness and tension, a situation that, over time, has been shown to be potentially harmful to a person's health (Mason, 1968). In fact, this imbalance between the chronic biochemical and physiological preparation of the organism resulting from emotional provocations and the generalized inactivity (flabby life) of the organism would seem to conjure up a most noxious combination. The long-term consequence of this condition, particularly in genetically susceptible individuals, can lead to elevated blood pressure, increased serum lipids, arterial lesions, ventricular arrythmias, myocardial infarction, sudden death, nephritis, and diabetes (Buel and Eliot, 1979; Pelletier, 1977; Engel, 1977; and Jenkins, 1971), as well as to a host of other problems: muscular aches, headaches, and migraines. Experimental evidence also indicates that chronic unrelieved stress can enhance susceptibility to infectious and neoplastic diseases due to a decrease in the immunological capability of the organism (Riley, 1981; Solomon, 1969).

Therefore, regular physical exercise is submitted as a fundamental activity in coping with emotional tension on three counts:

1.   As a basic component in the pursuit of health: to maintain optimal weight, to improve cardiorespiratory fitness (aerobic power) and physical working capacity, and generally to develop a high degree of resistance and resilience to emotional and physical provocation.

Table 10-2.   Factors Contributing to the Development of the Cortical Prism.

Genetic endowment
Early and on-going life experiences
Personality and habits
Values and priorities
Religious beliefs

2.   As a socially acceptable procedure for the organism to rid itself of potentially harmful biochemical secretions released during emotional stress and as a natural tranquilizer.
3.   As a leisure and social activity to provide general relaxation, dispel free-floating anxiety, and generally to provide a feeling of well-being.

It is realized that regular physical activity is but one component in the total arsenal of psychological and behavioral procedures that counteract the effects of stress. Since stress is basically the reaction of the organism to a psychological or environmental stressor that is perceived

Figure 10-1.   Stress and the Cortical Prism.

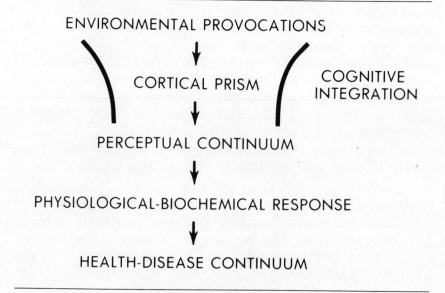

as demanding and consequential to one's well-being, the integrative role of our sociocultural brain becomes paramount. This center of cognitive integration, the outcome of a complex interaction of factors (Table 10-2), will thus act as a prism (Eliot and Buel, 1981). A stressor will be individually refracted and interpreted on a "perceptual continuum" as being either "overwhelming" (a narrow outlook, with limited alternatives), or "oblivious-chimerical" (as in Mr. McGoo, with his false sense of security and an unrealistic contact with the environment). (See Figure 10-1.) The extent of our emotional distress will determine the intensity of our physiological response, which can in turn reduce our sense of well-being, both physical and mental. The importance of fitness in counteracting the effects of stress can thus be fully appreciated.

PHYSICAL ACTIVITY IN COUNTERACTING THE EFFECTS OF STRESS

Emotional provocations will generally involve disproportionate cardiovascular and metabolic mobilization. However, if the adverse situation is removed or successfully dealt with, the healthy organism will regain its homeostasis and no undue anomalies will ensue. The ability of the organism to absorb with ease the physiological response, will, of necessity, be related to its degree of fitness. Furthermore, the capacity of the organism to dispel the hormonal secretions before they cause harmful effects will also be related in part to the extent to which the skeletal muscles can be activated.

Vigorous activity has been known for centuries to possess therapeutic and prophylactic effects on both mind and body. Physical activity is a fundamental component of health and well-being. The indivisibility of mind and body is well stated by Plato in his observation that "any defect of the psyche or soma is the occasion of the greatest discord and disproportion in the other." It is doubtful that we can fully achieve our full hereditary potential without a minimum degree of physical health: "Health is our best source of wealth. Without it happiness is almost impossible" (Schearer, 1975). We could also add that without health, optimal performance in our professional occupations is also most difficult to attain.

Table 10-3 summarizes experimental and clinical evidence with respect to the protective value of exercise in counteracting the potential

Table 10-3. Chronic Effects of Aerobic Exercise to Relieve Stress and Counteract the Disease Process.

1. Weight control	↓ serum lipids
	↓ blood pressure
	↓ insulin response
2. Lipid control	↑ high density lipoproteins (HDL-2)
	↑ cholesterol, triglycerides, very low density lipoproteins (VLDL)
3. Heart rate and blood pressure control	↓ heart rate, blood pressure
	↑ myocardial efficiency
	↓ myocardial irritability
	↓ myocardial oxygen consumption
4. Improvement in physical work capacity	↑ maximal oxygen uptake
	↓ fatigue
	↑ peripheral perfusion
5. Alterations in blood chemistry	↓ lactate response
	↓ platelet adhesiveness
	↓ platelet aggregability
	↑ fibrinolysis
6. Alterations in hormonal response	↓ catecholamines
	↓ glucocorticoids
	↑ immunology
7. Alterations in muscular contraction	↓ muscle tone action potential
	↑ relaxation
	↓ fatigue, anxiety
8. Alteration in bone mineral mass	↑ bone density
	↓ osteoporosis

harmful effects of stress. Exercise protects the individual by enhancing the state of resistance to any stimulus so that the individual is less susceptible to the effects of stress. A higher degree of health and physical fitness will provide the individual with an "armor plating" that can repulse and absorb, with less physiological intensity, the effects of a stressful situation.

This ability of exercise to enhance resistance was shown by Bajusz and Selye (1960) in their exercise pre-treatment experiments. Animals pre-treated with sodium acetate plus fluorocortisol (in doses harmless by themselves) and then exposed to forced muscular exercise, all died with massive infarctoid myocardial necrosis within 24 hours after the exercise period. Another group of animals, however, survived when similarly pre-treated but preconditioned by exercise. In these trained animals, no histological trace of cardiac necrosis was seen. Selye described this situation as a case of simple resistance, whereby the animals were protected from a specific stressor. He also demonstrated the value of exercise from a cross-resistance effect. Animals pre-treated and subjected to bone fractures suffered cardiac necrosis. When animals were first preconditioned by exercise and then subjected to bone fracture, they were spared the cardiopathies (Selye, 1966).

The beneficial effect of maintaining physical activity has also been shown indirectly in an experiment performed by Corley et al. (1975). Pairs of squirrel monkeys were restrained in a plastic chair at the neck and waist but allowed free limb movement. Each monkey was assigned the role of either "avoidance" or "yoked" monkey. The avoidance monkey was trained to manipulate a lever in order to avoid an electric shock, while the yoked monkey, which had no control, received each shock delivered to the avoidance monkey. The stress sessions involved eight-hour periods "on" avoidance alternated with eight-hour periods "off" avoidance. Results indicated that the avoidance monkeys, who were able to maintain some degree of physical activity during the stress periods, had less debilitation, fewer EKG abnormalities, bradycardia, and ventricular asystole than the helpless yoked monkeys.

One line of evidence favoring the role of exercise in protecting against coronary heart disease is the reported increase in high-density lipoprotein cholesterol (HDL_2) with physical training (Wood and Haskell, 1979). Low levels of HDL_2 have been shown to be strongly associated with an increased risk of coronary heart disease. The hypothesis is that HDL_2 may act as scavengers to remove cholesterol from coronary intimal cells (Eaton, 1978). If this theory is confirmed, and if exercise is shown to be a strong stimulis to an increase in HDL_2 cholesterol, the value of physical activity in counteracting the effects of stress will be greatly enhanced.

With respect to neoplastic diseases, an early experiment by Rusch and Kline (1944) documented the effect of exercise on the growth of a tumor. Albino mice were placed in a motor-driven rotating cage and subjected to forced exertion for a period preceding and following implantation of fibrosarcoma. When compared to implanted control animals receiving the same daily caloric equivalent of food, but not subjected to forced exercise, the exercised mice demonstrated a significantly lower rate of tumor growth. The hypothesis had been that neoplastic cells were not as likely to develop or to become established if little or no excess energy remained after the bodily requirements were met. The experiment of Rusch and Kline was motivated by an earlier report that increasing the metabolic rate by injection of thyroxin in mice retarded cancer growth (Gilroy, 1930).

Hoffman et al. (1962) also studied the effect of exercise to determine whether a substance produced by fatigued muscle would inhibit tumor growth. In establishing their hypothesis, they referred to the studies of Rusch and Kline (1944), Bullough (1949), and Heilbrun (1956). Bullough had reported that the number of mitosis in the skin was significantly diminished in mice forced to exercise vigorously, while Heilbrun interpreted his studies to indicate that fatigued muscles produced inhibiting effects on tumor-bearing mice.

Hoffman's results indeed indicated that the weight of the tumor in the inactive control group significantly exceeded that in the exercised group. In several instances there was complete tumor regression in the exercised animals. However, the nature of the substance through which the exercise had retarded tumor growth proved elusive (Hoffman et al., 1962).

In a recent study, Cannon and Kluger (1982) studied the increase in body temperature resulting from endurance (aerobic) exercise and its relationship to endogenous pyrogen released from leukocytes during infection. Such a reaction normally causes fever, depression of plasma iron and zinc, and elevation of plasma "acute phase" proteins which "makes it harder for enemy bacteria to make themselves at home" in the plasma (Weiner, 1982). The results indicated that, indeed, endurance exercise in animals, as well as in humans (70% of VO_2 maximum) resulted in the presence of an endogenous pyrogen-like substance in the plasma. This would suggest that exercisers may be in a better position to resist viral infections (and possibly even cancer) by exercise-induced enhancement of the immunological system.

TRANQUILIZER AND ANXIETY REDUCTION EFFECTS OF EXERCISE

DeVries (1981), after reviewing evidence from various sources, concluded that moderate rhythmic exercise (30–60% of maximum intensity) for five to thirty minutes duration can produce a significant tranquilizing effect. He emphasized the advantage of exercise over currently prescribed tranquilizer drugs, and in one of his own experiments, he reported that the exercise program had a significantly greater effect on the resting musculature than did meprofamate (deVries and Adams, 1972). DeVries hypothesized that the chronic tranquilizing effect of exercise is mediated by the random, intermittent, constantly changing proprioceptive stimuli that allows normal cortical activity and a state of relaxation. The acute tranquilizer action of vigorous exercise would be mediated by a rise in body temperature in appropriate structures of the brain stem or the whole body, thus resulting in decreased muscle spindle activity and synchronized activity in the cortex of the brain, both typical of a relaxed state (Haugen, Dixon, and Dickel, 1960).

A recent review by Ledwidge (1980) strongly suggested that routine vigorous activity (aerobic exercise) is an effective alternative strategy for moderating the intensity and duration of anxiety. He concluded that aerobic exercise has several advantages over drugs, psychotherapy, or change in lifestyle, in that it is free, it can be done alone, it has no deleterious effects, it takes little time, and, furthermore, that it provides a benefit no other method can claim: cardiorespiratory fitness. Exercise programs have also been employed successfully to prevent depression and promote mental health (Brown, Ramirez, and Taub, 1978; Jarrettt, 1980; Griest et al., 1978; Martin, 1977; Morgan, 1979; Young, 1979; Stern and Cleary, 1981). From these studies, there is sufficient evidence to indicate that when a person feels tense, constricted, anxious, and frustrated, a moderate to vigorous amount of aerobic exercise will provide beneficial results.

EXERCISES TO ALLEVIATE THE EFFECTS OF STRESS

A vast number of studies have indicated that if an exercise is to provide cardiovascular (aerobic) training effects, it must fulfill the requirements of type, frequency, duration, and intensity (American College of Sports Medicine, 1975). Activities most suited to developing aerobic power are those that employ the major muscle groups that are rhythmic in nature: walking, jogging, cycling, swimming, dancing, skiing, etc., and sports such as soccer and European handball. However, activities such as racquet sports, when combined with other aerobic exercise, can contribute to overall aerobic fitness while providing enjoyment. Anaerobic activities, such as weight lifting, while not specifically improving cardiorespiratory fitness, will increase muscular endurance and strength as well as produce a potent tension-relief mechanism.

It is necessary for the aerobic exercise stimulus to be maintained for a minimum of 15 to 20 minutes. However, if the intensity of the training program is increased, then a shorter duration can also provide a good training effect (Jetté and Mongeon, 1979). For the average person, training sessions beyond 30 to 40 minutes duration and in excess of 70 percent of maximum aerobic power will not markedly enhance cardiovascular fitness in proportion to the time and energy invested.

The frequency of participation will also vary with the needs and temperament of the individual. Aerobic training effects will be achieved by exercising two to three times a week. However, a person who experiences a high degree of stress in an occupation should consider exercising daily in order to dispel cardiovascular excitation and excessive energy substrates. The best time of day to exercise will be one that suits one's schedule and "metabolic preferences."

The intensity at which to exercise to obtain a training effect is the most important and difficult criterion to determine. In general, a minimum intensity of 50 to 60 percent of one's maximal working capacity (aerobic power) is required. Proper intensity of training can be best assessed by undergoing a maximal or symptom-limited stress test. However, such tests are not always available and they do involve certain risks. Submaximal tests, such as the Canadian Home Fitness Test, can provide a prediction of maximal aerobic power (Jetté, Campbell, Mongeon and Routhier, 1976) that can then be utilized to determine a walk-jog, rope skipping, or bench-stepping exercise prescription. The heart rate response to the submaximal test can also be employed to recommend a training exercise heart rate. General formulas that use age as the sole indicator of an exercise heart rate can provide erroneous information and can also be injurious due to the

Table 10-4.   Chronic Effects of Aerobic Training.

↑ Maximal oxygen consumption
↓ Blood lactate levels during sub-maximal exercise
↑ Percentage of energy from oxidation of fatty acids
↓ Percentage of carbohydrate utilization during sub-maximal exercise
↓ Blood flow to working muscles at absolute submaximal work
↓ Muscle myoglobin, total circulating hemoglobin
↓ Capacity of muscle to oxidize fat and carbohydrate
↑ Activity of mitochondrial enzymes
↓ Heart rate and blood pressure at absolute workload
↑ Resting stroke volume
↑ Heart size and volume
↑ Maximal cardiac output at absolute workload
↑ Mechanical function of the myocardium
↓ Cardiac catecholamine concentration
↑ Ability of the heart to withstand a period of ischemia

tremendous individual variability in exercise heart rate response (Hellerstein, Hirsch, Ader, Blott and Siegel, 1973).

In order for physical activity to be of value in counteracting the effects of stress, the selected aerobic exercises should therefore be:

1. Enjoyable and compatible with the personality, temperament, and body type of the individual;
2. Performed at an intensity of at least 50 to 60 percent maximum capacity for 20 to 30 minutes duration (the lower the intensity, the longer the duration);
3. Engaged in at least 2 to 3 times a week, although more frequent participation may be beneficial if a person is subjected to excessive stress.

Keeping physically fit will provide a sense of security and a feeling of well-being that few other activities can accomplish. A summary of the effects of aerobic training is shown in Table 10-4.

A particularly beneficial effect of regular exercise is the maintenance of optimal body weight. The effects of excess weight with respect to longevity, diabetes, cardiovascular, renal, gallbladder diseases, and sudden death are well documented (Bray, 1976). Ensuring that the body maintains an energy balance through regular physical activity will reduce one's innate susceptibility to these diseases, particularly when experiencing a high degree of stress.

GUIDELINES WHEN INITIATING AN
AEROBIC EXERCISE PROGRAM

In spite of all the medical advice offered prior to initiating an exercise program, the average person who is more or less healthy and fit can normally start exercising by following two basic principles: (1) starting very slowly and not over-exerting oneself; and (2) selecting an activity that primarily employs the leg muscles.

There are few people for whom a simple activity such as walking, cycling, or swimming cannot be of benefit. An investment in a good pair of shoes and 15 to 20 minutes daily of one's time will provide more benefit than harm, as long as the above common-sense rules are followed. If one's state of health is uncertain, medical advice should be sought before embarking on an exercise program.

It is advisable, particularly if one's experience with physical activity is limited or if one has not exercised for a number of years, to seek the services of a certified exercise specialist for an exercise stress test. As indicated, this is the best procedure to determine the intensity at which one should exercise to obtain a training effect. It is also the only method of detecting whether one's body can perform vigorous exercise without undue cardiovascular strain. An exercise prescription can then be tailored to one's specific needs. Again, whichever exercise program a person selects, one should start and progress slowly so that muscular pain does not ensue. One should avoid joining programs that foster a competitive environment to avoid overexertion.

A person can achieve all the benefits exercise can provide to counteract stress by participating in an aerobic type of activity, such as vigorous walking supplemented by calisthenics. In walking, a rule of thumb for a person of average height and weight is to increase one's pace progressively so that one can walk at 110–120 steps per minute. This pace should then be maintained for 15 to 20 minutes so that light perspiration ensues. There is a variety of excellent books available to assist one in safely initiating an exercise program (Vitale, 1973; Pollock, Wilmore, and Fox, 1978). If a person requires further advice, an exercise specialist should be consulted.

ORGANIZATIONAL FITNESS PROGRAM

Many organizations, appreciating the benefits of fit and healthy employees, have established corporate fitness programs. The services range from the very basic installation of shower facilities to the provision of fully-equipped gymnasiums. Other organizations subsidize employees who join local athletic clubs.

Fitness programs have also been shown to be excellent vehicles for lifestyle modification programs. Once a person is committed to a fitness program, other health habits, such as proper diet, sufficient sleep, abatement of smoking, and wise and moderate use of alcohol are normally enhanced (Haskell, 1980). Specific benefits of employee fitness programs have been documented (Collis, 1977; *Fitness: The Facts,* 1982; *Employee Fitness and Lifestyle Project,* 1979) and these include:

1.   Decreased on-the-job tension and stress
2.   Work perceived as more enjoyable, less of a routine, and less boring
3.   Improved rapport with supervisors
4.   Decreased absenteeism and employee turnover
5.   Improved work capacity and a decrease in fatigue
6.   Reduction of minor illnesses and medical claims.

"Fitness Canada," in its mandate to promote employee fitness, has prepared interesting material to assist companies in establishing health programs in the workplace. The Standardized Test of Fitness (STF) provides detailed information on equipment and procedures to perform a field test of fitness. The test involves anthropometric flexibility, muscular strength, and endurance measurements, and includes the Canadian Home Fitness Test to evaluate cardiorespiratory fitness. A calculator is used to predict aerobic power based on the step test and a walk-jog exercise program can be prescribed. Descriptive norms and percentile scores are provided for each test. A self-administered screening questionnaire, The Physical Activity Readiness Questionnaire (Par-Q), is also included. It provides a simple procedure to assess an individual's suitability to participate safely in a teaching and exercise program.

Also available from Fitness Canada is the Exercise Break package, designed for use in an office or plant, that includes four 6 to 7 minute sets of calisthenics performed to music.

A 35mm slide presentation, "Employee Fitness Slide Show," outlining the methods and principles of establishing and operating an employee fitness program, has recently been prepared by Fitness

Canada. It reviews planning, facilities, leadership, and cost considerations, as well as the benefits accruing from such a program.

An interesting guide to use in fitness and lifestyle modification programs is the "Health and Welfare Evalu Life." Following the completion of a questionnaire, it provides an individual with current risks of disease as compared to the average Canadian of one's age and sex. It is an excellent tool to assist the fitness and health professional in counselling and intervention programs.

Exercise is a fundamental activity for developing and maintaining health and fitness, and physical activity is becoming a most practical procedure for coping with stress, anxiety, and depression. There is, furthermore, an increasing amount of evidence indicating that regular exercise provides some degree of protection against disease. An active lifestyle that includes sufficient sleep and rest, a proper diet, maintenance of energy balance, moderate use of alcohol, and judicious use of medication is a most sensible and preventive approach to stress management.

REFERENCES

American College of Sports Medicine. 1975. *Guidelines for Graded Exercise Testing and Exercise Prescription.* Philadelphia: Lea & Febiger.

Bajusz, E., and H. Selye. 1960. "Adaptation to the Cardiac Necrosis-eliciting Effect of Stress." *American Journal of Physiology* 199: 453–456.

Bray, G.A. 1976. *The Obese Patient.* Philadelphia: W.R. Saunders.

Brown, R.S.; D.E. Ramirez; and J.M. Taub. 1978. "The Prescription of Exercise for Depression." *The Physician and Sports Medicine* 6: 35–45.

Buel, J.C., and R.S. Eliot. 1979. "Stress and Cardiovascular Disease." *Modern Concepts of Cardiovascular Disease* 48: 19–24.

Bullough, W.S. 1949. "The Effects of High and Low Temperatures on the Epidermal Mitotic Activity of the Adult Male Mouse." *Journal of Experimental Biology* 26: 76–82.

Canada Fitness Survey. 1982. *Canada's Fitness. Preliminary Findings of the 1981 Survey.* Ottawa.

Cannon, J.G., and M.J. Kluger. 1982. "Endogenous Pyrogenlike Activity in Human Plasma After Exercise." In *Proceedings of the Federation of American Societies for Experimental Biology.* Abstract (8228), March.

Corley, K.C.; H.P. Mauck; and F. O'Malley. 1975. "Cardiac Responses Associated with 'Yoked-Chair' Shock Avoidance in Squirrel Monkeys." *Psychophysiology* 12: 439–444.

Collis, M.L. 1977. *Employee Fitness.* Fitness and Amateur Sport, Ottawa.

Dawber, T.R.D. 1981. *Risk Factors for Atherosclerotic Disease.* Kalamazoo, Mich.: Upjohn Company.

DeVries, H.A. 1981. "Tranquilizer Effect of Exercise: A Critical Review." *The Physician and Sports Medicine* 9: 47-55.

DeVries, H.A., and G.N. Adams. 1972. "Electromyographic Comparison of Single Doses of Exercise and Meprobamate as to Effect on Muscular Relaxation." *American Journal of Physical Medicine* 51: 130-141.

Eaton, P. 1978. "High Density Lipoprotein—Key to Anti-Atherogenesis." *Journal of Chronic Diseases* 31: 131-135.

Eliot, R.S., and J.C. Buel. 1981. "Environmental and Behavioral Influences in the Major Cardiovascular Disorders." In *Perspectives on Behavioral Medicine,* edited by S.M. Weiss, J.A. Herd, and B.H. Fox. New York: Academic Press.

Employee Fitness and Lifestyle Project. 1979. "Toronto 1977-78." *Fitness and Amateur Sport.* Ottawa.

Engel, G. 1977. "Emotional Stress and Sudden Death," *Psychology Today,* November: 114-154.

Fitness: The Facts. 1982. "A Six-Part Fitness Communication Program." *Participaction.* Toronto.

Gilroy, E. 1930. "Comparison of the Effects of Arginine and Thyroxine Upon Tumor Growth Rate in the Mouse." *Biochemistry Journal* 24: 1181-1187.

Greist, J.H.; M.H. Klein; R.R. Eischens; and J.T. Faris. 1978. "Running Out of Depression." *The Physician and Sports Medicine* 6: 49-56.

Haskell, W.L. 1980. "The Physical Activity Components of Health Promotion in Occupational Settings." *Public Health Reports* 95: 109-118.

Haugen, G.B.; H.H. Dixon; and H.A. Dickel. 1960. *A Therapy for Anxiety Reactions.* New York: MacMillan.

Haut-Commissariat à la jeunesse, aux loisirs et aux sports. 1976. "Les Québécois et Leur Condition Physique: Evaluation Qualitative de l' Attitude des Québécois vis-à-vis des Activités Physiques et du Conditionnement Physique." *Québec, Gouvernement du Québec, Ministère de l' Education.*

Heilbrun, L.V. 1956. *Dynamics of Living Protoplasm.* New York: Academic Press.

Hellerstein, H.K.; E.Z. Hirsch; R. Ader; N. Green Blott; and M. Siegel. 1973. "Principles of Exercise Prescription for Normal and Cardiac Patients." In *Exercise Testing and Exercise Training in Coronary Disease,* edited by J.P. Naughton and H.K. Hellerstein. New York: Academic Press.

Hoffman, S.A.; K.E. Paschkis; D.A. DeBias; A. Cantarow; and T.L. Williams. 1962. "The Influence of Exercise on the Growth of Transplanted Rat Tumors." *Cancer Research* 22: 597-599.

Jarrett, P.S. 1980. Some Mental Aspects of Physical Fitness." *Journal of the Florida Medical Association* 67: 378–381.

Jenkins, C.D. 1971. "Psychologic and Social Precursors of Coronary Disease. Pt. I." *New England Journal of Medicine* 284: 244–255.

Jenkins, C.D. 1981. "Behavioral Factors in the Etiology and Pathogenesis of Cardiovascular Diseases: Sudden Death, Hypertension, and Myocardial Infarction." In *Perspectives in Behavioral Medicine,* edited by S.M. Weis, J.A. Herd, and B.H. Fox. New York: Academic Press.

Jetté, M. 1979. "An Analysis of the Lifestyle and Fitness of Male Employees: Implications for Physical Activity Programs." *Recreation Research Review* 6: 53–61.

Jetté, M. 1982a. "La santé, cuirasse par excellence pour résister au stress." *Entre nous* 14: 9–11.

Jetté, M. 1982b. "A Basis for Stress Management." *Optimum* 13: 35–46.

Jetté, M. J.; J. Campbell; J. Mongeon; and R. Routhier. 1976. "The Canadian Home Fitness Test as a Predictor of Aerobic Capacity." *Canadian Medical Association Journal* 114: 680–682.

Jetté, M., and J. Mongeon. 1979. "A Comparison Between the Effects of a Twelve-week Programme of Rope Skipping and a Walk-Jog Programme in Males and Females." *Canadian Journal of Applied Sports Sciences* 4: 268–273.

Ledwidge, B. 1980. "Run for Your Mind: Aerobic Exercise as a Means of Alleviating Anxiety and Depression." *Canadian Journal of Behavioral Science* 12: 126–140.

Martin, J. 1977. "In Activity Therapy, Patients Literally Move Toward Mental Health." *The Physician and Sports Medicine* 5: 85–89.

Mason, J.W. 1968. "A Review of Psycho-Endocrine Research on the Pituitary Adrenal Cortical System." *Psychosomatic Medicine* 30: 576–607.

Morgan, W.P. 1979. "Anxiety Reduction Following Acute Physical Activity." *Psychiatric Annals* 9: 36–45.

Pelletier, K.R. 1977. "Mind As Healer, Mind As Slayer." *Psychology Today* 35 (February).

Pollock, M.; J.H. Wilmore; and S.M. Fox, III. 1978, *Health and Fitness through Physical Activity.* New York: John Wiley and Sons.

Riley, V. 1981. "Behavioral Factors in Animal Work on Tumorigenesis." In *Perspectives on Behavioral Medicine,* edited by S.M. Weiss, J.A. Herd, and B.H. Fox. New York: Academic Press.

Rusch, H.P., and B.E. Kline. 1944. "The Effects of Exercise on the Growth of a Mouse Tumor." *Cancer Research* 4: 116–118.

Russek, H.I., and L.G. Russek. 1972. "Etiologic Factors in Ischemic Heart Disease: The Illusive Role of Emotional Stress." *Geriatrics* 27: 81–86.

Schearer, L. 1975. "Resolutions." *Fort Lauderdale News*, January 1.

Selye, H. 1966. *Thrombohemorrhagic Phenomena*. Springfield, Ill.: Charles C. Thomas Publishers.

Standardized Test of Fitness. *Fitness and Amateur Sport*. Ottawa.

Stern, M.J., and P. Clearly. 1981. "National Exercise and Heart Disease Project. Psychosocial Changes Observed During a Low-Level Exercise Program." *Archives of International Medicine* 141: 1463–1467.

Vitale, F. 1973. *Individualized Fitness Programs*. Englewood Cliffs: Prentice-Hall.

Weiner, J. 1982. "Running a Fever." *The Sciences* 22: 4–5.

Wood, P.D., and W.L. Haskell. 1979. "The Effects of Exercise on Plasma High Density Lipoproteins." *Lipids* 14: 417–427.

Young, R.J. 1979. "Effects of Regular Exercise on Cognitive Functioning and Personality." *British Journal of Sports Medicine* 13: 110–117.

11 STRESS AND THE MANAGER: PERSPECTIVES

John H. Howard

Marked by rapid rates of change and greater complexity, the turbulent environment of modern society is placing increasing demands on the individual's capacity to adapt (Dubos, 1965; Phillips, 1968). The resulting difficulty in finding a harmony between the individual and his environment has led to greater stress and an ascendancy of those illnesses and diseases consequent to an overtaxing of the individual's psychophysiological capacity.

Most people understand stress intuitively. It is usually an emotional discomfort accompanied by feelings of not being able to cope, that things are falling apart, that one is not in control, or just a general uneasy feeling that all is not well without any particular cause being apparent. At the physical level, it includes loss of appetite, sleeplessness, sweating, ulcers, and other illnesses of varying degrees.

In general, stress is the result of the body preparing itself for an activity without the activity following. Consequently the body's systems are thrown out of balance with excess acid secreted in the stomach, adrenalin in the blood, higher heart rates, and other inappropriate reactions. Chronic physiological preparation for action, without the action, leads to disease and disorder.

Stress is fundamentally a psychophysiological phenomenon. It has to do with our thoughts, feelings, and emotions and how our body reacts to these. In general, the disturbances we experience as stressful tend to be transitory. They can also, however, be chronic. In addition, some types of experiences are more stressful than others, and the same experience can be more or less stressful depending on the individual.

Unfortunately, as we live each day and encounter each new stressful experience, there is a residual effect to these experiences that accumulates. The daily wear and tear of living serves to remind us that our bodily resources are not infinite and that we use them at a slower or faster pace as a matter of choice.

Of course, not all the stress in our life can be controlled. Some of it is unexpected and beyond our control. The remainder, however, is the product of events about which we daily make decisions. During most of our life, the controllable experiences predominate, but the total stress in our life is the sum of these two kinds of experiences. If the total stress we experience in living exceeds our capacity, we become candidates for the onset of illness and disease.

In any disease, some factors are more important than others, and scientists are beginning to find that stress has more and more importance to our overall health. Stress disorders tend to be basically psychosomatic and do not involve germs and viruses. Thus, the older concept of illness as being basically the result of disharmony between the individual and his environment is taking on increasing importance.

SOME STRESS PATTERNS AMONG CANADIANS

In recent stress research on over 2,000 management and professional people in a single Canadian organization, five basic stress-symptom patterns were developed (Zaleznik et al., 1977). These patterns were labelled: (1) emotional distress; (2) medication use; (3) cardiovascular symptoms; (4) gastrointestinal symptoms; and (5) allergy respiratory symptoms. Each pattern was composed of a number of symptoms that are typical stress reactions. The emotional distress pattern included symptoms such as insomnia, fatigue, loss of appetite, moodiness, and depression. Medication use included the taking of sleeping pills, diet pills, pain relievers, vitamin pills, and tranquilizers. The cardiovascular pattern consisted of high blood pressure, rapid heart beat, and heart disease. The gastrointestinal pattern included ulcers, colitis, digestion problems, diarrhea, and nausea. And the allergy respiratory pattern included hay fever, a number of respiratory problems, and skin problems such as eczema and psoriasis. Each of these patterns represents typical ways in which people react to stress-producing experiences.

It is not entirely clear why people react to stress in different ways, but factors such as age, sex, culture, and education seem to be strongly related to the symptoms an individual is likely to develop. For example, emotional distress seemed to be particularly high among the young, while medication use and cardiovascular symptoms were found to be more common among older individuals. Gastrointestinal problems and allergy-respiratory problems did not seem to be aged-related. Women were higher than men in the categories of emotional distress, medication use, and allergy-respiratory symptoms, whereas cardiovascular symptoms afflicted men more often than women.

The study included a large group of French Canadians in addition to English Canadians. It was found that the French were higher than the English on emotional distress and medication use, while the English were higher on gastrointestinal and cardiovascular disorders. Higher levels of education were associated with medication use, gastrointestinal symptoms, and allergy-respiratory symptoms, while lower levels of education were associated with emotional distress and cardiovascular disease.

These types of symptom patterns indicate that the way individuals respond to stress is in part determined by social and cultural traditions. If, for example, we consider the visible expression of symptoms, the findings indicated that French Canadians reacted to the stress they experienced in a very visible way: the symptoms they developed were highly visible to the outside world. The English Canadians, on the other hand, were repressors. The stress they experienced was turned inward; consequently, the symptoms they developed tended to be associated with the gastrointestinal and cardiovascular systems. The phenomenon of the "stiff upper lip" seemed to prevail across their total physical reaction. Men, as compared to women, also tended to be repressors, and the higher educated, as compared to the lower educated, seemed to handle the stress they experienced in a less visible way.

These are just a few of the patterns that seem to be associated with stress. There seems to be a degree of learning associated with the ability to cope successfully with stressful experiences. In general, it is found that individuals with higher education experience fewer stress symptoms than those with lower education levels. The reasons for this difference appear to be based on an increased sensitivity to situations that have the capacity to be stress-producing and a greater repertoire of coping responses.

STRESS SITUATIONS

In the broadest psychological sense, the stress we experience in life is a function of what we long for and the amount of striving we are willing to endure to achieve it. The issue of longing and striving is acted out in our jobs, our careers, and our families.

There are many jobs and careers that are characterized by the stress levels the incumbents are expected to endure. In industry, the job of foreman has long been recognized as an ideal example of a situation with considerable conflict and ambiguity (Wray, 1949; Balma, Maloney, and Lawshe 1958). The foremen have been described as the "master and victim of double-talk," "the man in the middle," a position in which, on the one hand, they are expected to identify with and represent the workers' point of view, and on the other, be responsible to management (Roethlisberger, 1944). It is interesting that associated with the dual and conflicting loyalty of this kind of role is a rather high incidence of ulcers. Foremen are found to have more ulcers than either the workers below them or management above them.

Similar roles are found throughout organization life. The salesman is another example. Here the individual is caught between the customer's demands and the organization's willingness to respond. In these types of roles or situations the individual generally experiences the simultaneous occurrence of two or more sets of pressures so that compliance with one makes compliance with the other more difficult.

The level of job responsibility is another factor that has considerable consequences in terms of stress. Interestingly enough, most research on corporate organizations finds that the top jobs are the least stressful. The further up the hierarchy you are the less stress there seems to be. There are a number of possible explanations for this finding, but the most probable relates to the individual's capacity to influence the job environment. The individual at or near the top has more power to manipulate this environment so as to contain or allocate some of the stress that arises. Managers at lower levels in the organization lack this ability and consequently experience a higher burden of adaptation. This factor, coupled with unfulfilled aspirations for mobility, often makes mid-management jobs most stressful. Having the power and freedom to influence one's work environment, rather than continually having to adapt to the environment, is a critical factor in evaluating the stress inherent in certain occupations.

STRESS AND THE MANAGER'S JOB

There are a number of reasons why managers in particular should be aware and concerned about stress. In the first place, stress is associated with change; the amount of change in our life has been increasing, and managers tend to be at the leading edge or focal point of much of the change in our society. Secondly, the industrial corporation, which is a pervasive characteristic of modern society, and which is designed, built, and operated by managers, is one of the principle sources of stress in the lives of many people. Many executives fail to understand or consider the consequences certain policies and procedures have in terms of the health of managers and employees.

These two factors determine the principle roles that managers have to play in understanding and coping with the stress involved in organizational life. The first involves the structure and operation of the manager's own organization, and the second involves the manager's personal ability to deal with the stress associated with the job itself. In the first case the manager needs to be aware of the situations in organizational life that seem to have the greatest capacity for producing stress. In the second case, the manager's own sensitivity and capacity for alternate responses are the issues that should be of concern.

In a recently completed study, we asked 300 managers from twelve major Canadian companies what they found to be the principle sources of stress on the job and how they dealt with it (Howard, 1980). In both cases, their answers covered situations and techniques that were both interesting and diverse. An analysis of their responses indicated four very general characteristics of management jobs that seem most stress-producing:

1. *Feelings of impotence or helplessness*. Managers often understand problems and have reasonable solutions, but feel powerless

to act because of organizational constraints. Feeling helpless and unable to influence a situation can be particularly stressful. In contrast, being able to act is greatly therapeutic. Power is definitely an antidote for stress.

2. *Too much work.* Management jobs are often characterized by a large amount of work at an unrelenting pace. Managers can be overloaded in both a quantitative and a qualitative sense, but the sheer quantity of work is most often the problem.

3. *Urgency.* In a recent study, we found that, on average, managers do something different every seven minutes (Ross, 1979). Their jobs are characterized by brevity and fragmentation and stress. Many other studies show similar patterns.

4. *Ambiguity and uncertainty.* Not only are problems usually undefined, but company policies can also be just as ambiguous. Uncertainty characterizes both the environment and the potential outcomes of alternate courses of action. This is the key factor that makes decisionmaking difficult.

These, then, are the major underlying dimensions of stress in a manager's job, and they originate in many different situations. We have categorized these situations as follows:

1. Poor Management
2. Lack of Authority or Blurred Organizational Relationships
3. Promotion and Recognition Concerns
4. Basic Business Problems
5. Company Politics
6. Personnel Problems
7. Heavy Work Volumes
8. Unfamiliar Work, Job, People, Moves
9. Miscellaneous

Poor Management

Poor management ranked top on the list of sources of stress. Managers described lack of adequate planning and direction along with chronic indecisiveness as causing the most tension. These themes were mentioned in a large number of situations.

"In my opinion, the Chairman is sometimes inconsistent, impractical and unrealistic in his attitudes."

"I feel frustrated that top management cannot or will not air certain pockets of discord in the organization."

Poor communication by top management was also included in this category. Although it was mentioned specifically a few times, it was implied in many other responses. Frequently, top management fail to communicate their total plans. A certain amount of stress produced from this communication gap may be a positive force in the organization. But it appears that the failure to communicate plans and actions may lead to feelings of stress by managers and a decreased respect for top management.

Lack of Authority or Blurred Organizational Relationships

Second on the list were lack of authority and blurred organizational structures. Most of the comments focusing on lack of authority also highlighted the other side of the coin—total responsibility. These managers had the responsibility but not the authority to complete the job adequately.

"It is most frustrating to be accountable for solving certain tasks or problems, if you are not given the authority which is needed to properly carry out such an assignment."

Some of the managers described a "do-or-die" situation. Their supervisors would set unrealistically high standards for the department. If these standards were not met, the manager would be the scapegoat and pay the penalty. If the standards were achieved, the supervisor would receive credit:

"My organization is a small division of a very large multinational company. Lack of authority at the local level is a very serious deterrent to the successful development of our business. Top management has 'apparent' authority but in reality is completely controlled by the parent hierarchy."

These authority problems were also linked to political issues. Often the managers could define the problem and devise possible alternatives, but they were not in a "political position" to take action.

Blurred organizational structure was often blamed on conflicting demands caused primarily by too many bosses. Unclear job descriptions were a contributing factor to the confusion.

"The majority of my work is with the Chief Executive Officer. However, my staff is basically involved with the Chief Operating Officer. Both men are significantly different and the blurred organizational structure produces many problems."

The roots of these problems owe to the very nature of a corporation that is constantly changing and evolving to meet new situations. Often the informal lines of authority are a truer reflection of the situation than the formal structure. Job descriptions and organizational charts are frequently designed after the situation has developed.

Promotion and Recognition Concerns

Promotion and recognition concerns and basic business problems were each mentioned the same number of times. Promotion and recognition concerns centered around the uncertainty of future advancement and the frustration from lack of praise and recognition by top management. Many of these comments were first-hand testimonials from executives who had been passed over for younger people with more formal education.

"In our organization, they tell you that they like to promote from within but they seldom do. They usually bring in new people and promote them quickly."

Most managers have in mind a position that they would like to be promoted to in the "next round of musical chairs." They don't know, however, the criteria by which they currently are being judged nor the prerequisites for the next position. For nonmanagement jobs, the requirements are usually posted. Interested parties can evaluate their chances of promotion and strive to do the right things or achieve the necessary qualifications to be awarded the job. This is not the case with management. The jobs and necessary qualifications are not posted. Potential applicants do not know which "hoops to jump through," and their efforts for promotion are frequently misdirected. When a new person is brought in for the job, managers still don't know what they did wrong, nor what they didn't do to get the job. They are left with feelings of frustration that often surface as apathy or resentment toward top management.

Stress is also a by-product of the ignorance about how new jobs and positions are developed. Inexperienced managers wait for top management to take the initiative and "give" them the job. Experienced managers are aware that the development of new tasks or a new job is done by small steps. Often the manager perceives that a certain task needs to be done and takes over the duties. This manager soon becomes responsible for the task and frequently becomes the authority on the subject. Although it is not part of the job description, it has become the manager's job. When top management perceives the need to put someone in charge of that area, the natural contender for the position is the person who has the most experience. The other managers are out of the running before the race has begun. It is often this misconception of how jobs develop and companies evolve that produces much frustration and disqualifies many managers. Initiative is a key ingredient in ambition.

Basic Business Problems

Stress related to basic business problems was described in terms of deadlines, volume of paper, and budgets. These types of problems seem to be fairly common to all business and, at times, become a major source of stress.

"We operate on very stringent copy deadlines which cause friction between customer, advertising and production. This necessitates frequent bargaining sessions with production—who cannot or will not understand there are occasions where deadlines must be broken."

When the managers were given a list of daily work problems and asked to identify the major sources of stress, six work-related problems ranked closely:

1. Never being able to really center in and concentrate on a single problem for very long.

2. Contacts with subordinates who don't understand my goals or don't perform to my expectations.
3. Constant telephone interruptions.
4. Scheduled meetings constantly taking up too much valuable time.
5. Contacts with my supervisors.
6. Having to supervise and coordinate the work of many people on varied tasks.

These findings seem to reflect Henry Mintzberg's description of managerial work as being characterized by brevity, fragmentation, and urgency (Mintzberg, 1973). In other words, "much work at an unrelenting pace." Unfortunately, these same basic characteristics of the managerial job produce stress. Never being able to really center in on a problem and constant telephone interruptions are inherent to the job, and are perceived as frustrating and stressful.

Company Politics

Company politics were well recognized by the participants and were always seen as a source of stress. It appears that more politicking is done at the higher levels of management.

"The major problem in this organization is the office politics. You must support the right party. It's 'who you know' not 'what you know or do' that really counts."

"Some decisions by upper management seem to be self-serving rather than directed to the best interests of the corporation."

The existence of corporate politics is like beauty—it's often in the eye of the beholder. Some situations, however, are prone to include political influences. A study done by Gandz and Murray (1980) found that office politics most often plays a part in the following situations: promotions or transfers; allocation of supplies and equipment; division of authority; and coordination between departments. This was reflected in some of the comments.

"There is a type of 'buddy' system among top management as they are very protective of each other. This results in the wrong people in key jobs and the right people in a position of no authority."

Personnel Problems

Problems with personnel were cited as some of the most difficult to handle. One group of comments centered around employees unsuited to their work. Another group of managers described the difficulty of handling personal problems of employees. These problems are usually addressed by the managers only when work was affected.

"It is very difficult to know when and how to draw the line on personnel problems which occur from time to time."

Work Volume

The heavy volume of work was described in terms of time limits and staff shortages. Some of the managers mentioned that these conditions were temporary, but others said it was a chronic source of stress.

"Excessive demands on my time tend to create stress and tension. I tend to do some jobs which should be done by my subordinates, partly because I enjoy it occasionally and, secondly, because it would overload one of my people if I didn't do it. Unfortunately, the job doesn't justify hiring another full-time employee."

Most managers initially blame themselves for this lack of time. They often see their inability to delegate work adequately as the culprit. However, after considerable soul searching, managers come to realize that it is frequently impossible to complete all the work. It is only when this realization occurs that the situation can be solved or coping strategies devised.

Unfamiliarity

Stress due to change was described in terms of unfamiliar work, jobs, people, and moves. Being placed in situations out of the manager's expertise was perceived as generally stressful. Some managers felt that any change produced stress. It was when the "people element" of the decision was forgotten that the stress became too great.

"Tension and stress are created when being placed in particular situations in which you have little experience or knowledge."

Miscellaneous

The miscellaneous category included problems concerning personal shortcomings and the price paid for being a perfectionist. Fear of decisionmaking was also a concern, especially when it involved the careers of others. It was interesting to find that in some companies, government regulations and the power held by unions were producing stress at a number of management levels.

JOB SATISFACTION

Recent research on Canadian managers has revealed the critical role of job satisfaction (Howard, Rechnitzer, and Cunningham, 1978). This study found that the greater the job dissatisfaction the greater number of stress symptoms. In addition, the following five factors, in order of importance, were found to be the most significant as contributors to stress and dissatisfaction.

1. A lack of awareness with regard to the opportunities for advancement and promotion.
2. A lack of awareness with regard to how performance is evaluated.
3. A feeling that the job interferes unduly with the individual's personal life.
4. A feeling that the individual lacks the authority and influence needed to carry out assigned responsibilities.
5. Too heavy a workload.

The first two items are the most important and strongly reflect the issue of uncertainty. They are also issues over which management has control and reflect policies, or the lack of policies, within the organization.

The feeling that a job interferes with an individual's personal life and the heavy workload likely represent extra hours spent on the job. In the case of managers it is often difficult to judge whether they are simply living up to expectations or following self-imposed work habits, but in either case the outcome is increased stress.

The lack of authority to match responsibilities is an age-old complaint of managers, but it reflects a central issue in terms of stress.

This is the issue of influence—a feeling of being able to influence the events that have meaning and importance to the individual. Being without the feeling that you have some control over the important events in your job can only lead to stress and the development of stress symptoms.

Uncertainty has always had a significant effect on the emotional and physical health of the individual, but for two principle reasons its psychological importance seems to be increasing. In the first place, scientific and technological change seems to have created more, not less, uncertainty in life. Our society is characterized by an ever-increasing complexity of tasks and technology, a rapidity of organizational change, and a resulting high rate of job and geographic mobility. Combined with the resulting strains on family life, these factors make adaptation to and maintenance of the delicate balance between biological and psychological forces an ever-growing burden. This view was clearly put by Alvin Toffler in his book *Future Shock*.

The second reason why uncertainty is increasing in importance is because the means and institutions that people had traditionally used to help cope with uncertainty have either begun to disintegrate or have lost much of their value as effective psychological support. The family and religion are two of the most important institutions fitting into this category, and while their importance has often been downgraded, little new has come along that has proven its effectiveness in supporting the individual during times of high uncertainty. It is somewhat ironic that in a period of increasing uncertainty we are losing our traditional means of coping with the stresses involved.

COPING WITH STRESS

In general, people differ in their ability to cope with stress-producing situations. What seems to differentiate the more successful from the less successful is the awareness of the stress potential in a situation, a sensitivity to an individual's own reactions, and a capacity for alternate responses. Successful coping seems to be a skill in which there is some potential for learning and development on the part of the individual. In a deeper sense, however, our coping abilities are tied to the development of our personality, become a part of our character, and are very difficult to influence.

An understanding of the techniques that people use to cope with stress is an area where research work remains to be done. Are some techniques more effective than others? Are some more appropriate depending on the type of experience and symptoms the individual tends to encounter? There are few answers to these types of questions, and what little information does exist seems to be mostly intuitive and available to the individual only after an illness has developed.

One researcher who asked a group of managers how they coped with stress and tension on the job was able to group their replies in the following ten basic categories (Burke, 1971).

1. Change to an engrossing non-work or play activity such as reading, community affairs, coaching sports, hobbies, and outdoor activities.
2. Analyze the stress-producing situation and change the strategy of attack. Decide on what's worth worrying about and what is not. Accept less perfection. Delegate tasks when tension builds.
3. Withdraw physically from the situation for awhile. Take a break.
4. Engage in physical exercise.
5. Work harder. Take work home. Work longer hours.
6. Talk with others on the job. Discuss with contemporaries. Have a bitching session with peers.
7. Compartmentalize work and home life. Work hard on the job, but when at home learn to "blank out" job problems.
8. Change to a completely different work task or job activity.
9. Talk with spouse.
10. Build resistance to frustration by regular sleep, regular exercise, and good health habits.

In follow-up studies, the effectiveness of each technique was determined by relating the usage of the technique to the incidence of somatic complaints (Hoard et al., 1975). In terms of the average number of stress symptoms reported, the five best techniques for coping with job tension were as follows:

1. Build resistance by regular sleep, exercise, and good health habits.
2. Compartmentalize work and non-work life.
3. Engage in physical exercise.

4.   Talk with peers on the job.
5.   Withdraw physically from the situation.

The most effective mechanism, building physical resistance, is highly significant in designing an action plan for coping with stress. It reflects an awareness of job demands, a sensitivity to one's own limited physical resources, and a readiness to deal with tension as it arises. An individual who has a preventive concern about his health will have available energy that can be used to help him deal with problems rationally and effectively. The individual who is healthy and alert has a much greater success potential as a "manager of stress" than the one who neglects his health and, consequently, his readiness to deal with stress.

BECOMING A "MANAGER OF STRESS"

What can the individual do today to begin training in the management of stress? The following steps might be considered:[1]

1.   Consciously assess your own pace of life at present. Take inventory of all recent changes, include current or upcoming change events. Analyze job situations and identify those which you find particularly stressful. Ask yourself if you feel generally tense, overloaded, unsure about your job status, or confused by your state of affairs.
2.   Try to become aware of your own psychophysiological threshold. Practice sensitivity in detecting stress symptoms (i.e., heart palpitations, headaches, rapid pulse, insomnia, etc.). Learn to recognize a state of stress within yourself so you can begin to deal with it directly.
3.   Simplify your life. Attempt to foresee the occurrence of specific stress-producing job events and try to schedule these so they do not occur simultaneously. In the same way, budget change events in such a way that they remain within your perception of controllable limits. Don't suppress all change and tension; merely "manage" them. Leave job tensions at the office; compartmentalize work and home life.
4.   Leave room within your coping range for those unanticipated stress situations. Don't load your time and budget your energy

[1]For considerable elaboration on these issues see (Howard et al., 1978).

completely to its quota. Maintain a state of readiness by staying healthy and alert. Develop a preventive concern about your health.

5. When an unexpected stress situation or major change event arises, stop and think about it. Is it really as serious as it appears to be on the surface? Is it worth the expenditure of valuable energy resources in worrying and tension? Or, with the application of a little imagination and flexibility, can you adapt easily and readily?

6. Evaluate the various alternative mechanisms at hand for coping with tension. Are the "old ways" still working effectively? Or is it time to take a break, get away from it all, and evaluate new courses of action objectively? Begin to design and apply a broad repertoire of alternate responses, and shy away from stereotypical reactions. Follow through by analyzing the implications and range of consequences in your responses.

7. Above all, be in conscious control of your life. Participate actively, imaginatively, and with flexibility. Become an "active participator" in controlling your life rather than a "passive reactor" to fate.

THE NEED FOR STRESS

Some stress in our jobs, as well as in our life, is both inevitable and necessary. The very nature of the process of maturation implies a mastery of the stresses inherent in life. The issue, in fact, is not the elimination of stress, but its containment and allocation. In response to the challenge of improving our abilities and performance, stress is a necessary part. Without stress, there is no improvement. Increasing stress, however, results in improved performance only up to a point, and impairment thereafter.

For the individual, what is most important in life often has the capacity to be the most stressful. The key issue in stress is the balance we strike between longing and striving. The goals we set and the energy we invest in their pursuit are becoming the most important determinants of the stress, illness, and disease we experience.

We are beginning to know the price we pay in illness for a given way of life, and we should profit by the opportunity to make our choices with better information. Since our health is now more significantly a product of our thinking, it is within our own mind that the defenses against illness have to be constructed.

REFERENCES

Balma, M.; J. Maloney; C. Lawshe. 1958. "The Role of the Foreman in Modern Industry, I, III." *Personnel Psychology* II.

Burke, R.K. 1971. "Are You Fed-Up with Work?" *Personnel Administration* (January–February).

Caplan, R.D.; S. Cobb; J.R.P. French; R.V. Harrison; and S.R. Pinneau. 1980. *Job Demands and Worker Health.* Research Report Services, University of Michigan.

Dubos, R. 1965. *Man Adapting.* New Haven: Yale University Press.

Gandz, J., and V.V. Murray. 1980. "The Experience of Workplace Politics." *Academy of Management Journal* 23, no. 2: 237–251.

Howard, J.H.; P.A. Rechnitzer; D.A. Cunningham. 1978. *Rusting Out, Burning Out or Bowing Out: Stress and Survival on the Job.* Toronto: Macmillan/Gage.

Howard, J.H. 1980. "Stress and Today's Manager," *Journal of the International Institute of Stress* 1, no. 1, 24–27.

Mintzberg, H. 1973. *The Nature of Managerial Work.* New York: Harper & Row.

Phillips, L. 1968. *Human Adaptation and its Failures.* New York: Academic Press.

Roethlisberger, B. 1944. "The Foreman: Master and Victim of Double-Talk." *Harvard Business Review* 23: 283–298.

Ross, G.H.B. 1979. "Work Activities and Physiological Stress: Monitoring Managers on the Job." Ph.D. dissertation, University of Western Ontario.

Wray, D. 1949. "Marginal Men of Industry: the Foreman." *American Journal of Sociology* 54: 298–301.

Zaleznik, A. M.F.R. Kets de Vries; J.H. Howard. 1977. "Stress Reaction in Organizations: Syndromes, Causes and Consequences." *Behavioural Science* 22: 151–162.

12 ORGANIZATIONAL STRESS MANAGEMENT AUDIT

Manfred F.R. Kets de Vries

We are beginning to realize that industrial development, urbanization, and social change do not come without their price; they are accompanied by many dysfunctional side effects. The knowledge revolution, the information explosion, and the associated acceleration of changes in technology, social structure, occupations, and organizations make for an increasingly complex living environment. Postindustrial society not only puts incredible pressures on the individual; it places high demands on individual coping behavior, thereby contributing to the incidence of diseases of adaptation.

Throughout history man has been exposed to stress, but it is only in this century, after the almost successful elimination of infectious diseases, that we are beginning to realize the increase of this threat to health. Chronic diseases have replaced contagious diseases as the major contributors to mortality. Coronary disease has become the new scourge of mankind. Heart attacks are now the main cause of mortality, accounting for more than 50 percent of all deaths in most developed societies. Hypertension, gastrointestinal disorders, alcoholism, drug addiction, depression, and suicide are also taking their toll.

The fact that organizational factors play a significant role in the causation of stress has become recognized. Variables such as career stagnation, demotion, unemployment, job obsolescence, transfers, long and irregular working hours, work overload, and intense competition can produce stress. The cost to society of the side effects of organizational stress can be staggering. The U.S. National Clearing House for Mental Health Information estimated a decrease in productive capacity of $17 billion for the United States alone through factors such as excessive absenteeism, excessive unemployment, inefficiency on the job, and working below capacity (Rogers, 1975). Stress, given its growing influence on society, can no longer be ignored.

One way of approaching stress in an organizational context is to consider it as a social indicator reflecting the impact of organizational variables on the individual. In comparison with more traditional organizational measurement tools (e.g., attitudinal studies), the monitoring of stress reactions seems to be a far more accurate and meaningful way of assessing an organization's overall well-being. Physiological and emotional reactions tend to be more reliable indicators of the quality of the organization's working environment than simplistic answers on attitude scales. Hence, the addition of stress audit to the traditional financial audit can create a more discriminating base from which to make individual and organizational adjustments. The stress audit thus bcomes an essential part of the overall management process. The results of a stress audit can be used to identify problem areas that contribute to an impairment of organizational performance. Better intervention strategies can therefore be created that make for more efficient and effective organizational functioning.

A MULTIFACTORIAL STRESS MODEL

Many researchers interested in stress in organizations may have recognized its multifactorial nature, but for the sake of convenience have limited the sphere of inquiry. All too often research boundaries have been narrowly defined and have focused exclusively on the work situation, thus substituting the notion of stress reactions (with its associations with illness and psychiatry) for more neutral indicators less fraught with highly emotional connotations. Instead, scales of job satisfaction, organizational climate, job attitude, alienation, and morale have been used extensively. But despite the proliferation of these studies the results have been disappointing. The frequent simplicity of research design, owing to narrowly defined boundaries, has probably been a main reason.

Figure 12-1. A Multifactorial Approach to Stress.

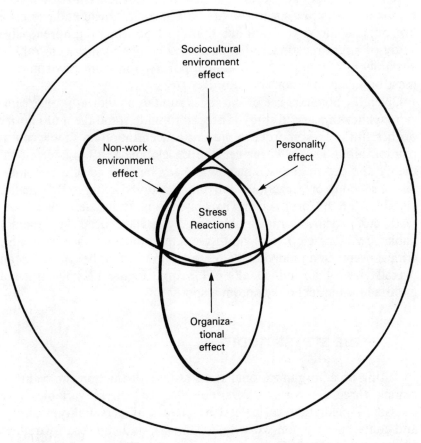

It can be argued that job variables in isolation have not been able to explain adequately the interface of personality and organization. The ways in which an individual can express his dissatisfaction and frustration with organizations (apart from responding to various measurement scales of satisfaction, alienation, career aspirations, or the like), seem to be of a greater complexity than originally envisioned. In addition, the observation that many other factors, besides organizational variables, are responsible for stress reactions has not simplified the matter. The effects of the organizational environment in the etiology of stress has to be viewed in its proper perspective. Stress in organizations does not occur in a vacuum. Individuals have their own personal history in a specific sociocultural environment and possess a life outside the organizational setting. Thus, in a comprehensive study of stress reactions other factors such as the sociocultural environment, personality, and contemporary non-work environment must be taken into consideration.

Given the potential use of the stress audit as an indicator of organizational health, careful study is needed to understand the multiplexity of these influences in order to prevent concentration on simple causal relationships. This will further the development of organizational theory and design and will narrow the gap between ideal conceptualizations about organizations and organizational reality. Personality variables (life history, personality dimensions, traits, defensive structures, etc.), sociocultural variables (e.g., ethnicity, social class, dietary habits, religion, etc.), and non-work environmental variables (e.g., critical events in an individual's personal life) cannot be ignored in an overall view of an individual's well-being.[1] Figure 12–1 illustrates a multifactoral model of symptom response.

THE STRESS AUDIT

In setting up an organizational stress audit a distinction can be made among three categories of variables: causal stress variables (the stressors), mediating variables (the effects of personality, culture, and contemporary non-work environment), and end-result variables (the stress reactions). Causal organizational variables are independent variables that can be effected by the organization and its management. We can summarize these stressors under the headings of organizational design variables, interpersonal variables, and career variables.[2] The end result variables reflect the outcome of the combined effect of stressors and mediating variables on organization and individual. We are referring here to both individual stress reactions of a psychosomatic and psychoneurotic nature, and to dysfunctional

[1]For a discussion of the personality, culture, and non-work environment effect see Kets de Vries (1977).

[2]Excellent examples of summaries of organizational stressors are the reviews of French and Caplan (1973), Cooper and Marshall (1976), Beehr and Newman (1978), and Schuler in this Handbook.

Figure 12-2. Organizational Factors Contributing to Stress.

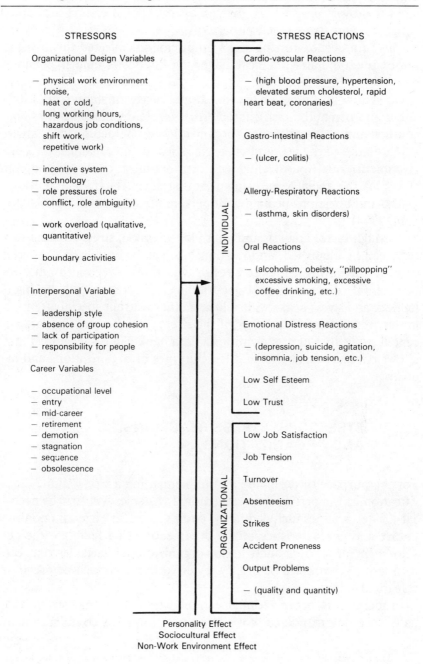

organizational patterns such as morale, absenteeism, strikes, and labor turnover. Figure 12–2 gives an overview of stressors, mediating variables, and stress reaction patterns.

The data needed for the stress audit can be collected through the use of questionnaires, clinical-diagnostic interviews, and if possible, physiological examinations. A typical questionnaire should include a stress-symptom survey, an organizational survey (including questions about job demands, task characteristics, role demands such as role conflict and role ambiguity, organizational characteristics, career, performance variables, and characteristics of the organization's environment), questions dealing with extraorganizational variables, for example, the social readjustment rating scale (Holmes and Rahe, 1967), and questions dealing with personality (Friedman and Rosenman, 1974).[3]

Through factor analysis and multiple regression, stress-reaction patterns can be identified, and relationships can be established between causal, mediating, and end-result variables. Occupational, departmental, divisional, and geographical differences will be highlighted, and stress peaks will be located that warrant special attention in the organization. Moreover, if the stress audit becomes a more accepted procedure in organizations a data bank can be developed that allows comparisons between different types of organizations and industries.

STRESSORS, STRESS REACTIONS, AND ORGANIZATIONS

For the purpose of designing and implementing a stress audit, identification of the pertinent organizational variables will first be necessary. The variables included in the audit will differ depending on the nature and characteristics of the organization. To facilitate the development of a stress audit major organizational variables that can turn into stressors will be briefly reviewed in the context of previous research findings.

In identifying organizational variables we realize that an individual's specific attitude to work is a reflection of a combination of

[3]For an example of a completed stress audit and specific instruments used see Kets de Vries et al., 1976; Zaleznik et al., 1977.

factors in which occupational level, socialization patterns, position in the career life cycle, and work content are important. Technological changes put additional pressures upon the individual. Employees of organizations in transition or organizations experiencing rapid growth can be subjected to severe hardships. Turbulence in the environment has its own repercussions in organizations. The vicissitudes of organizational life may come with feelings of isolation, frustration, and helplessness. The increasing demands for mobility and travel placed upon executives can also cause problems at home. Managers have to make choices between work and leisure time. The process of aging is not without its strains, given the premium placed upon youth. Job obsolescence and redundancy can become a grim reality for middle-aged executives.

We should realize too that a certain amount of stress in organizations is necessary. An organization completely without stress becomes complacent, disregards environmental danger signs, and may soon be on the road to bankruptcy. Excessive stress, though, can be dysfunctional. Naturally, the threshold of stress varies with the individual. We may find that specific types of people flock to particular occupations with the most compatible stress levels. Misfits drop out and find more agreeable types of jobs, or, if they persist in stressful occupations (in cases of an inadequate fit between individual and position), they may suffer from coronary heart disease and die prematurely. It is these personality differences that make "stress engineering" such a difficult endeavor.

The infra- and supra-structure of organizations, which involve such relationships as hierarchy of authority, departmentalization, organizational goals, control and information systems, workflow, technology, and degree of differentiation or integration, can be a great source of stress. These design parameters raise questions about the nature of the work environment, role pressures, work overload, and boundary spanning activities.

The Nature of the Work

Physical conditions of the work environment can produce stress, and this has been indicated by many physiological experiments and observations of work under adverse conditions (Landy and Trumbo, 1976). Factors such as noise, heat and cold, long working hours, shift work, repetitive work, and hazardous work can be stressful. In addition, the way in which incentive systems are designed can be stress-producing. Piece-rate renumeration and rapidly changing technology in the work setting have their own stress-inducing effects.

Ferguson (1973), for example, has described how Australian tele-graphists complained that the monotony, repetitiveness, and machine-pacing of their job was responsible for such stress reactions as insomnia, headaches, peptic ulcers, indigestion, heart attacks, high blood pressure, and asthma. When the symptom rate of the telegraphists was compared to that of a group of mail sorters operating under more relaxed working conditions, the rate of stress symptoms among the telegraphists proved to be substantially higher.

Another study found that the incidence of hypertension, peptic ulcers, and diabetes among air-traffic controllers was higher than among a control group consisting of second-class airmen (Cobb and Rose, 1973). Stress symptoms were particularly substantial among those working in high-density traffic centers. There thus seems to be a consistent body of research indicating that the nature of the work, conditions under which work takes place (such as the incentive system), and technology play a role in the etiology of stress reactions.

Role Pressures

The way in which organizations are structured can also contribute to stress: infra- and supra-structure will determine the degree of conflict and ambiguity experienced by the individual. For example, Kahn and his associates (1964) introduced the concepts of role conflict and role ambiguity in the study of stress reactions in organizations. They defined role conflict as "the simultaneous occurrence of two (or more) sets of pressures such that compliance with one would make more difficult compliance with the other" (p. 19). Role ambiguity was conceived as "the degree to which required information is available to a given organizational position" (p. 25). Kahn discovered that if the information is insufficient to assist an individual in the execution of his job, role ambiguity is experienced:

> The emotional costs of role conflict for the focal person include low job satisfaction, low confidence in the organization, and a high degree of job-related tension. A very frequent behavioral response to role conflict is withdrawal (p. 380).

The individual consequences of ambiguity are in general comparable to the individual effects of role conflict. These include . . . low job satisfaction, low self-esteem, a high sense of futility, and a high score on the tension index (p. 254).

The high incidence of ulcers among foremen (compared to skilled and unskilled blue-collar workers, and executives) is a good example of stress reactions where the effects of role conflict and role ambiguity are noticeable (Vertin, 1954; Dunn and Cobb, 1962). Foremen usually are exposed to conflicting demands from both superiors and subordinates. This, in combination with ambiguity about their position, puts them under considerable pressure.

In a study carried out at the Goddard Space Flight Center the original research strategy of Kahn and his associates was expanded by taking physiological measures of job strain such as pulse rate, blood pressure, and blood samples. A strong relationship was found between degree of role conflict and heart rate. In addition, there was an association between role conflict and a number of physical symptoms indicating anxiety, such as insomnia, nervousness, and hard breathing (Caplan, 1971).

House and Rizzo (1972) in a study of research, development, and engineering personnel discovered that a high degree of role conflict was related to low satisfaction with adequacy of authority, job security, and recognition. In addition, these individuals reported a higher level of job-induced anxiety, tension and feelings of uneasiness, and general fatigue. Individuals subjected to a high level of role ambiguity reported similar experiences.

These studies suggest that role conflict and role ambiguity can be stress-producing. The degree to which role pressure affects stress remains unclear because of the influence of the intervening personality, and sociocultural and non-work environment effects.

Work Overload

This conflict can be divided into quantitative overload (the sum total of all the work that has to be done) and qualitative overload (what the job requires in skills, ability, and knowledge beyond the person's capacity). In both cases, extremes of either too much or too little work, or too easy or too difficult work, can be stress-inducing.

A study involving professors and administrators concluded that both quantitative and qualitative work overload was related to job tension (French, Tupper, and Mueller, 1965). A high association was also discovered between achievement orientation and serum uric acid (related to gout and possibly associated with coronary heart disease).

In a laboratory experiment performed by Sales (1969), overload was related to an increase in serum cholesterol. Underload was also associated with mean increases in cholesterol. When underload as such was not experienced by the subjects, a decrease in serum cholesterol level was observed. The Goddard study (Caplan, 1971) found a relationship between cigarette smoking and overload. Moreover, overload was substantially related to heart rate and serum cholesterol.

The association of overload and stress concurs with the Type A individual who habitually lives under time pressures and is very achievement-oriented (Friedman and Rosenman, 1974). The achievement orientation of Type A personalities may result in acceptance of increasingly larger and more difficult tasks that are impossible to complete. This will put these individuals under continuous strain, and eventually lead to stress reactions.

Boundary-spanning Activities

Individuals occupying positions at the organization's boundaries are potentially susceptible to a considerably higher degree of conflict and ambiguity. We refer here both to external boundaries (the dividing line between organization and environment) and intra-organizational boundaries. In the latter case, we are dealing with individuals who interact regularly with more than one organizational sub-unit. A project manager in a matrix organization is a typical example. The nature of the job requires continually crossing the boundaries of such departments as research and development, engineering, production, marketing, and sales, in addition to coordinating activities with people from outside the organization. Another typical example would be the systems analyst.

Boundary-spanning activities performed by these examples of "integrators" may be stressful. Ambiguity is an intricate part of these individuals' lives. And the potential for conflict tends to increase with the degree of organizational differentiation (Miles, 1976). Moreover, as indicated in discussing role conflict and role ambiguity, a relationship with stress symptoms exists. For example, in the Goddard study, individuals in an alien environment (administrators in an engineering environment) showed higher blood pressure and faster pulse rate than the predominating occupational group (Caplan, 1971). A word of caution, however, is needed. A boundary state does not necessarily imply an adverse situation. It can also be looked upon in a positive way—as a reward for demonstrated excellence with quite different effects. Here, again, we should not lose sight of the multifactorial nature of stress. Studies on boundary activities and stress indicate that particular personality variables are as important as intermediate factors (Keller and Holland, 1975; Miles, 1976). Individual threshold to stress will affect incidence of stress reactions.

Interpersonal Processes

From the time of the Hawthorne study onward, literature on organizational behavior has emphasized the importance of interpersonal relations, group processes, and leadership style as variables influencing motivation, attitudes, satisfaction, and productivity. These studies suggest an association between interpersonal relations and stress reactions. A dominant theme in many of them has been that members of cohesive groups are more capable of dealing with stressful conditions than members of loosely structured groups (Stouffer et al., 1949; Janis, 1958; Golembiewski, 1965).

Signs of organizational stress can be manifold. Sudden increases in vertical and lateral interpersonal communication can be taken as warning signs of problems related to interpersonal processes. Complete withdrawal from interaction would be another indication. In some instances we find a change in the content of interaction. The nature of participation and responsibility are other examples of the interdependency between interpersonal processes and stress.

Participation

Apart from supportive-group interaction acting as a buffer against the development of stress symptoms, relationships between stress and leadership style can be found. For example, Oaklander and Fleishman (1964) found a negative relationship between inter-unit stress and considerate leadership (defined as participation in decisionmaking and encouragement of two-way communication). This finding has been supported by a number of other studies (Hall and Lawler, 1970; Cummings and DeCotiis, 1973). French (1973) emphasized the buffering function of good superior-subordinate relationships. He discovered a significant positive relation between role ambiguity and serum cortisol in those who had poor relationships with their subordinates. This pattern disappeared when relationships were good.

French and Caplan (1973: 51) argued that increased "participation is an efficient way of reducing many other stresses which also lead to psychological strain." Referring to the Goddard study, they reported that individuals who participated intensively in decisionmaking were satisfied and scored high on feelings of self-esteem and self-worth. These researchers emphasized the importance of participation in decisionmaking, but only if the participants were dealing with substantive issues, as opposed to engagement in ritualistic, non-essential forms of decisionmaking. Participation offers control over one's destiny, and this mastery of uncertainty seems to have a stress-reducing effect.

We might add, though, that participation can also cause stress. Some individuals may be frustrated by the delays often associated with shared decisionmaking. Moreover, managers may view shared decisionmaking and delegation of responsibility as a threat to the traditional rights of management. Depending on the intensity of this experience, stress may be the consequence. In addition, participation can lead to new forms of confrontation, again with possible stress.

The Nature of Responsibility

Other studies indicate that responsibility for people can be stress-producing. A prime example is the high incidence of stress reactions among physicians. Alcoholism and suicide rate is unusually high among this occupational group (Lamott, 1975). Drug addiction is estimated as being between thirty to sixty times greater than that of the general population (Rensberger, 1977). Variations in stress symptoms occur within the medical profession depending on specialization. An increase in life and death responsibility seems to coincide with an increase in symptom rate. For example, anesthesiologists and general practitioners report a coronary heart disease rate that is two to three times higher than the rate in dermatologists and pathologists (Russek, 1960). Suicide rates are more than three times as high among psychiatrists than among radiologists (Lamott, 1975). These differences may reflect the fact that psychiatrists have a very high life and death responsibility, but only limited control over the actions of their patients. This can be a source of great frustration and may be a contributing factor to stress reactions.

The Goddard study (Caplan, 1971) showed a strong relationship between degree of responsibility for others, and intensity of cigarette smoking and high diastolic blood pressure. If an individual's responsibility was more directed toward things rather than toward people, diastolic blood pressure declined. It was also observed that in situations where a person had either more responsibility for the work of others than desired, or less responsibility than desired, serum cholesterol levels tended to be higher than when desired responsibility matched given responsibility. Apparently, both the nature of the responsibility and the match between desired and given responsibility are related to stress reactions. These studies also suggest that control over the organizational environment makes for congruence of aspirations and achievement. The outcome can be a lessening of frustration and limitation or absence of stress symptoms.

That responsibility for people can be stressful has been seen in the previously cited examples of foremen and air-traffic controllers, both occupations with a high responsibility for others. Cobb (1973: 13) argued that there exists "scattered evidence that diabetes, hypertension, and myocardial infarction as well as peptic (presumably duodenal) ulcer are unduly common among persons subject to heavy, close personal responsibility for the lives of other people."

Occupational Level

In studying all first-admissions in the state of Ohio's prolonged-care mental hospitals, Frumkin (1955) found a much higher incidence of psychosis, schizophrenia, and alcoholism among individuals in lower-level occupations.[4]

---

[4]The argument can be used that problems in diagnosis might have biased these results. The higher occupational brackets may have easier access to more intensive medical care which makes for more reliable diagnoses.

Gurin and his associates (1960), after classifying eight occupational levels, discovered that people in the lower-level occupations had high scores on the physical health symptom factor, but he also found that professionals and technicians possessed a relatively high incidence of psychological anxiety symptoms. Another stress reaction, respiratory problems, appears to have a much higher occurrence among lower-level occupations than among the higher professional and managerial ones (Fuentes and Kendrick, 1968). Naturally, unsafe and unhealthy working conditions can be contributing variables.

In the three-year study of coronary thrombosis by Pell and D'Alonso (1961), the lowest incidence of this disorder was found to be among executives and the highest incidence among lower-salaried clerical workers. This finding has not been unique. A coronary disease study of the Bell Telephone System suggested that employees "who attain the highest level of management as a group do not have a higher risk of coronary heart disease than (those) who remain at lower levels" (Hinkle et al., 1968: 245; Jenkins, 1971). In addition, this study indicated that education seemed to play a role in the etiology of cardiovascular disorders. Individuals who entered the organization with a college degree had a lower coronary symptom rate. Moreover, "men promoted to high levels, men promoted rapidly, men promoted recently, and men transferred to new jobs, to new departments, or to new companies in new geographic areas have no higher rates of coronary heart disease than comparable men who have not had these experiences" (Hinkle et al., 1968: 243). Given the pressures associated with the uprooting experience, this finding seems even more remarkable. Other forces seem to neutralize the stressful effects of uprooting. An important one seems to be career progression, an experience that can create a degree of resistance to stress. Success in one's career may be perceived as control over one's destiny and can serve as a buffer to lessen frustration and combat stress.

In comparing 1,171 executives with 1,203 nonexecutives in the New York City area over a five-year period, Lee and Schneider (1958) discovered that the incidence of hypertension and arteriosclerotic heart disease was lower in the executive group. In a factory study Kornhauser (1965) found poorer mental health among the lower echelon of factory workers. Kasl and French (1962), in studying two companies, found an inverse relationship between skill level and dispensary visits, the latter interpreted by them as a measurement of mental and physical health.

As far as coronary heart disease is concerned, the amount of physical activity on the job becomes an important intervening variable and may disprove the general trend of a higher symptom rate among lower-level occupations. Occupations requiring physical activity have lower rates of coronary heart disease than those occupations at the same status level where this is not a factor (Kasl and French, 1962: 70). A recent study of California dock workers underlines this point. The workers with low-energy-demanding jobs had a disproportionately high percentage of fatal heart attacks as compared to the group engaged in heavy physical activity (New York Times, 1977: E7). In addition, we should not de-emphasize (particularly in relationship to coronary heart disease) differences in dietary practices by occupational and educational level or social class.

We can find a consistent pattern among these various studies: a higher incidence of stress reactions seems to occur among the lower-level occupations. The reasons for these differences can be manifold. We can blame variations in dietary practices by occupational level, unhealthy and unsafe working conditions, diagnostic problems, or the experience of helplessness in controlling the events of the working environment. An exception is the unusually high incidence of peptic ulcers among foremen who are exposed to an extremely high degree of role conflict and role ambiguity, and therefore seem to be in a special position.

Career Obstacles

Three points in the career life cycle seem to be particularly stressful, entry, mid-career, and retirement (Hall, 1976; Kets de Vries, 1980). Many individuals experience career entry with a sense of reality shock. A conflict arises between high expectations and frustrating, on-the-job experiences. Frequently, the new recruit is exposed to very little challenge, and the predictable outcome is boredom with the job. Stress reactions may result. A poor "fit" between individual and job also can be the result of a wrong choice of occupation, or caused by a job is beyond the capabilities of the individual.

Mid-career stress can be considered an outcome of what is sometimes described as the mid-life crisis. It is a time when a person becomes more aware of physical aging and the increasing proximity of death. With this realization comes an assessment of one's accomplishments in meeting original career goals. Many managers are left with feelings of disappointment and frustration, because a plateau has been reached in their career. The executive's position accentuates the notion of being "early" or "late" on the "career clock" (given Western society's emphasis on career progression) and emphasizes this sense of frustration. In addition, competition for a limited number of positions, given the organizational pyramid, is unavoidable and will be stressful for the majority of managers. Mid-career is also the period when job obsolescence becomes noticeable. Low job satisfaction and morale, absenteeism, and decreased productivity will be side effects. For some it will mean that their role in the organization has become untenable.

Approaching retirement creates other forms of stress. With society's association of career with personal identity, retirement can be traumatic. It raises images of being useless, of being discarded on the scrapheap. It is also a time when one reviews one's own career. For some managers this is a despairing experience when the feeling prevails that one's one and only life has been a failure and a waste.

Demotion or dismissal is often associated with stress reactions (Kasl, Gore, and Cobb, 1975), because these incidents raise questions about self-worth and identity. Depending on an individual's threshold to stress, these events may be the last ones in a string of incidents pushing the person to illness.

Anticipation of job loss or demotion can be even more stressful than the event itself (Kasl and Cobb, 1970; Kasl et al., 1975). This has been demonstrated in a study of parachute jumpers. Greater stress was experienced before these parachutists left the airplane, not while falling through the air (Fenz and Epstein, 1967). Another fairly common example of anticipatory stress is the period before exams. Possessing accurate information reduces anticipatory fear and the "work of worrying." This results in expectations that are more accurate, and the dramatic impact of hostility, depression, and other stress symptoms is subsequently cushioned (Janis, 1958).

Career change can be extremely stressful. Often a major re-orientation in lifestyle is in order, especially if a geographical move is involved. Retraining is not without its stress since it usually brings the individual into unknown domains and promotes a sense of helplessness. Job rotation can have the same effects.

In describing possible sources of organizational stress, we have emphasized the intervening effects of the personality, society, and nonwork environment in a stress audit. Simple causal relationships between organizational variables and stress do not exist. An important organizational variable that can influence an individual's threshold to stress, however, does stand out. This seems to be the degree of control a person can exert over his work environmént. If the individual experiences a sense of powerlessness in affecting organizational life, susceptibility to stress seems to increase. We will elaborate on this phenomenon using a Canadian study as illustration.

THE THREAPEUTIC NATURE OF THE POSSESSION OF POWER

In two Canadian studies (Kets de Vries et al., 1976; Zaleznik et al., 1977) differences were found in stress-reaction patterns among occupational groups. These differences were compatible with findings in the previously-mentioned organizational studies describing stress levels according to occupational groups. In those studies the higher-level occupational groups showed the lowest incidence of stress symptoms (compared to staff and the lower level operations group).

These findings do not conform to the popular image of the manager as the primary victim of stress reactions. In the Canadian studies this difference in relative health was largely explained by introducing the notion of a "power effect." According to Zaleznik, Kets de Vries, and Howard (1977: 159):

> Power may be viewed as the potential to induce change in organizational processes in a formal and informal sense and to affect goal achievement. Clearly management perceives itself favorably in the expectation of not only retaining the power it now holds, but of realizing an increase in the future. Apart from the reality of new power accumulated, the positive expectation asserts the sense of self-esteem derived from a belief in one's strategic location in the social space of an organization. Obviously, expectancy ultimately depends on reality, suggesting that management's conviction of its power position squares with the actual outcomes of changes in the distribution of power.

Managers (particularly the successful ones) have a considerable amount of control and influence over their environment; they have the greatest opportunity to decrease the distance between aspirations and achievement. Reduction of uncertainty, through control over information and people can be considered a countervailing force to feelings of helplessness. It encourages self-esteem and seems to have considerable therapeutic value. This concurs with an earlier statement that control over one's environment may have a stress-reducing impact. We can draw a similar inference from our previous comments on stress reactions and personality and from our overview of organizational variables. The notion of a "giving up–given up complex" can be considered another piece of supportive evidence (Engel, 1971; Schmale, 1972). Studies using locus of control over environment point in the same direction. In these studies a strong relationship is suggested between low self-esteem, anxiety, and externality.[5] An experimental study by Pennebaker et al. (1977) that looked at the relationship between control over the environment and incidence of stress symptoms arrived at a similar conclusion. Experimentally-induced lack of control was a cause of reported physical symptoms. These findings concur with Seligman's conclusion that control over the environment acts as a countervailing force to helplessness. In an extensive review of both experimental work on animals and case histories of individuals, Seligman discovered that "when subjects believe they are controlling events, even when they are not, anxiety is lessened" (1975: 129). Predictability and controllability seem to reduce anxiety and prevent the manifestation of stress symptoms. Other studies have supported the notion that power and control over organizational environment lessen stress reactions. Tosi (1971) indicated that in fairly stable, predictable environments a higher level of influence will reduce job anxiety.

In one experimental setting the role of feedback in avoiding stress reactions has been emphasized (Weiss, 1972). This study suggests that the power effect operates only adequately if relevant continuous feedback is part of the process. Control alone, without feedback, is insufficient in combatting stress. Lack of feedback increases uncertainty and is associated with a sense of helplessness and frustration that can give way to stress reactions.

In the Canadian study management had the most power and control in the organization. Managers were more aware and better informed of the realities of organizational life. They knew how to use organizational variables to their advantage and, consequently, experienced limited frustration within the work environment as compared

---

[5]Externals experience a great sense of powerlessness perceiving themselves to be at the mercy of the environment versus internals who view themselves as to be in control of their destiny (Phares, 1976).

to other occupational groups. Dysfunctional side effects of the bureaucracy, such as ritualistic attachment to rules, depersonalization of work, the avoidance of face-to-face confrontation, alienation, apathy, and general resistance to change, were more easily dealt with by this group. In contrast, the other occupational groups felt burdened by considerable pressure, high accountability, red tape, uncertainty, lack of coordination, ambivalence about leadership, and performance evaluation. Their problems in dealing with the organizational task environment (the perceived unpredictability of events, their inability to handle the power effect, and their frustration in finding a way through the maze of the organizational bureaucracy) contributed to the high incidence of stress reactions.

We are faced here with a kind of paradox. Bureaucratic practices would seem to restrict or set safeguards against the abuses of power (Crozier, 1964). But confrontations with the bureaucracy, its red tape, and its rules and regulations, may result in reactions of helplessness and stress. Through the abuse of power, managers can induce stress in their subordinates, and for the person in charge, control over subordinates can have a stress-reducing effect. It is responsibility without control that gives rise to stress. Sudden, unanticipated alterations in the organizational environment or unpredictable actions on the part of superiors contribute to the onset of stress.

We are all familiar with the quietly aggressive supervisor who picks an ulcer-prone subordinate. For the supervisor, the possession of power may serve as a buffer against stress, but apparently at the subordinate's expense. The superior is not the one who suffers from ulcers or a heart attack; rather, the superior is the one who gives them.

This paradoxical situation raises a number of questions about the prevention of stress. Some people may argue that organizational stress is unavoidable. Actually, a moderate amount of stress is necessary for organizations to continue functioning. An excess though is to be avoided. But even in situations of moderate organizational stress, wide discrepancies can occur in its distribution. Some individuals will be victimized. The name of the organizational game becomes one of gaining control over the organization's environment. This contributes to the competitiveness of life in organizations.

If we view power in organizations as a zero-sum game, the inevitable conclusion is that some individuals lose out—the ones most susceptible to stress. However, a counterargument is occasionally heard.

Real power-sharing and participation in decisionmaking is viewed by some as a realistic alternative that can reduce competitiveness. These advocates consider participation as the only way to limit the incidence of stress reactions for everybody without the need for "losers" and "winners." In their opinion this makes for more effective organizations where the value of cooperation is recognized.

Apart from its democratic appeal, these statements carry an element of truth and have important implications for organizational design and development. Some people, however, are more cynical about the role of power and warn about the dangers of co-optation and the addiction of people to positions of power (Mulder, 1975). Participation may degenerate into a ritual without any substantive meaning.

The truth about ways of dealing with the power effect probably lies somewhere in between. Whatever the answer might be, a better understanding of it will be helpful in finding new ways of adapting to stress and reducing a manager's susceptibility. The power effect seems to be a very important organizational variable in combatting stress and should be taken into consideration in a stress audit.

CONCLUDING COMMENTS

We have emphasized the importance of the power effect in the etiology of organizational stress. Role conflict, role ambiguity, and work overload are closely related stress-inducing factors. Boundary activities have to be considered as another source of conflict. All these factors should be covered in a stress audit.

Many of these stress-inducing conditions evolve from the nature of the infra- and supra-structure which in turn are strongly influenced by the power effect. But regardless of the organizational design, uncertainty over organizational processes will always remain; only the degree of uncertainty can be modified. To combat the harmful effects of these structural arrangements we may need a reallocation of workload that is compatible with capability, a restructuring of organizational units, and a clarification of tasks and responsibilities. Openness and trust in organizations become a priority. A free flow of information reduces uncertainty and has an impact on the incidence of stress. Realistic feedback on performance is also advisable. And it should be kept in mind that the avoidance of honest feedback (because of fear of confrontation) will, in the long-run, have a far more stressful impact than the cost of doing unpleasant "housecleaning" immediately. Criteria for evaluation and promotion should be clearly spelled out.

The physical design of work environments, compensation standards, work flow, and technology may need modifications. Responsiveness to complaints is another important issue. Changes in decisionmaking patterns and leadership style is in some instances advisable, particularly when leadership is perceived as unpredictable. Distribution of authority and participation in decisionmaking can have beneficial effects in view of what we know about the consequences of the power effect. This change can be difficult, however, given the addiction to power that often occurs.

As we can see, many factors seem to be responsible in the etiology of stress reactions. Organizational life is only one of the elements. Although the stress audit is a more sensitive indicator of an organization's health than the traditional attitude scale, the introduction of the stress audit does not simplify the life of the manager. On the contrary, it introduces the manager to a new dimension of management with a far greater degree of complexity. But it will make the manager also aware of the futility of resorting to overly simplistic, patch-up approaches to organizational design and development devoid of any realistic assessment of organizational functioning. An understanding of the complexity of the interchange between individual and environment that is guided by a stress audit will make for more effective intervention strategies and contribute to better performance and improved quality of work life.

REFERENCES

Beehr, T.A., and J.E. Newman. 1978. "Job Stress, Employee Health, and Organizational Effectiveness: A Facet Analysis, Model, and Literature Review." *Personnel Psychology* 31.

Caplan, R.D. 1971. *Organizational Stress and Individual Strain: A Socio-Psychological Study of Risk Factors in Coronary Heart Disease Among Administrators, Engineers, and Scientists*. Ph.D. dissertation, University of Michigan.

Cobb, Sidney. 1973. "Role Responsibility: The Differentiation of a Concept." *Occupational Mental Health* 3, no. 1: 10–14.

Cobb, Sidney, and Robert M. Rose. 1973. "Hypertension, Peptic Ulcer, and Diabetes in Air Traffic Controllers." *Journal of the American Medical Association* 224, no. 4.

Cooper, C.L., and J. Marshall. 1976. "Occupational Sources of Stress: A Review of the Literature Relating to Coronary Heart Disease and Mental Ill Health." *Journal of Occupational Psychology* 49: 11–18.

Crozier, Michael. 1964. *The Bureaucratic Phenomenon*. Chicago: University of Chicago Press.

Cummings, L.L., and T.A. Decotiis. 1973. "Organizational Correlates of Perceived Stress in a Professional Organization." *Public Personnel Management* July-August: 275–282.

Dunn, James P., and Sidney Cobb. 1962. "Frequency of Peptic Ulcer Among Executives, Craftsmen, and Foremen." *Journal of Occupational Medicine* 4, no. 7: 343–348.

Engel, George L. 1971. "Sudden and Rapid Death During Psychological Stress." *Annals of Internal Medicine* 74: 771–782.

Fenz, W.D., and S. Epstein. 1967. "Gradients of Physiological Arousal in Parachutists as a Function of an Approaching Jump." *Psychosomatic Medicine* 29, no. 1.

Ferguson, D. 1973. "A Study of Occupational Stress." *Ergonomics* 16: 649–664.

French, John R.P., Jr. 1973. "Person Role Fit." *Occupational Mental Health* 3, no. 1: 15–20.

French, John R.P., Jr., and Robert D. Caplan. 1973. "Organizational Stress and Individual Strain." In *The Failure of Success*, edited by Alfred J. Marrow. New York: AMACOM.

French, John R.P., Jr.; C.J. Tupper; and E.F. Mueller. 1965. *Working Load of University Professors*. Cooperative Research Project No. 2171, University of Michigan.

Friedman, Meyer, and Ray H. Rosenman. 1974. *Type A Behavior and Your Heart*. New York: Alfred A. Knopf.

Frumkin, Robert M. 1955. "Occupation and Major Mental Disorder." In *Mental Health and Mental Disorder*, edited by A. Rose. New York: W.W. Norton.

Fuentes, Roberto, and Mildred A. Kendrick. 1968. "Occupations Associated with Disabling Respiratory Conditions." *Journal of Occupational Medicine* 10, no. 8: 386–391.

Golembiewski, Robert T. 1965. "Small Groups and Large Organizations." In *Handbook of Organizations*, edited by James G. March. Chicago: Rand McNally.

Gurin, Gerald; Joseph Veroff; and Sheila Feld. 1960. *Americans View Their Mental Health*. New York: Basic Books.

Hall, Douglas T. 1976. *Careers in Organizations*. Pacific Palisades: Good-year Publishing Company.

Hall, Douglas T., and E.E. Lawler, III. 1970. "Job Characteristics and Pressures and the Organizational Integration of Professionals." *Administrative Science Quarterly* vol. 15: 271–281.

Hinkle, Lawrence E., Jr.; L.H. Whitney; and E.W. Lehman. 1968. "Occupation, Education, and Coronary Heart Disease." *Science* 161: 238–246.

Holmes, Thomas H., and Richard H. Rahe. 1967. "The Social Readjustment Rating Scale." *Journal of Psychosomatic Research* 11: 213–218.

House, R.J., and J.R. Rizzo. 1972. "Role Conflict and Ambiguity as Critical Variables in a Model of Organizational Behavior." *Organizational Behavior and Human Performance*, 7: 467–505.

Janis, I.L. 1958. *Psychological Stress*. New York: John Wiley and Sons.

Jenkins, C. David. 1971. "Psychological and Social Precursors of Coronary Disease, Part II." *The New England Journal of Medicine* 284, no. 6.

Kahn, R., D.M. Wolfe; R.P. Quinn; and J.D. Snoek. 1964. *Organizational Stress*. New York: John Wiley and Sons.

Kasl, Stanislav V., and John R.P. French, Jr. 1962. "The Effects of Occupational Status in Physical and Mental Health." *Journal of Social Issues* 43, July.

Kasl, Stanislav V., and Sidney Cobb. 1970. "Blood Pressure Changes in Men Undergoing Job Loss: A Prelminary Report." *Psychosomatic Medicine* 32, no. 1: 19–38.

Kasl, Stanislav V.; Susan Gore; and Sidney Cobb. 1975. "The Experience of Losing a Job: Reported Changes in Health, Symptoms and Illness Behavior." *Psychosomatic Medicine* 37, no. 2: 106–122.

Keller, R.T., and W.E. Holland. 1975. "Boundary-Spanning Roles in a Research and Development Organization: An Empirical Investigation." *Academy of Management Journal* 18: 388–393.

Kets De Vries, Manfred F.R. 1977. "Organizations and Stress Reactions." In *Behavioral Issues in Management*, edited by R. Kanungo and H. Jain. Toronto: McGraw-Hill.

Kets De Vries, Manfred F.R. 1980. *Organizational Paradoxes: Clinical Approaches to Management*. London: Tavistock.

Kets De Vries, Manfred F.R.; Abraham Zaleznik; and John Howard. 1976. "Stress Reactions and Organizations: The Minotaur Revisited." McGill University Faculty of Management Working Paper, no. 7530.

Kornhauser, A. 1965. *Mental Health of the Industrial Worker: A Detroit Study*. New York: John Wiley and Sons.

Lamott, Kenneth. 1975. *Escape from Stress*. New York: Berkley Medallion Books.

Landy, Frank J., and Don A. Trumbo. 1976. *Psychology of Work Behavior*. Homewood, Ill.: The Dorsey Press.

Lee, R.E., and R.A. Schneider. 1958. "Hypertension and Arteriosclerosis in Executive and Non-Executive Personnel." *Journal of the American Medical Association* 167: 1447–1450.

Miles, Robert H. 1976. "Role Requirements as Sources of Organizational Stress." *Journal of Applied Psychology* 61, no. 2: 172–179.

Mulder, Mauk. 1975. *Het Spel om de Macht*. Meppel: Boom.

New York Times. 1977. "The Life of Vigor." March 27, p. E8.

Oaklander, H., and E.A. Fleishman. 1964. "Patterns of Leadership in Hospital Settings." *Administrative Science Quarterly* 8: 520–532.

Pell, S., and C.A. D'Alonso. 1961. "Three Year Study of Coronary Thrombosis in Employed Populations." *Journal of the American Medical Association* 175: 463–470.

Pennebaker, James W.; M. Audrey Burnam; Marc A. Schaeffer; and David C. Harper. 1977. "Lack of Control as a Determinant of Perceived Physical Symptoms." *Journal of Personality and Social Psychology* 35, no. 3: 167–174.

Phares, E. Jerry. 1976. *Locus of Control in Personality*. Morristown, New Jersey: General Learning Press.

Rensberger, Boyce. 1977. "The Doctors Who Need the Care of Other Doctors." *The New York Times*, May 1, p. E8.

Rogers, Rolf E. 1975. "Executive Stress." *Human Resource Management*, Fall.

Russek, H.I. 1960. "Emotional Stress and Coronary Heart Disease in American Physicians." *American Journal of Medical Sciences* 240.

Sales, Stephen M. 1969. "Organizational Role as a Risk Factor in Coronary Disease." *Administrative Science Quarterly* 14, no. 3: 325–335.

Schmale, A.H. 1972. "Giving up as a Final Common Pathway to Changes in Health." *Advances in Psychosomatic Medicine* 8: 20–40.

Seligman, M.E.P. 1975. *Helplessness: On Depression, Development, and Death*. San Francisco: W.H. Freeman.

Stouffer, Samuel A.; Arthur A. Lumsdaine; Marion Harper Lumsdaine; Robin M. Williams, Jr.; M. Brewster Smith; Irvin L. Janis; Shirley Star; and Leonard S. Cottrell, Jr. 1949. *The American Soldier: Combat and its Aftermath: Studies in Social Psychology in World War II*, Vol. II. Princeton: Princeton University Press.

Tosi, Henry. 1971. "Organization Stress as a Moderator of the Relationship Between Influence and Role Response." *Academy of Management Journal*, March: 7–20.

Vertin, P.G. 1954. *Bedrijfsgeneeskundige Aspecten van het Ulcus Pepticum*. Groningen: Thesis.

Weiss, Jay M. 1972. "Psychological Factors in Stress and Disease." *Scientific American*, June: 104–113.

Zaleznik, Abraham; Manfred F.R. Kets De Vries; and John Howard. 1977. "Stress Reactions in Organizations: Syndromes, Causes, and Consequences." *Behavioral Science* 22: 151–162.

13 STRESS COPING RESEARCH: METHODOLOGICAL ISSUES

Terry A. Beehr

Knowledge about stress[1] in both the work and nonwork domains of individuals' lives has been increasing dramatically in recent years. There is scarcely an adult in North America today who has not heard of stress and who does not believe that he or she knows what it is to be stressed. Reports of studies on occupational stress often lead us to the tempting conclusion that there is no job that is exempt from the pressures of stress. While it appears that there is a common belief that many aspects of life are stressful, stress researchers, the professionals working to reduce harmful effects of stress, and the consumers of both the research information and the professional services need to know what to believe and what not to believe about this mushrooming topic. This is why it is important for many groups of people to understand some of the most basic aspects of research in the behavioral sciences. Without this basic understanding, even the most dedicated and concerned people among us cannot be wise consumers, researchers, or practitioners in this complex area.

---

[1]The use of the word stress in the scientific and applied literature has been inconsistent (Beehr and Newman, 1978). In this chapter, stressor refers to an environmental characteristic or event that is thought to cause adverse physical or psychological consequences for a person. Strain refers to these adverse consequences to the individual. Stress is the term used to refer to the general domain of research and professional practice regarding stressors and strains.

It is obvious that researchers need to know the techniques of behavioral investigation in order to do their work, but it is also important for the rest of the public interested in stress to understand it to some extent. The practitioner must choose from among a myriad of coping techniques those that are most likely to be successful with a particular client or group of clients and in a specific situation, and the consumer of such services must be able to choose a self-help technique or a professional consultant intelligently. A basic understanding of research methods can help both these types of people to ask intelligent questions and to evaluate the answers, the advertising, and the other information available about stress coping or stress management. It is evaluation research that helps lead to improvement in techniques for coping with or managing stress. As new techniques are developed, they need to be evaluated in their various forms in order to determine the relative usefulness of each.

TRADITIONAL RESEARCH METHODS

There are two traditional divisions of research in the behavioral sciencies: experimental versus non-experimental research, and laboratory versus field research. Each has its own strengths or weaknesses.

Experimental Versus
Non-experimental Methods

A true experiment differs from a nonexperiment in several ways, but this discussion will focus on the concept of manipulation of the independent variable. In traditional terms, the independent variable is the one manipulated and the dependent variable is the one measured to see what the effect of the independent variable has on it. For example, in order to test the effects of an individual coping technique such as progressive relaxation, the researcher would manipulate relaxation (the independent variable) by having some people learn and practice relaxation and have another group of people go about their daily lives without learning or using this technique. The effects of relaxation on one or more dependent variables (e.g., occurrence of headaches) would be recorded or measured. If the group of people employing relaxation reported fewer headaches than those reported in the other group (often called the "control" group), the researcher would be tempted to conclude that relaxation is an effective coping technique for headaches, and presumably for headaches due to stress. This would be a strong conclusion to the extent that the researcher also was able to control all the potential extraneous variables in the experimental situation and to eliminate the potential for the placebo effect.

The other variables would be controlled by keeping them the same for everybody in this experiment. In a true experiment, for example, the participants in both the experimental and control groups would be kept in the same environment with the same potential stressors in order to control aspects of the situation. The participants themselves would be randomly assigned to the two groups in order to control for possible differences (e.g., previous experience with relaxation or other coping techniques, physical or psychological hardiness, etc.). The two groups in the true experiment, then, would be equal in terms of the personal factors and the environment except for the independent variable that was being manipulated, in this case, progressive relaxation techniques. If the two groups differed on the dependent variable (number of headaches), it would be likely that the difference was caused by the only other thing distinguishing the groups, namely, relaxation as a coping technique. If one were to evaluate one of the organizational coping techniques, for example, the use of social support groups, social support groups would become the independent variable in a true experiment, and headaches or some other relevant measure of strain could be the dependent variable.

The placebo effect occurs when the participants' measures of strain (e.g., headaches) show improvement simply because the participants in the experimental (e.g., relaxation) group *expected* to improve, rather than because of the effectiveness of relaxation itself. The strength of the placebo effect can be assessed to some extent either by changing the control group in order to make it also expect to improve (by inducing in them the expectation that their headaches will diminish even though they are not using a coping technique), or better still, by having a group in which this is done in addition to a more traditional control group. By making comparisons between specific groups, then, the researcher can get some idea whether a placebo effect can occur for the dependent variable under investigation (e.g., headaches) and whether the independent variable (e.g., relaxation) can have an effect beyond the strength of the placebo effect.

The non-experimental study differs from the experimental study, for our purposes, in its lack of manipulation of the independent variable. Since the independent variable is the one that is manipulated, there is no true independent variable in the non-experimental study. In many fields, however, the term independent variable has come to be used rather loosely; in studies with non-experimental designs, it has been applied to the variable that the researcher believes is a causal factor. Since this can lead to confusion, use of the term independent variable will be avoided in this chapter when referring to non-experimental studies.

In a non-experimental study, therefore, the researcher manipulates nothing (makes no intervention), and measures whatever seems to be important. Relationships among variables are then investigated. As a result of this type of study, the researcher can conclude that certain variables are related to each other.

It should be noted here that many people refer to non-experimental studies as "correlational," and that this sometimes leads to confusion. Using the term correlational in this way means, generally, that two or more things are related. Unfortunately, it is easy to infer that use of the term refers more specifically to the statistic correlation. Although this statistic is usually used in non-experimental studies, it, and most inferential statistics, can actually be used regardless of the method (experimental or non-experimental). This chapter will therefore avoid using the term correlational to refer to the non-experimental method.

Laboratory Versus Field Research

While the terms experimental and non-experimental describe *how* the research is conducted, the terms laboratory versus field describe *where* the research is conducted. Because much experimental research is conducted in the laboratory and most non-experimental research is conducted in the field, it is often assumed that this must be the case. In theory, however, the laboratory/field distinction is independent from the distinction between experimental and non-experimental research.

In general, laboratory research is conducted in settings that are relatively easy to control, and the researcher can eliminate the potential effects of distracting variables not intended for study. Along with this ability to control, the laboratory setting also tends, in practice, to be somewhat artificial, that is, the people being studied know that they are being studied and feel as if they are involved in something other than a normal part of their lives.

Field research, on the other hand, is considered to be conducted in the "real world," and it should give the subjects of the study more of a feeling that they are currently involved in their normal, everyday life. Thus, one might study occupational stress by observing people as they work or by inspecting a company's personnel record to search for patterns of sick leave.

The Fourfold Classification of Traditional Research Methods

Figure 13-1 illustrates the four possible research methods, using the laboratory/field and experimental/non-experimental dimensions. Although it is easiest to describe and consider these dimensions as dichotomies, it often happens in research on stress and coping that a particular method may be somewhat laboratory and somewhat field, or somewhat experimental and somewhat non-experimental. Such studies indicate that the fourfold distinction is overly simple. Nevertheless, it is a helpful tool for understanding important methodological principles.

Platt (1964) has noted that all science is not equal—some investigation methods allow stronger inference than others. Although he was interested in a wide variety of issues regarding investigation in the natural sciences, one of his concerns is especially important here and another will be dealt with later. Each of the four methods in Figure 13-1 is characterized by its own particular strengths and weaknesses. Two of the most important issues in examining these methods are (1) the probability that the research can provide proof regarding causation, and (2) the probability that the results of the research can be generalized to include real-world situations.

It is usually desirable to establish causation in stress research because one wants to know (1) whether a given personal characteristic or environmental situation is the cause of the individual's strain, and (2) whether a particular intervention strategy causes

Figure 13-1.   The Fourfold Classification of Traditional Research Methods.

WHERE THE RESEARCH
IS CONDUCTED

	Laboratory	Field
Non-experimental	non-experimental laboratory study	non-experimental field study
Experimental	laboratory experiment	field experiment

HOW THE RESEARCH IS CONDUCTED

harmful stress to be reduced. If one can be quite certain what the cause of a problem is, it is easier to develop solutions; and if one can be certain that the coping intervention caused improvement in the condition of the person, it would be wise to consider using that intervention again in similar situations in the future.

Traditional wisdom claims that experimental methods allow stronger inference regarding causation than non-experimental methods, and that field methods allow stronger inference regarding generalization than laboratory methods. Because the true experiment manipulates one or more independent variables, allows the dependent variable to vary and then measures it, and controls all other extraneous variables, there is strong evidence that the independent variable has caused the changes in the dependent variable. Because the field study is conducted in a real-world setting, there is strong evidence that its results will generalize to the real world. Applying these principles to Figure 13-1, the non-experimental laboratory study should provide only weak evidence regarding either causality or generalization; the non-experimental field study should provide weak evidence regarding causality, but strong evidence regarding generalization; the laboratory experiment should provide strong evidence regarding causality, but weak evidence regarding generalization; and the field experiment should provide strong evidence regarding both causality and generalization. Thus, in designing a study, or in deciding what to conclude from a study done by someone else, the person interested in stress and coping can classify the nature of the study, know something about the strength of evidence provided for the proposition that something is a cause of stress or strain, and that the results of the study are likely to apply to a particular field setting or to the real world in general. Since the field experiment appears to be the best overall method to use, it might be supposed that it is used predominately. This is usually not the case, however, because it is sometimes unethical to do field experiments in stress (for reasons to be discussed shortly), and because it is very difficult to do a true experiment in the field. As a result, much of the evidence regarding stress and coping has come from laboratory experiments, from non-experimental field studies, or from hybrid designs that incorporate the best principles possible in a given situation. Many of these hybrid designs have been labeled quasi-experimental (e.g., Campbell and Stanley, 1963; Cook and Campbell, 1976), and a selected set of these will be discussed shortly.

There is little point in discussing the non-experimental laboratory study in detail, since it provides very little evidence on either of the two criteria of interest (causality and generalization). But it should be noted in passing that it may be possible to make some observations in such a setting that could lead to the formation of hypotheses that would then need to be tested by one of the methods offering stronger evidence.

Examples Investigating Stress with Three Methods

An example of a study of stress with many of the principles of a *laboratory experiment* is provided by a portion of a study by Sales (1969). Using paid subjects from a voluntary pool of university underclassmen, Sales had them work on an experimental task of solving anagrams while sitting in a cubicle with a chair, a table, and a one-way mirror. One of the independent variables was workload—some of the subjects were overloaded by being given more anagrams than they could solve in the time available, and others were given a number of anagrams that they could easily solve in the time available. One of the dependent variables was the change in serum cholesterol levels in blood samples taken from subjects just prior to the start and just after the end of the experiment. Sales reported that the subjects in the overload condition had an increase in their serum cholesterol levels, while those in the underload condition had a slight decrease in cholesterol. To the extent that all laboratory experimental procedures were followed, it can be concluded that it is certain that the workload on this anagram task caused the changes in serum cholesterol levels, but it is not as certain that this result would apply to real-life tasks and situations (e.g., to workload on a job, a hobby, or in one's chores around the home).

An example of a set of studies of stress that incorporates many of the principles of a *non-experimental field study* is described in Kaufmann (1982) and Kaufmann and Beehr (1982). These researchers administered a questionnaire and measures of blood pressure and heart rate to nurses while on duty and also collected data regarding these nurses from the hospital's personnel files. Based upon this information, it was concluded that an interaction between role stressors (e.g., quantitative workload in the job) and social support was associated with the nurses' psychosomatic strain. To the extent that this study succeeded in collecting real-world data in the field, it can be concluded that an interaction between nurses' workload and social support in their jobs is *related to* psychosomatic problems at work, but it cannot be concluded with strong evidence that the workload and the social support caused the strain to be at certain levels for these nurses.

True *field experiments* on stress or coping are more rare, but there are studies that use many of the same experimental principles. One example is provided by Lahner and Lahner (1981), who conducted two interventions among patrolmen in three police departments. As with most field experiments, this was actually a quasi-experiment because there were some uncontrolled variables. The two interventions consisted of (1) a series of workshops designed to increase individuals' awareness of stress, to increase individuals' sense of mastery over stress, and to increase a sense of mutual support among the individuals, and (2) an organizational intervention with the police administrators and supervisors designed to (among other things) improve the quality of feedback and role clarity within the organization. Some officers received the individual intervention and some did not, while administrators in one department received the organizational intervention and some did not. These two interventions were both independent variables. The dependent variables included quantitative overload of work among the patrolmen which was measured via a questionnaire administered just prior to the interventions, just after the interventions, and again several months after the interventions. It was found, based on this dependent variable, that the group of policemen receiving both the individual and the organizational interventions reported the lowest levels of quantitative workload just after the conclusion of the interventions. To the extent that this field experiment met all of the requirements of a true experiment (which it did not), it could be concluded that the interventions caused the reduction of workload and that the results would probably be applicable to police officers in their real-world jobs.

SPECIAL ISSUES IN RESEARCH ON STRESS

Research on stress has faced particular issues, has tended to utilize certain designs more than others, and has the potential to use certain designs more in the future. These issues include: (1) the ethics of stress research, which are a problem in some designs and in studying some stress characteristics more than in others; and (2) the search for intermediary mechanisms.

Ethics In Stress Research

Some types of research on stress can be criticized as constituting invasions of privacy. For example, if questionnaires are administered in which people are asked to report their physical health and their past or present behavioral tendencies related to psychological health, some will see this as unduly invading an individual's personal life. Similarly, obtaining data from records of mental or medical health clinics or business organizations can also be considered unethical invasions of privacy. It is currently common practice to obtain informed consent from the subjects involved before undertaking such projects in order to be sure that the person has volunteered for participation in the research. This volunteerism, combined with the practice of keeping the individuals' data confidential, is usually expected to reduce this potential ethical problem to acceptable proportions.

While the potential for invasion of privacy is present in nearly any type of methodological design for the study of stress, a second ethical problem germane to the study of stress is especially related to the use of experimental designs, that is, those in which there is intervention by an independent variable. Such manipulation is a direct intrusion into the individual's life (if it is a field experiment) or into a small, temporary part of the individual's life (if it is a laboratory experiment). Suppose that a researcher wished to determine whether the death of a spouse could result in greater susceptibility to harmful disease for the surviving spouse, as might be suggested for research on stressful life events (see Holmes and Rahe, 1967; Sarason, Johnson, and Siegel, 1978). A straightforward experimental test of this hypothesis would involve killing the spouses of the experimental group. While this example is absurd because of its extremity, many other potential experimental designs in stress research involve the manipulation of independent variables that are expected to be harmful to the individual to varying degrees. These differ from the example of the death of a spouse only in their degree of severity—not in the concept that something harmful is being done to the experiments' participants. An example is a study by Sales (1970) in which he again manipulated workload on an anagrams task. One of his dependent measures was heart rate, which was thought to be a measure of strain. When a researcher manipulates independent variables that are expected to be stressors (e.g., workload) because they may lead to strain or adversive consequences for the individual, there is always the possibility that ethical problems may arise regarding potential harm to subjects. In Sales's experiment, it seems unlikely that the temporary increase in heart rate (to an average of 80 to 81 beats per minute) was very harmful, but ethical judgment is always necessary when stressors are being manipulated.

Some experimental studies of stress are likely to pose less of an ethical problem, however. One of these is represented by certain types of studies in which the independent variable is thought to reduce harmful stressors or strain, that is, when coping techniques are manipulated. Providing subjects of an experiment with the skill to reduce their own stress is often less likely to be harmful than putting stress on them. Some of the experiments described by Brown (1960), in which people were taught relaxation techniques using biofeedback, are examples of such research. In this case, the independent variable would be skill with the potential for improving the subjects' conditions, rather than a manipulation with the potential for increasing their stress.

Even when the independent variable in an experiment on stress is a coping technique, however, there is sometimes a potential ethical problem. This would occur mainly when the subjects of the experiment have come to the researcher not as volunteers for an experiment, but as "clients" seeking relief from stressful experiences. If some of these clients are assigned to a control group receiving no treatment, there is an ethical question.

In the special area of occupational stress, there is often another party with a vested interest in experimental manipulations of stress-related variables—the organization employing the subjects. The researcher also must be aware of and take into consideration the fact that some of the manipulations could affect the organization as well as the individual. This question is seldom asked in discussions of research on stress, but it can be argued that organizations deserve the same considerations that individuals do. This would be especially true if many individuals in the same organization are the objects of study, so that large changes in each of them may significantly affect the organization's functioning.

It is for these ethical reasons, as well as for some more practical reasons, that true experiments are somewhat rare in the field of stress.

Research on Intermediary Mechanisms

Intermediary mechanisms are thought to have their effects in the causal chain of stress between stressors and strains. Figure 13-2 shows two types of intermediary variables that have been of interest to researchers and practitioners in the stress domain. In Causal Situation A, a stressor (e.g., a stressful life event such as the death of a spouse) directly causes some changes in the type of intermediary mechanism that will be called an intervening variable in this chapter. It is this intervening variable that directly causes individuals to experience strains. Selye (1976) has proposed that there are physiological

Figure 13-2. Intermediary Mechanisms.

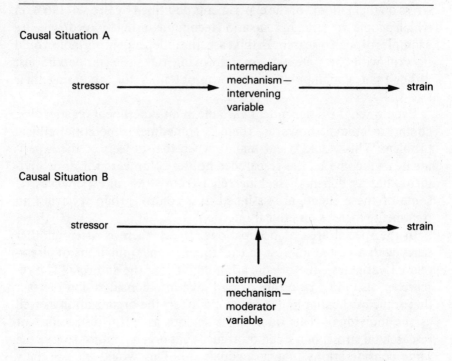

"first mediators" of stress that carry messages to various parts of the body to start the stress syndrome. Thus, environmental stressors cause changes in the first mediators (intervening variables), which in turn cause changes in the strains (stress responses). Selye's first mediators are intervening variables in the language of this chapter.

In Causal Situation B, the intermediary mechanism operates in a different manner. This mechanism, here called a moderator variable, does not directly cause changes in individuals' strains, but instead, it alters the relationship between stressors and strains. Social support has been proposed as operating in this manner by some researchers and practitioners (for examples, see House, 1981). It is sometimes proposed that stressors, such as the death of a spouse or the loss of one's job, tend to cause strain but that the presence of social support can lessen this negative effect. The moderating or buffering effect works by somehow breaking the causal relationship between the stressor and the strain.

It should be noted that the two types of intermediary mechanisms may be closely related in the domain of stress. For example, it may well be that moderator variables have their effect by causing changes in the intervening variable that counteract the influence of the stressors on the intervening variable.

Depending upon which of the two types of intermediary mechanisms one is studying, a different methodological approach may be best. In the study of intervening variables, for example, experimental studies of two sorts are appropriate: (1) those in which stressors are the independent variables, and (2) those in which the intervening variables are the independent variables and the strains are the dependent variables. In the study of moderator variables, appropriate experiments would manipulate stressors and moderating variables simultaneously as independent variables in the same experiment in order to search for a statistical interaction effect that they might have on the dependent variable (strain).

Methods for Research on the Effects of Stress

Documeting the effects of stress involves an investigation into the effects of stressors on strains. Non-experimental field studies are most often performed for this purpose because of the practical and ethical problems that arise in experimental field studies. Thus, to determine the effects of stressors, role ambiguity, role overload, and role conflict on strains, researchers commonly administer questionnaires, investigate company or clinical records, and in some cases, take measures of the physiological functioning of employees in organizations (e.g., Beehr, Walsh, and Taber, 1976; Gupta and Beehr, 1979; Caplan et al., 1975). Such studies may find that role overload, for example, is *related to* strains, but because of the weakness of non-experimental methods, these studies provide little strong evidence to support the hypothesis that role overload *causes* strain.

Some of the non-experimental stress research in the past has relied heavily upon the use of a questionnaire or survey to measure all of the variables of interest to the study (e.g., both stressors and strains). Many researchers, however, are becoming aware of the problems inherent in an over-reliance on surveys for measurement. Since much of the stress research is weak because of other problems (e.g., the inability to make strong inferences regarding causality because of heavy reliance upon non-experimental methods), the measures need to be as accurate as possible. Thus, it is best if studies utilize multiple methods of measurement, including at least some measures that are objective. In stress research, variables that are amenable to measurement by non-survey methods include characteristics of the employee's work environment (e.g., physical conditions, location of the job in relation to organizational boundaries, frequency of work interruptions), and some strains (e.g., medical records, absenteeism, and turnover). Total reliance upon the survey is seldom necessary.

A somewhat unusual non-experimental design, but one that is useful for stress research, is the use of *longitudinal studies.* Studies that take measurements over a period of time are likely to lead to a fuller understanding of the phenomena. Cook and Campbell (1976) have recommended several designs that can be used with longitudinal data in organizational research. I will review here briefly the specific techniques that are particularly useful for the study of the effects of stressors or strains. Interested readers should refer to Cook and Campbell (1976) and Campbell and Stanley (1963) for more details on these and other designs. The primary purpose of this chapter is to indicate how stress variables can fit into some of the designs.

One non-experimental longitudinal design that is frequently recommended is *cross-lagged panel correlation,* a non-experimental method since no independent variables are manipulated. Measures of relevant variables are taken at several points in time, and correlations are then computed between all variables measured at all points in time. In order to infer causality, the researcher assumes, among other things, that there is some type of causal relationship among the variables measured and that causation is not instantaneous. It might be concluded, for example, that a stressor causes strain if the correlation between the stressor measured at an earlier point in time and the strain measured at a later point in time is stronger than the correlation between any other combination of the two variables (especially the correlation between the strain measured at the earlier point in time and the stressor measured at the later time). This method is especially useful in the study of stress because it is a "passive" design (i.e., it does not require manipulation of independent variables). Although researchers have traditionally considered passivity to be characteristic of weak designs, it is actually helpful or often necessary for stress research because of the ethical reasons cited earlier.

A Note on Statistics.   Simple correlations and more complicated inferential statistics based on correlations are often used in non-experimental field studies of stressors and strains. Although it is not the intent of this chapter to develop the skill of the reader in using statistics, readers may be interested to know that there are a few statistical methods that have been employed quite often in past non-experimental research on stress and that are likely to be encountered in reading research reports on the subject. This section is intended to help readers understand the general purpose of some of these statistics.

Simple *correlations* (e.g., Pearson "r") indicate whether two variables (e.g., a stressor and a strain) are related to each other and the strength of the relationship.

Factor analysis (or *cluster analysis*) is often used to determine whether a large set of variables (e.g., questions on a long questionnaire) are measuring a limited or a large set of constructs. In questionnaires, for example, it frequently occurs, intentionally or otherwise, that two or more questions are asking the same thing in different ways. If so, a factor (or cluster) analysis might discover that these two questions are part of the same factor (or cluster). Often, answers to such questions would then be combined into a single "index" thought to measure only one construct.

Whereas a simple correlation indicates the relationship between two variables, *multiple regression* is used to show whether a set of variables are related to a single criterion variable. Thus, for example, the researcher may wish to know the strength of the relationship between a set of stressors, such as losing one's job, failing a college examination, and getting married, and a single strain, such as psychological anxiety. As a set, a number of stressors may "predict" the anxiety better than any single stressor alone. Multiple regression can be useful in determining this.

Each of the statistics described above can be found in virtually any standard statistics book, but the reader may wish to refer to Cohen and Cohen (1975) for details on the final one, *moderated multiple regression.* House (1981), in an appendix to his book on social support as a technique for coping with occupational stress, also describes the computation of this statistic in simple terms. Moderated multiple regression is a multiple regression technique that allows for the testing of interactions, much as the more traditional analysis of variance does. This technique has been used widely in studying the effects of social support as a moderating or buffering variable in the relationship between stressors and strain in the workplace (Beehr, 1984; House, 1981). It can help to test any coping technique, however, for its moderator effects in a non-experimental design.

Methods for Research on the Effectiveness of Coping Strategies

When possible, the best way to evaluate the effects of coping techniques is to use experimental methods since they can provide the strongest evidence of causality. The ethics problem in manipulating variables related to job stress is smaller when studying coping strategies because the variable being manipulated is an attempt to help individuals and their organizations. Presumably, there is less inherent evil to manipulating a variable in a way expected to result in benefits than there is in manipulating a variable in a way that is expected to result in adverse consequences. In addition, many professional helpers and organizational employers are likely to treat symptoms of stress (stressors or strains). In these cases, the researcher can take advantage of naturally occurring events to study the phenomena involved in job stress.

Laboratory experiments have the weakness of allowing uncertainty regarding the degree to which the results generalize to the real world. True field experiments, while the ideal method of research for both inferring causation and generalizing to real-life situations, are nearly impossible to do. Therefore, what is often done is referred to as quasi-experiments, that is, studies in which some but not all of the principles of experimental design are used. In quasi-experiments, there is usually a lack of control over one or more types (e.g., control of individual difference variables, or control of unwanted events occurring to one or more groups in the study).

Cook and Campbell (1976) have described several quasi-experimental methods in detail. This chapter will focus on three of these designs that appear to have the greatest utility for studying the effectiveness of stress coping strategies: (1) non-equivalent control group design, (2) regression-discontinuity designs, and (3) interrupted time series designs.

The non-equivalent control group designs are not true experiments primarily because the sample of people between treatment and control groups is not randomly selected. The most obvious of these designs is the untreated control group design with pre-test and post-test (Cook and Campbell, 1976). If, by chance, the two groups were roughly equivalent on relevant variables on the pre-test, the researcher is fortunate enough to have nearly the advantage of a true experiment. When they are not, however, matching of people within each group or co-variance analysis is often attempted to minimize the effects of the non-equivalence on the interpretation of the results of the experiment. This design is quite well-known among field researchers.

"Selection cohort designs" (as termed by Cook and Campbell) are also included in the category of non-equivalent control group designs. In organizational stress research the non-equivalence between treatment and control groups would be reduced by taking advantage of natural movements of personnel within an organization. If, for example, new managers regularly move from an entry-level job into a second-level job in a given company, this type of design can be useful. Suppose a treatment aimed at alleviating the stress of new managers is attempted with managers in the entry-level jobs. In this design, managers who had not received the treatment because they had cycled through this job prior to the implementation of the treatment program would be the "cohorts" (control group). Any records kept of their job performance, physical complaints, absenteeism, etc., at the end of their time in the entry-level positions or even in their second jobs could be compared with the same measures for the treatment (experimental) group of managers when they are at the end of their stay in the entry-level positions or in their second jobs. The treatment and cohort groups are likely to have some equivalence as long as the company uses consistent selection techniques for its managers. One way to strengthen this design even more in job stress research is to anticipate the introduction of the treatment early enough to administer to the cohort group some specific measures that are especially relevant for job stress research. This would be an advantage since the researcher would not have to rely on whatever measures the company records happen to contain.

Regression-discontinuity designs could be used when a treatment program is given only to the people (individuals seeking treatment in a clinic or an organization) who appear to need it the most. It should normally be expected that a stress-related measure (e.g., a measure of a stressor, of an individual strain, or of an organizational consequence) taken at one point in time would be positively related to the same measure for the same people or organizational units taken at a later time. Thus, a regression line with a positive slope could be drawn. A regression line is developed statistically, but it can be understood easily with a visual example, as in Figure 13–3. With the regression-discontinuity design, a cutoff score on a stress-related measure (e.g., the strain illustrated in Figure 13–3, anxiety) taken at the first point in time would be used to determine which people or units get the treatment (i.e., those who are on the high-stress side of

Figure 13–3. A Sample Regression Line Representing the Relationship between the Same Strain (Anxiety) Measured at Two Points in Time.

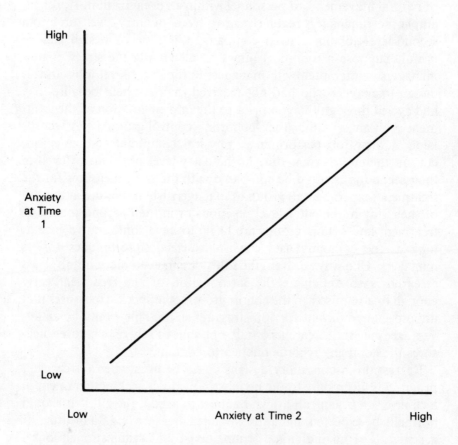

the cutoff would ordinarily receive the treatment program). If the treatment program is successful, the regression line for the treatment group might still have a positive slope, but its lower end would not meet the upper end of the regression line for the nontreatment group. Instead, it would be below the end of the other slope. In essence, the mean of the post-test stress measure for the treatment group is lower than expected based on this group's pre-test scores. In Figure 13–4, the broken line is the relationship that would have been predicted if the high-stress group (on the pre-test) had received no treatment.

Interrupted time-series designs are among the most powerful of the quasi-experimental designs (Cook and Campbell, 1976). Using Cook and Campbell's notation, it is diagrammed as:

$O_1 O_2 O_3$ $O_4 O_5 O_6 O_7 O_8 X O_9 O_{10} O_{11}$ Delayed Treatment Group

$O_1 O_2 O_3 X O_4 O_5 O_6 O_7 O_8$ $O_9 O_{10} O_{11}$ Initial Treatment Group

---

In this diagram, "X" stands for the stress treatment program, "O" (observation) stands for the stress measure, subscripts 1 through 11 refer to the sequential order of the measurements of stress, and the broken line separates the two non-equivalent groups. The groups are not equivalent (i.e., it was not practical to assign people to groups randomly), and the treatment is delayed for one group. This delayed treatment group serves as a control group while the initial treatment group undergoes the stress-treatment program. The process is reversed when the delayed treatment group undergoes the program and the initial treatment group serves as the control. This type of design is obviously useful when it is possible or necessary to introduce changes or treatment programs to only some of the people at a time—perhaps due to inadequate resources to treat everyone at once. In addition, it would be most feasible when unobtrusive measures are available or when periodic measures have been gathered for so long a time that they have become a routine and accepted part of the peoples' lives (so that the relatively large number of observations will not disrupt their lives). This is often the case with certain measures of organizational stress kept by employers (e.g., number of sick days taken) or with some measures kept by clinics.

In all of these quasi-experimental field designs there is some confidence both in the inferences of causality that can be made and in the ability to generalize to the real-world. The problem that each design

Figure 13-4. Regression-Discontinuity Research Design Using Anxiety as a Sample Strain.

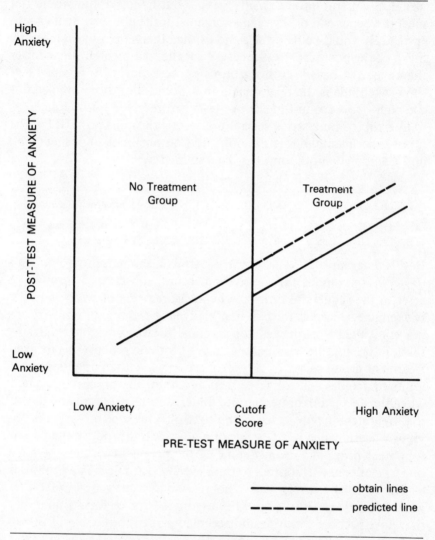

Source: Adapted from Cook and Campbell (1976).

attempts to reduce is the lack of control over extraneous variables. This cannot be done completely in most situations, but these designs are often the best available under the particular circumstances of research on stress and coping.

A Note on Statistics. Some of the most common inferential statistics used with designs aimed at testing the effects of coping techniques are variations of *analysis of variance* (ANOVA). ANOVA is used for testing differences in means (e.g., mean levels of stressors or strains) between groups of people (e.g., an experimental and a control group). Since most of the quasi-experimental designs involve the use of non-equivalent groups, *analysis of co-variance* (ANCOVA) is often used to control for the original differences between the groups. The co-variate in ANCOVA is usually the pre-test measure of the stressors or strains.

Since many studies of coping are interested in more than one measure of stressors or strains, it is often appropriate to use *multiple analysis of variance* (MANOVA). MANOVA tests the probability that the coping technique had an overall effect on the dependent variables (stressors or strains) as a set. It is also possible and helpful to compute *multiple analysis of co-variance* (MANCOVA), which will statistically control for variables that were uncontrolled by the experimental design (e.g., due to lack of random assignment to groups).

Many studies on the effects of coping with stress do not use any inferential statistics at all. The belief is that if there is an effect of any real consequence, it will be obvious by graphing the data to provide a visual inspection. This is not always the case, however, and inferential statistics should always be used where feasible since two or more visual inspectors may not agree with each other. It is not very useful to rely on inferential statistics in one particular situation, however, when the experiment has a small number of participants ("small-N"). The usefulness of inferential statistics is dependent upon the number of subjects to some extent. As noted by Robinson and Foster (1979), small-N research seldom uses inferential statistics, but relies heavily on visual graphing to determine whether there is an effect.

One of the factors lending credibility to experimental results is replicability. Large-N studies replicate the effects of the stress treatment across many subjects; small-N studies, because of their small number of subjects, cannot. Some small-N methods, therefore, utilize a technique in which the subjects are given repeated treatments in order to determine whether the dependent variables (e.g., stressors or strains) change with each administration of the treatment. A version of this is often described as a "reversal" design (e.g., Komaki, 1977; Robinson and Foster, 1979), since the treatment may be given at one point in time, taken away later (a reversal of the treatment), and given at a future point. This is an attempt to replicate the treatment's effects over time with the same subjects, thus giving more confidence to the results.

CONCLUSION

Research on stress and coping is very important for practitioners and for the researchers themselves. Most of what we know about the topic today is a result of more or less systematic research. Without testing the effects of individual and organizational coping techniques, there would be no improvement in the treatments afforded for those in need of it. The basics of classical research designs and of research designs that are practical in the context of stress and coping have been presented with an eye toward strengthening inferences of causality and generalization. The quasi-experimental designs appear to have the most utility for studying stress and reducing the potential ethical and practical problems involved.

The information contained in the other chapters of this *Handbook* is the result of various types of research. The reader may benefit from this chapter by evaluating the information in some of the other chapters in light of the research design used to form the chapters' conclusions. Depending upon whether the methods used were experimental or non-experimental, laboratory or field, for example, the conclusions will have particular strengths or weaknesses (e.g., in the ability to generalize or to infer causality). Many times the studies from which conclusions are drawn are hybrid designs (e.g., quasi-experimental methods). In those instances, judgments will have to be made regarding the probable success in capitalizing on strengths and reducing weaknesses.

The reference to weaknesses in the various other studies on stress and coping is not meant to detract from the usefulness of the information obtained for research. It is simply an acknowledgement that stress and coping are difficult areas to study. The accumulation of many studies with different strengths and different weaknesses eventually allows investigators to ascertain patterns that are consistent enough to lend confidence to our best judgments about causes of and cures for stress.

REFERENCES

Beehr, T.A. 1984. "The Role of Social Support in Coping with Organizational Stress." In *Human Stress and Cognition in Organizations: An Integrated Perspective,* edited by T.A. Beehr and R.S. Bhagat. New York: John Wiley and Sons.

Beehr, T.A., and J.E. Newman. 1978. "Job Stress, Employee Health, and Organizational Effectiveness: A Facet Analysis, Model and Literature Review." *Personnel Psychology* 31, no. 4 (Spring): 665–99.

Beehr, T.A.; J.T. Walsh; and T.D. Taber. 1976. "Relationship of Stress to Individually and Organizationally Valued States: Higher Order Need Strength as a Moderator." *Journal of Applied Psychology* 61, no. 1 (February): 41–47.

Brown, B.B. 1960. *Stress and the Art of Biofeedback.* New York: Bantam Books, Inc.

Campbell D.T., and J.D. Stanley. 1963. *Experimental and Quasi-Experimental Designs for Research.* Chicago: Rand-McNally and Company.

Caplan, R.D.; S. Cobb; J.R.P. French, Jr.; R. Van Harrison; and S.R. Pinneau, Jr. 1975. *Job Demands and Worker Health.* Washington, D.C.: U.S. Government Printing Office.

Cohen, J., and P. Cohen. 1975. *Applied Multiple Regression/Correlation Analysis for the Behavioral Sciences.* Hillsdale, N.J.: Erlbaum.

Cook, T.D., and D.T. Campbell. 1976. "The Design and Conduct of Quasi-Experiments and True Experiments in Field Settings." In *Handbook of Industrial and Organizational Psychology,* edited by M.D. Dunnette. Chicago: Rand-McNally and Company.

Gupta, N., and T.A. Beehr. 1979. "Job Stress and Employee Behaviors." *Organizational Behavior and Human Performance* 23: 373–87.

Holmes, T.H., and R.H. Rahe. 1967. "The Social Readjustment Scale." *Journal of Psychosomatic Research* 11: 213–18.

House, J.S. 1981. *Work Stress and Social Support.* Reading, Mass: Addison-Wesley.

Kaufmann, G.M. 1982. "The Effects of Social Supports on Job Stressors and Strains in Police and Nurses." Psychology Dissertation Project, Central Michigan University.

Kaufman, G.M., and T.A. Beehr. 1982. "Social Support as a Moderator of the Relationship between Job Stressors and Strains among Nurses." Paper presented at the meeting of the American Psychological Association, Washington, D.C., August 23–27.

Komaki, J. 1977. "Alternative Evaluation Strategies in Work Settings: Reversal and Multiple-Baleine Designs." *Journal of Organizational Behavior Management* 1, no. 1 (Summer): 53–77.

Lahner, D.L., and M.H. Lahner. 1981. "Burnout: An Evaluation of Organizational Development Strategies with Police." Psychology Disserttion Project, Central Michigan University.

Platt, J.R. 1964. "Strong Inference." *Science* 146, no. 3642 (October): 347–53.

Robinson, P.W., and D.F. Foster. 1979. *Experimental Psychology: A Small-N Approach.* New York: Harper and Row.

Sales, S.M. 1969. "Organizational Role as a Risk Factor in Coronary Disease." *Administrative Science Quarterly* 14: 325–26.

Sales, S.M. 1970. "Some Effects of Role Overload and Role Underload." *Organizational Behavior and Human Performance* 5, no. 5: 592–608.

Sarason, I.G.; J.H. Johnson; and J.M. Siegel. 1978. "Assessing the Impact of Life Changes: Development of the Life Experiences Survey." *Journal of Consulting and Clinical Psychology* 46: 932–46.

Selye, H. 1976. *The Stress of Life,* Revised Edition. New York: McGraw-Hill.

14 ORGANIZATIONAL STRESS COPING: RESEARCH ISSUES AND FUTURE DIRECTIONS

Amarjit S. Sethi and *Randall S. Schuler*

Although each of the authors in this *Handbook* has suggested a definition or model of stress and coping, we conclude here by presenting research directions and future issues in the form of testable hypotheses based on the transactional models of stress and coping examined in Chapter 3. Consistent with the previous chapter by Beehr, however, we think that the testable hypotheses offered here are sufficiently general so as to apply to many other chapters in this *Handbook*. For example, the third hypothesis explicitly incorporates both individual and organizational categories of coping. This level of generality is somewhat limited, however, in the sixth hypothesis where only *our* specific definition of stress is used.[1] After presenting these stress coping hypotheses, several recommended research topics for stress are presented.

RESEARCH HYPOTHESES FOR STRESS COPING STRATEGIES

Developing research hypotheses may not only be desirable but a necessity if an understanding of coping and stress is to emerge. Hypotheses

[1]The discussion of the six hypotheses is taken in part from Schuler (1984).

can suggest a research focus and thereby potentially stimulate research in the area. But even with several hypotheses and a definition and model of coping, research on coping strategies is still "fraught with difficulties" (Burke and Weir, 1980). This is because coping is a complex and dynamic process that may evolve as slowly over time as does stress itself. In addition, coping involves multiple decision points that may be difficult to capture (Folkman, Schaefer, and Lazarus, 1979). Nevertheless, such research efforts are underway in an attempt to capture the richness and complexity of the coping process (Folkman and Lazarus, 1980).

Hypothesis 1   Individuals who engage in the process of gathering information, generating alternatives, selecting and implementing an alternative, and finally evaluating the implemented strategy will be more effective and efficient at coping with stress than individuals who do not take this methodological approach.

Partial support for this hypothesis is based on the work of Howard, Rechnitzer, and Cunningham (1975); Antonovsky (1979); Lazarus (1978); and Gal and Lazarus (1975). These studies suggest that when individuals are methodical in their analysis of a stressful situation they are more likely to produce a wide range of potentially effective coping strategies than if they do not. Anderson's (1976) findings suggest that individuals should try to avoid situations in which they are facing too much stress since this may preclude engaging in problem-solving activities.

Hypothesis 2   Individuals who have a higher self-esteem, higher cognitive complexity, better problem-solving and decisionmaking skills, and who have a high sense of personal efficacy are likely to be more methodical than individuals without these attributes.

Hypothesis 3   A specific coping strategy is more likely to be effective when it is selected after a thorough analysis and consideration of the feasibility of organizational and individual coping strategies.

Obviously, a strategy to change the organization when it is not likely to change will be less successful than if it is likely to change.

Furthermore, it is likely that more stress will result if the inappropriate strategy is chosen than if none is chosen. Thus it is important to be able to analyze stress situations and successfully identify the realistic constraints. In addition to the identification, it is necessary to develop a repertoire of strategies that can be matched and evaluated in comparison with different stressful situations. A consequence of this matching and testing may be a contingency or situational approach to coping. Current research suggests that a broad, general contingency approach may not only be an effective and efficient way of coping, but may in fact describe what individuals do, at least those who are successful (see, for example, the work of Folkman and Lazarus, 1980; Jackson and Maslach, 1982).

These first three hypotheses imply that for individuals to engage in effective coping they must be not only perceptive but adaptable as well. Making individuals aware of this cognitive-diagnostic approach to coping strategies will not ensure that they will actually select or implement the most effective strategy. But even if individuals are completely adaptable, it is possible that they will not maximize or select the most effective strategy. Because of time and information processing capabilities, it is more probable that individuals will satisfy or select a coping strategy that produces a satisfactory resolution at best (Simon, 1976). Some individuals, however, will be more capable of developing coping strategies that produce more satisfactory solutions than others.

Hypothesis 4   Only when organizations perceive that a sufficiently large number of its employees are experiencing stress will they implement or strongly support the implementation of coping strategies that involve organizational change.

It is likely to be inappropriate and dysfunctional for organizations to make organizational changes to improve conditions for a relatively small group of employees. The stress experiences of a limited number of employees could largely reflect conditions associated with the individual more than the organization. Thus, although organizational change could prove to be a successful coping strategy for a few employees, it may prove harmful to those who were previously not in need of coping.

Hypothesis 5   Individuals under similar conditions are likely to adopt very dissimilar coping strategies.

This hypothesis suggests that there are likely to be very substantial individual differences (due to attributes, experiences, cognitive abilities, and behaviors) that influence which coping strategy individuals use. These individual differences may also influence how individuals perceive the same situation, and thus explain some of the differential in strategy selection.

Hypothesis 6   Coping strategies can be effective to the extent that they (1) reduce the uncertainty associated with a situation, (2) reduce the importance of the situation, or (3) reduce the duration of the stress. The less effective strategy reduces only the effects of stress on the individual.

This final hypothesis is critical. Upon this hypothesis rests the usefulness of the entire model of coping as presented in Chapter 3. Some individuals are thought to be more effective in their coping with stress than others because of their personal ability to deal with the essence of stress: uncertainty, importance, and duration. Not only is it hypothesized here that some individuals will be more effective than others in dealing with stress, but also that those individuals who deal with stress by addressing uncertainty, importance, and duration will be more effective than those who only deal with the results of stress.

RESEARCH ISSUES FOR STRESS

In addition to these specific hypotheses to direct future stress coping research, we think that there are several stress research topics that should be investigated. A better understanding of stress, we think, is essential to a better understanding and examination of stress coping. First, it is recommended that more interdisciplinary research be undertaken on job stress (Beehr and Newman, 1978; Cooper and Marshall, 1976; Schuler, 1980). Without interdisciplinary teams of researchers (including, for example, people from business, medicine, and psychology), it is difficult to broaden the types of consequences studied.

Our first recommended research topic is the effect of combinations of different stressors in or out of the workplace. It is easy to assume that employees with two stressors experience greater consequences than employees with only one stressor It may be, however, that the effects of stressors are not additive, and that someone with many types of stressors is not in a much worse position than somebody with only one stressor. This possibility is very seldom addressed.

Some combinations of stressors however may be additive. Each individual stressor will need then to be investigated in combinations with each of the other stressors in order to come to an overall conclusion regarding stressor additiveness. This will be an enormous task. Since such research would be informative, however, it is recommended that the task be begun. It is further recommended that the task proceed initially by investigating the accumulative nature of relatively diverse types of stressors—specifically, psychosocial and physical stressors in the organization, and non-organization stressors. The psychosocial stressors are primarily the role, task, and interrelationship characteristics of an employee's job; the physical stressors are characteristics of the physical work environment such as heat and noise; and the non-organizational stressors refer to any stressful event that occurs in one's life that is not directly attributable to one's employment. House et al. (1979) have begun work in this area by investigating combinations of psychosocial stressors with physical health hazards among blue-collar workers in the rubber industry. They are finding that there are indeed interactive effects to some psychosocial stressors and some physical stressors. The relationship between the psychosocial stressors and the individual consequences were strongest for those workers who were exposed to noxious physical stressors. More research investigating the effects of combinations among the types of stressors is thus recommended.

The whole area of work and nonwork relationships is recommended for more research within the area of job stress. The popular life-stress scales (e.g., Holmes and Holmes, 1970) contain both work and nonwork events. Stressors are thus thought to exist either at work or in one's nonwork life, or in both places. In addition, the consequences of stress can become evident at work (e.g., absenteeism) or in other areas of one's life (e.g., divorce). Finally, adaptive, coping responses to stress may occur in either work or nonwork areas of one's life (e.g., seeking social support at work or elsewhere). These possibilities are all in need of research. It is therefore recommended that research be conducted to determine the relationships between the work and nonwork locations of stressors, consequences, and coping responses. There are many variations on this theme of work/non-work stress relationships, and nearly all of them are relatively unexamined.

SUMMARY

Stress in organizations is becoming an important concern for individuals and organizations because of its severe deleterious effects. By reducing or managing stress, these effects may be significantly reduced, thus benefiting both individuals and organizations. Since reducing or managing stress is the essence of coping, an understanding of coping can aid in attaining the benefits of dealing with stress successfully. By examining the specific coping hypotheses presented in this chapter, as well as our more general research topics for stress, this understanding can be enhanced.

REFERENCES

Anderson, C.R. 1976. "Coping Behaviors and Intervening Mechanisms in the Inverted-U–Stress Performance Relationship." *Journal of Applied Psychology* 61: 3–34.

Antonovsky, A. 1979. *Health Stress and Coping.* San Francisco: Jossey-Bass Publishers.

Beehr, T.A., and J.E. Newman. 1978. "Job Stress, Employee Health, and Organizational Effectiveness: A Facet Analysis, Model and Literature Review." *Personnel Psychology* 31: 665–699.

Burke, R.J., and T. Weir. 1980. "Coping with the Stress of Managerial Occupations." In *Current Concerns in Occupational Stress,* edited by C.L. Cooper and R.L. Payne, pp. 229–335. London: John Wiley and Sons.

Cooper, C.L., and J. Marshall. 1976. "Occupational Sources of Stress: A Review of the Literature Relating to Coronary Heart Disease and Mental Ill Health." *Journal of Occupational Psychology* 49: 11–28.

Folkman, S., and R.S. Lazarus. 1980. "An Analysis of Coping in a Middle-Aged Community Sample." *Journal of Health and Social Behavior* 21: 219–239.

Folkman, S.; C. Schaefer; and R.S. Lazarus. 1979. "Cognitive Processes as Mediators of Stress and Coping." In *Human Stress and Cognition,* edited by V. Hamilton and D.M. Warburton. Chilchestor, England: John Wiley and Sons.

Gal, R., and R.S. Lazarus. 1975. "The Role of Activity in Anticipating and Confronting Stressful Situations." *Journal of Human Stress* 2: 4–20.

Holmes, T.S., and T.H. Holmes. 1970. "Short-Term Intrusions into the Life Style Routine." *Journal of Psychosomatic Research* 14: 121–132.

House, J.S.; A.J. McMichael; J.A. Wells; B.H. Kaplan; and L.R. Landerman. 1979. "Occupational Stress and Health among Factory Workers." *Journal of Health and Social Behavior* 30 139-160.

Howard, J.H.; P.A. Rechnitzer; and D.A. Cunningham. 1975. "Coping with Job Tensions—Effective and Ineffective Methods." *Public Personnel Management* 1: 317-326.

Jackson, S.E., and C. Maslach. 1982. "After-Effects of Job Related Stress: Families as Victims." *Journal of Occupational Behavior* 3: 63-77.

Lazarus, R.S. 1978. "The Stress and Coping Paradigm." Paper presented at a conference on the Critical Evaluation of Behavioral Paradigms for Psychiatric Science, Glendon Beach, Oregon, November 3-6.

Schuler, R.S. 1980. "Definition and Conceptualization of Stress in Organizations." *Organizational Behavior and Human Performance* 24: 115-130.

Schuler, R.S. 1984. "Integrative Transactional Process Model of Coping with Stress in Organizations." In *Human Stress and Cognition in Organizations,* edited by T.A. Beehr and R.S. Bhagat. New York: John Wiley and Sons.

Simon, H.A. 1976. *Administrative Behavior* (3rd ed.). New York: The Free Press.

INDEX

Act Respecting Occupational
  Health and Safety (Canada), 5
Adrenal(s), 20, 146
Adrenaline, 4, 22, 38, 168
Aerobic exercise, 222-26
Aging, 21, 25-30, 257, 265
Air-traffic control, 44-45, 263
Alcohol use, 2, 96-97, 262, 263
Animals, 16-17
ANS activity, 199-200
Anticipatory socialization pro-
  grams, 99-101
Arousal mechanism, 202
Autogenic training, 160, 188, 195,
  197-98

Bell Telephone System, 264
Biofeedback, 183-208; applications, 190-93; augmented,
  187-90, 193-96, 200; as
  cognitive therapy, 202-205;
  defined, 183; EEG, 197-98,
  203-5; EMG, 196-97, 203, 205;
  and endocrine disorders, 206;
  information, 195; learning,
  194-95, 204; and meditation,
  148, 160; methodologies,
  187-90; modalities, 188-89, 198;
of muscle activity (motor
  response), 186-87, 188-89, 191,
  192-93; and neural re-education,
  204-5; and patient-therapist
  communication, 205-6; procedures, 187, 188, 192; roots of,
  185-87; and stress, 191-202;
  temperature, 191
Biofeedback Society, 191
Blood sugar, 38, 168
Blue collar workers, 45
Burnout, 10, 89-90; and alcohol
  use, 96-97; aspects of, 91-93;
  and caseloads, 106-8; coping
  strategies, 97-98; consequences
  of, 93-97; and performance
  feedback, 108-9; prevention
  programs, 98-110; and role am-
  biguity/conflict, 102-3, 106;
  support conditions for, 103

Caliphylaxis, 28-29
Calories/caloric energy, 21, 29
Canada, 5; fitness programs, 227;
  stress research, 234-36
Canada Fitness Survey, 11, 216-17
Canadian Centre for Occupational
  Health and Safety, 5

309

Cardiovascular disorders, 2, 27, 264
Career/mid-career crisis, 41–42
Catecholemine levels, 147
Client Feedback Survey, 109
Communication behaviors, 78–84
Consciousness: levels, 173–74; research, 167
Coping/organizational stress coping, 1–6, 114–40, 245–47; attempts, 138; defined, 7–8, 45–61, 114–18; results, 138; telic character of, 115; trigger, 49. *See also* Stress coping strategies
Coronary heart disease, 2, 130, 147, 147, 215, 221, 251, 257, 260, 262, 264–65
Corticoids, 9, 20, 22
Cybernetics, 185, 187

Depressions, 91–93
Drug use, 2, 9, 96, 115, 262

EEG alpha activity, 186–87, 188–89, 192, 197–98, 203–4
Ego, 174–75
Electrocardiogram (EKG), 183
EMG (muscle) activity, 186–87, 188–89, 191, 196–97, 203
Emotional arousal, 16
Emotional exhaustion/disorders, 91–93, 102–3, 200
Energy substrates, 217
Exercise. *See* Physical activity/exercise

Flight or fight response, 37, 199
Foremen and stress, 236, 259, 263, 265
Free association, 160
Future Shock, 245

Gantt chart, 72
General adaptation syndrome (GAS), 9, 20–25, 26
Giving up-given up complex, 268
Goddard Space Flight Center, 259

High blood pressure, 2
High-density lipo-protein cholesterol (HDL$_2$), 221
Homeostasis, 9, 19, 22, 24, 219; disruption of, 37–38

Human service professions, 89–91, 103–4
Hypnosis, self, 160
Hypothalmus, 16

Imagery, 195, 197, 201–2
Importance, 36–37, 46–47, 49
Individual stress coping strategies, 6, 8, 58–61
Information: cognitively useful, 195; psychologically supporting, 195; strategy, 195

Learned helplessness, 98–99
Life-stress scales, 305
Low personal accomplishment, 91–93

Managers and stress, 237–244, 267–270, 271
Mason, John W., 17
Medical profession and stress, 262–63
Meditation, 167, 195, 196; and biofeedback, 148, 160; clinically standardized (CSM), 152–53; defined, 145; diagnostic (DM), 156–59, 162; and gestalt, 160–61; physiological effects of, 149–51; relaxation response, 153; research on, 148–52; Sikh, 155–56; techniques, 152–59; and time management, 161–62; transcendental (TM), 150, 151–52, 156, 170, 197; Zen, 153–55
Muscle rehabilitation procedures, 185

Nanak, Guru, 155
National Clearing House for Mental Health Information, 252
National Institute of Occupational Safety and Health (NIOSH), 5
Nervous tension, 16, 17, 21
Neurophysiology, 185
Neuroses, 2, 204
Noradrenaline, 4, 38, 168

Organizational Safety and Health Act (OSHA), 4–5

Organizational stress. *See* Stress/ organizational stress; Stress coping strategies
Operant conditioning, 185–86, 187–90, 192, 200

Pareto Principle, 72–73
Participatory decisionmaking, 102–6
Patanjali, Master, 167
Pathogens, 24–25, 44
Physical activity/exercise: aerobic, 222–26; and anxiety reduction, 223; organizational fitness programs, 226–28; and stress, 11, 215–25; tranquilizer effect of, 223
Plants, 16–17
Primary social relationships, 114
Progressive Relaxation (P.R.), 160, 188, 195, 197–98
Psychology, 185
Psychoses, 263
Psychotherapy, 202–3

Rama, Swami, 177
Reality Shock, 98
Relaxation response, 196–98
Respiratory problems, 264
Role ambiguity/conflict, 39–42, 71–72, 102–3, 106, 130, 258–59, 260–61, 265, 270

Salesmen and stress, 236
Schizophrenia, 263
Serum cholesterol, 260, 263
Social perceptual activity, 201–2
Social support: and coping, 120–21, 137–40; defined, 114–18, 137; effects of, 121–38; elements of, 117–18; recipients of, 118–19; sources of, 118–20; and stress, 120; studies, 124–40; from subordinates, 119–20; from supervisors, 120; and workload, 130
States of constraint, 36
States of demand, 36
States of opportunity, 36
Stress/organizational stress, 1–6, 35–38, 44–45, 55, 57–58, 61–62, 251–52, 306; additive concept of, 37; and aging, 21, 25–30; and alcohol use, 2, 96–97, 262, 263; in animals, 16–17; anticipatory, 266; audit, 252, 254–56, 267, 271; avoidance of, 18; behavioral reaction to, 53; biochemical reaction to, 217; biologic, 15, 19, 20; and burnout, 10, 89–90; bodily reaction to (*See* physiological reaction to) and boundary-spanning activities, 260–61; and career life cycle, 265–67; chronic, 234; and chronic disease, 113–14, 251; cognitive factors of, 199–200; concept, 18–25; and coronary heart disease. *See separate listing.* and death, 18; defined, 6–7, 15–18, 36–45, 146, 168, 218, 277fn; and diseases of adaptation, 24–25, 38, 114, 168, 251, 263–65; disorders, 235; and drug use, 2, 9, 96, 115, 262; and energy utilization, 17; financial impact of, 2–3; 236, 259, 263, 265; and health, 1–2, 235; hormonal reaction to, 4, 22–25; immunologic reactions to, 25, 215, 217; integrative transactional process model of, 38–39; and interpersonal processes, 261; and job qualities, 42–43, 257–58; and job satisfaction, 244–45; local, 28; management, 8, 32; and managers, 237–44, 267–70, 271; and men, 235; multifactorial model of, 252–54; need for, 248–49, 257, 269; negative, 36, 38, 168; neuroendocrine reaction to, 146; nonphysical, 199–200; nonspecific, 21; and occupational level, 263–65; and organizational structure/conditions, 44, 69–70, 257; and participation, 261–62; and personality, 268; physical conditions for, 37–38, 44; physiological reaction to, 20–25, 38, 49, 53, 217, 233; and pituitary-adrenal system, 146; in plants, 16–17; positive, 36, 38, 168; prevention, 8, 269; and productivity

Stress/organizational stress (cont.)
in organizations, 3–4; psychological reaction to, 53, 168;
psychoendocrine reaction to,
148; psychoneuroendocrine
research on, 145; psycho-
neurotic, 254; psychophysiological reaction to, 233;
psychosocial reactions to, 114;
psychosomatic, 254; reaction
patterns, 256; and relationships
at work, 43; repression of, 235;
research (Canada), 234–36;
response/reaction, 19, 24,
234–36; and responsibility,
262–63; and retirement, 31–33,
266; and role characteristics,
39–42, 71–72, 102–3, 106, 130,
258–59, 260–61, 265, 270; and
salesmen, 236; social, 200–1;
and social support, 120–21;
sociophysiological, 168; sociopsychological, 37–38; sources
of, 69, 266–67; and sym-
pathetic adrenal system, 146;
symptoms, 35, 234–36; systemic,
28; and time management, 77–
78; and type A personalities, 59,
60, 260; types of, 17; unrelieved, 217; variables, 256–67;
and women, 235; and work
overload, 259–60, 270; worker
compensation benefits for, 4–6.
See also Stressor(s)/organiza-
tional stressor(s)
Stress coping research, 277–78; on
effectiveness of coping strategies, 292–98; on effects of stress,
289–92; ethics in, 285–87;
hypotheses for coping strategies,
301–4; on intermediary mechanisms, 287–89; issues, 304–5;
method classification, 281–83;
methods, 278–85; statistics, 291,
297–98
Stress coping strategy(ies)/organiza-
tional stress coping strategy(ies),
2–3, 6–8, 46, 61–62, 84, 117–18,
202, 247–48; analysis/evaluation
of, 47–48, 53–54, 61–62, 84;
biofeedback, 191–208; for burnout, 97–98, 106–8; communica-

tion behaviors, 78–84; decisionmaking participation, 270, 271;
detachment/withdrawal, 91, 95,
115; development of, 51–52, 61;
exercise. (See physical activity);
feedback from, 54, 108–9, 116,
268, 270–71; implementation of,
52–53, 84; integrative transactional process model, 48–54, 61;
long-term, 60; management, 8;
meditation, 146, 151; and the
organization, 55–58; palliative,
59; and physical activity, 11,
215–28; prevention, 8; primary
appraisal of, 49–51, 70, 115–17,
120; problem-solving, 160; reduction of importance of stress,
59; reduction of uncertainty,
58–60; research. See Stress coping research. secondary appraisal of, 51, 116–17; selection
of, 47, 51–52, 59–61, 84; short-
term, 60; and social support,
120–21, 137–40; structural ambiguity determinant of, 46–47;
support conditions for, 52, 84,
120–21; time management,
70–78, 160, 161–62; types of,
55–61, 69–70; yoga, 167–81. See
also Coping/organizational
stress coping
Stress of Life, The, 9
Stressor(s)/organizational stressor(s):
defined, 8–9, 16, 277fn; effect,
16–18, 22; emotional, 217; interdependent, 58; organizational
environment as, 35–36, 70;
physical, 200; research on,
39–44; variables, 256–67. See
also Stress/organizational
stress
Suicide, 262

Time management, 70–78, 160,
161–62
Toffler, Alvin, 245
Transcendental Meditation (TM),
150, 151–52, 156, 197
Type A personality, 59, 60,
260; and meditation, 147–48,
162

Ulcer(s), 2, 20, 22, 236, 265
Uncertainty, 36–37, 46–47, 49,
    58, 70, 202, 270–71; coping
    strategies to reduce, 58–60

White collar workers, 45
Work-nonwork relationship, 41–
    42, 305
Workplace Safety and Health Act
    (WSHA) (Canada), 5
World Health Organization, 1

Yoga, 169, 177–80; Bhakti, or
    devotional, 170–71; defined,
    167–69; Gnana, or philo-
    sophical, 170, 174; Hatha, 172,
    177; Karma, 169; Kundalini,
    171–72; Raja, 172–73; Tantric,
    171; Vendantic, 169

ABOUT THE EDITORS

Amarjit Singh Sethi is Associate Professor of Health Administration, Faculty of Administration, University of Ottawa. During the past twelve years Professor Sethi has taught labor relations, personnel management, health administration, and organizational behavior at the University of Ottawa. Dr. Sethi's interests include executive stress management, collective bargaining, human resource management, meditation, and comparative sociology. He is the author of two books: *Industrial Relations and Health Services* and *Role of Collective Bargaining in Industrial Relations in India.* He is also chief editor of the *Journal of Comparative Sociology and Religion* and has co-authored a special issue on *Stress Coping and Religion.* In addition he has contributed a chapter on "Stress Coping Strategies: The Role of Meditation" in *Selye's Guide to Stress Research,* Vol. 3, and has written several articles on stress, including "Stress Coping" in the *Canadian Journal of Public Health.*

Dr. Randall S. Schuler is Associate Professor, Graduate School of Business, New York University. Dr. Schuler's interests are stress and time management, role conflict and ambiguity, task design, quality of work life, leadership, communications, performance appraisal, compensation, staffing, and human resource planning. He is the author of a textbook entitled *Personnel and Human Resource Man-*

agement and the co-author of *Case Problems in Management, Book of Readings in Human Resource Management, Effective Personnel Management,* and *Managing Job Stress.* In addition he has contributed numerous chapters to various books, including "Teaching Personnel and Human Resource Management," (with Elizabeth Zubritzky) in *Management Education: Issues in Theory, Research and Practice,* and "Current and Future Perspectives on Stress," with Terry Beehr, in *Personnel Management.*

ABOUT THE
CONTRIBUTORS

Dr. Terry A. Beehr received his Ph.D. in Organizational Psychology from the University of Michigan and is currently Professor of Psychology at Central Michigan University. He has formerly held positions at Illinois State University and the Institute for Social Research. He has written several articles on work-related stress and is co-editor (with Rabi S. Bhagat) of the book, *Human Stress and Cognition in Organizations: An Integrated Perspective.*

Dr. Barbara B. Brown is an expert in psychiatry, pharmacology, and cardiovascular physiology. She has been associated with the Sepulveda Veterans Hospital and with the UCLA Medical School. Recognized as a creative researcher and in wide demand as a lecturer, she was one of the pioneers in the work that resulted in the development of the stress-reducing techniques of biofeedback. Dr. Brown has edited two reference books, *The Bio-Feedback Syllabus* and *The Alpha Syllabus,* the latter with J. Klug. She is the author of the first comprehensive book on biofeedback, *New Mind, New Body,* and *Stress and the Art of Biofeedback.*

Dr. John H. Howard is an Associate Professor of Business Administration, School of Business, University of Western Ontario. Professor Howard has been involved in research and teaching at both

317

Harvard and the University of California at Berkeley. During the past twelve years Professor Howard has been engaged in extensive studies of the problems of stress on people at work. He has published widely on this topic and with two colleagues recently published *Rusting Out, Burning Out or Bowing Out: Stress and Survival on the Job.*

Dr. Maurice Jetté is Professor at the Department of Kinanthropology, Faculty of Health Sciences, University of Ottawa, Canada. Dr. Jetté has been a researcher in the field of health, fitness, and stress for the last ten years. He has published widely in the areas of fitness and stress. He has also served as a director of the Cardiac Prevention and Rehabilitation Programme at the Ottawa Civic Hospital, Ottawa, Canada.

Dr. Susan E. Jackson is Assistant Professor in the Department of Management at New York University. She has published several articles on the topics of burnout, role commitment, role conflict and ambiguity, and the effects of job stress on family life. Her articles have appeared in the *Journal of Applied Psychology, The Journal of Personality and Social Psychology,* and *The Journal of Occupational Behaviour.*

Dr. Manfred F.R. Kets de Vries is a Professor of Management Policy and Organizational Behaviour at McGill University and is a practicing psychoanalyst and member of the Canadian Psychoanalytic Society. Before coming to McGill, Prof. Kets de Vries was a Research Fellow in Social Psychology of Management at the Harvard Business School. He is the author and co-author of various books and articles, including *Power and the Corporate Mind* and *Organizational Paradoxes: Clinical Approaches to Management.* His latest book, *The Irrational Executive,* is in press. He has published in a wide variety of journals, including the *Harvard Business Review, Human Relations, Behavioral Science,* and *Academy of Management Journal.*

Dr. Hans Selye pioneered the research of stress and opened countless new avenues of treatment through the discovery that hormones participate in the development of many degenerative diseases, including coronary thrombosis, brain hemorrhage, hardening of the arteries, high blood pressure, kidney failure, arthritis, peptic ulcers, and cancer. Over the course of his career, Dr. Selye devoted most of his research toward formulating a code of behavior based on the laws governing the body's stress resistance.

Born in Vienna in 1907, Dr. Selye studied in Prague, Paris, and Rome, and received his medical degree and Ph.D. from the German University in Prague. He held doctorates in medicine and science from universities around the world and in recognition of his outstanding achievements, earned nineteen honorary degrees.

James A. Wells, B.A. (Marquette), M.A. and Ph.D. (Duke) is Assistant Professor of Sociology at Washington University in St. Louis. He is currently on leave as a Postdoctoral Fellow in the Department of Epidemiology and Public Health, Yale University School of Medicine. In addition to stress and social support, his interests include research methodology, psychiatric epidemiology, and health care utilization. He has published on these topics in journals such as the *Journal of Health and Social Behavior, Journal of Occupational Medicine, Medical Care,* and *Journal of Occupational Behavior.* He is currently designing a longitudinal study of psychosocial factors and blood pressure.